Psychoanalysis in Fashion

Psychoanalysis in Fashion

Anita Weinreb Katz
Arlene Kramer Richards

International Psychoanalytic Books (IPBooks)
New York • http://www.IPBooks.net

International Psychoanalytic Books (IPBooks)
Queens, New York
Online at: www.IPBooks.net

Interior book design by Maureen Cutajar, www.gopublished.com

Fabulous Fashionistas Photo courtesy of Sue Bourne, Producer and Director and Tony Miller, cinematographer of *Fabulous Fashionistas* © 2013.

To order *Fabulous Fashionistas* please go to
www.wellparkproductions.com/filmography/fashion.html

Front cover photo by Elsa Blum

ISBN: 978-0-9985323-6-3

Anita Katz dedicates this book to her mother, Minna Banges Weinreb,
her father, Samuel Weinreb, her grandmother Lisa Banges,
and her brothers, Marvin and Joe Weinreb.

Lisa Banges　　　　　　　　**Minna Banges Weinreb**

Samuel Weinreb　　　　　　　　**Joe and Marvin Weinreb**

Arlene Kramer Richards dedicates this book to the memory
of her mother, Edith Burstein Kramer,
her father, Emanuel Kramer,
her grandmother, Rebecca Rosental Burstein,
and her grandfather, Joseph Burstein.

Table of Contents

I

Introduction

1. *Anita Weinreb Katz*

When I was a child, like all children, I grew every year. Each year my mother bought me new clothes because I was growing. I connected growing up with dreaming about the future. I had high hopes that the future would bring me love, achievement, and recognition. My insight into the connections between growing up, buying new clothes, and imagining future fulfillments inspired my desire to write this book.

I have a vivid memory of being eight years old and getting a beautiful plaid dress as a present from my father. To me it meant that he cared about me and about how I looked. He wanted to take part in supporting my being a cute little girl, and that made me happy. It was no longer a teddy bear (that he had given me when I was three years old) but a beautiful dress that both affirmed and enhanced my appearance and significance to him.

When I was a teenager my father's offer to buy me a winter coat resulted in my mother's screaming at him with jealousy. My response was to say to him, "No, don't give me a coat." Of course my mother wanted me to have a winter coat, but she wanted to be the one who took me shopping for it. I still remember the beautiful winter coat that she bought me. It was black wool with a gold velvet lining. I also remember when I was in my teens I impulsively went into a very fancy store where my mother shopped for herself. I guess I was striving to be a grown-up lady like my mother. Playing the role to the hilt, I asked the saleslady to show me some outfits. I picked out two beautiful, very expensive dresses, tried them on, and loved how I looked in them. I still remember them—one was a padded, light blue, elegant two-piece dress, and the other was a sophisticated burgundy dress. I did not have the money to pay for them of course, so I went home fearful that my mother would be angry with me for thinking I was entitled to shop in her store. To my great surprise she went to the shop with me and asked me to try on both outfits. She loved both of them and bought them for me. She was not threatened or jealous of my emerging self; instead, she embraced and participated in my fantasies about being an elegant woman like herself.

When I was 11½ years old I got the measles and was quarantined in my bedroom. I spent the sequestered two weeks designing paper-doll clothes and listening to the radio, either to music or soap operas. It was a wonderful time. Paradoxically, even though I was ill and alone, I was completely engrossed in the newfound pleasure of designing and making clothes for my paper dolls. A later version of my creative relationship to designing clothes for my paper dolls was to buy clothes for my daughter; I delighted in dressing her up and making her look cute.

Although I do not design or make clothes any longer, I learned to knit when I was eight years old and continue to do so. My grandmother was a beautiful knitter and made me some wonderful outfits, some of which I still have, and one or two that I have given to my daughter. My grandmother and I knit squares with unique and sometimes quirky designs. We put them together to make a blanket.

Fashion has remained a passion of mine: it is a way of enhancing and/or presenting myself to the world as well as an art form that I enjoy looking at and fantasizing about. I was inspired to write this book to learn more about what fashion means to myself and to other people. This includes how fashion affects mood and a person's relationship to self, others, and society.

I was surprised and pleased to learn that the significance of fashion in the culture and in the individual is part of a serious academic curriculum. My daughter alerted me to the March 2016 bulletin of Reed College, which featured an article on fashion called "Patterns of Power," subtitled "How fashion reveals—and enforces—the hidden hierarchies of society." This affirmed my belief in the cultural and psychoanalytic significance of fashion in the psyche and the culture.

I want to express my deep appreciation to Arnold Richards, who was not only enthusiastic about my idea to write a book about fashion, but also encouraged my dear friend and his wife, Arlene Kramer Richards, to compose the book with me. Without Arlene as my partner, I could not have done this. I also would like to express my deepest gratitude to Arlene for encouraging me many years ago to learn how to use a computer as a way to facilitate the presentation and publication of my clinical papers and psychoanalytic studies of film. I am extremely grateful for the theoretical, technical, and editorial help that Dee Polyak gave me every step of the way in giving birth to this book. And to my daughter, Jennifer Katz, I am deeply grateful for her enthusiastic support of all my creative endeavors. I am moved by her adventurous pursuit of new paths in both her career and her personal life, and by her being who she is.

2. Arlene Kramer Richards

I have been interested in fashion for as long as I can remember. My family used to laugh about my getting up very early one morning, putting on my grandmother's shoes, taking her pocketbook and marching down the hall to "go shopping." I learned to read in kindergarten in order to see what was going on in a Sunday morning series in the New York *Daily News* called "Ladies of Fashion." I knew that my mother worked in the fashion trade as a hat designer and maker, and that she supported us by her work.

My first vocational interest was in fashion, but when that did not work out, I became a schoolteacher, a psychologist and finally a psychoanalyst. For the years of my education and analytic training, I thought as little about fashion as I could; I kept the shopping down to the Sears catalogue and made many of my own and my children's clothes.

Having been redirected in my own career to become a psychoanalyst, I could only indulge in my interest in fashion as a knitter and mainly as a consumer of fashion. The intersection between psychoanalytic thinking and fashion led me to write two papers on shopping and to think about the role of fashion and shopping in the lives of my patients, colleagues and friends. My two daughters taught me a lot about fashion and about shopping.

A vivid demonstration of how fashion can convey meaning in therapy happened early in my practice. A high school student who was causing trouble in class was referred to me by the school psychologist. He arrived at my office on roller skates and in tight running shorts, a long sleeved T-shirt, a yarmulke, and long, curly sidelicks. The doorman rang me up to ask if he really was my patient. I said yes with some trepidation. When I saw

6

him at the door to my office, I had a pretty good sense that this young man was in conflict. Was he religious? Or an athlete? Could he hold it together to be both? It turned out that he had one parent who was religious and one who was not. As he saw it, he had to live by pleasing both of them, but he could not make that work. He had to choose, but he could not. I worked with him for several months, and then he went off to a secular college. A year later he came to see me to let me know that he was doing well. He had gotten a franchise to sell a line of high end Italian athletic clothing in the United States. He was staying in college while running his business and was proud that he was paying his own college and living costs. No longer dependent on his parents, he was dressed in an athletic outfit that was appropriate for someone his age. He had decided to keep his yarmulke and his religion. Even my doorman was approving.

Later I read an article (Friedman 2016) about first ladies' choosing fashion for political reasons. By wearing the clothes designed by Canadians, Mrs. Trudeau, the wife of Canada's Prime Minister, showed the onlookers that Canada is "a melting pot of nationalities, ideas and aesthetics, which could be a coincidence but probably is not. When it comes to fashion and politics, clothes are never just clothes. They are a strategic tool." (P.13)

So when my colleague and friend Anita Katz asked me to work on a book about fashion and psychoanalysis, I demurred at first, but then welcomed the opportunity. I thank her for the idea and the persistence with which she has carried it out. Thanks to Tamar and Lawrence Schwartz for their unflappable cheerfulness in the face of the demands of authors and editors. And most of all, thanks to Arnold Richards, my husband, partner, and colleague. So here it is.

II

Fashion Journeys on the Couch and Off

1. Ladies of Fashion: Pleasure, Perversion or Paraphilia

ARLENE KRAMER RICHARDS

Full nakedness! All joys are due to thee;
As souls unbodied, bodies unclothed must be
To taste whole joys. Gems which you women use
Are like Atalanta's ball cast in men's views;
That when a fool's eye lighteth on a gem,
His earthly soul might court that, not them.
Like pictures, or like books' gay coverings made
For laymen, are all women thus arrayed.
Themselves are mystic books which only we
(Whom their imputed grace will dignify)
Must see revealed. Then, since that I may know,
As liberally as to a midwife show
Thyself: cast all, yea, this white linen hence;
There is no penance due to innocence.
To teach thee, I am naked first; why then,
What needst thou have more covering than a man?

(From: John Donne "To his Mistress Going to Bed." In *The Love Poems of Robert Herrick and John Donne*. New York: Barnes & Noble, 1994, p. 246.)

Why are dress, fashion and shopping for clothing so important to women? Freud (Rose, 1988) stated that:

All women … are clothes fetishists … It is a question, again, of the repression of the same drive, this time, however, in the passive form of allowing oneself to be seen, which is repressed by clothes, and on account of which, clothes are raised to a fetish. Only now can we understand why even the most intelligent women behave defenselessly against the demands of fashion. For them, clothes take the place of parts of the body, and to wear the same clothes means only to be able to show what the others can show, means only that one can find in her everything that one can expect from women (p. 156).

At that time, Freud thought that clothes were overvalued because they covered ("repressed") the naked body that women wished to display in what he then thought of as a passive kind of perverse pleasure. But he went on to say that clothes are prostheses for parts of the body. Did he mean that they were substitutes for the penis? He said that he meant that clothes give the message that the wearer possesses all that can be expected of a woman. This is a display of all of the erotic parts of the feminine body. This view, unlike some of his later ideas, seems to refer to a woman's wish to possess an erotic body that is the essence of female allure and function.

For a woman, the act of dressing and display are not passive pursuits. They are activities with many steps and many pleasures. The female body is displayed as part of courtship; can be flaunted aggressively to frighten and humiliate men; and can be the center of a woman's consolidated sense of self. In this regard, Freud's comment that not even the most intelligent woman is free of the dictates of fashion suggests that the motivation for that interest is not frivolous, but has psychological import.

Clothing has been of interest to psychoanalysts as an expression of feelings and thoughts of which the patient is not necessarily aware. Clinical case reports often mention that the patient began treatment dressed sloppily or inappropriately and came to look better-groomed and more appropriately dressed as treatment progressed. Schwaber (1977), for example, has used grooming as a measure of her patient's self-regard and therefore as a measure of his mental health. Similarly, Bergmann (1985) used femininity of dress and adornment as an indicator of her patient's ease with her gender identity and therefore of her mental health. Bergler (1953), writing in the heyday of conformity, cited many cases of what he believed to be improper or unfashionable dress as evidence of the presence of neurosis.

Bergler also took issue with Flugel's (1930) idea that female clothing was used for modesty. While Flugel believed that there is an essential tension between decoration and modesty in dress, Bergler thought that feminine clothing was always used to draw attention to female sexuality. Even when apparently modest, it enhances attractiveness by allaying men's fears of the unclothed female genitals. Flugel pointed out that clothing was used to enhance the body by enlarging salient features of it. The skirt, he noted, would make the female body appear wider and therefore more powerful, especially when it was extended by crinolines, hoops, or bustles. Flugel also showed that by enlarging a body part somewhat, but not too much, a maximally enhancing effect was achieved.

Protective functions of clothes are noted by Flugel in that a mother will always suggest to her child that he or she should wear more, but rarely less, clothing. According to Flugel, strict differentiation between male and female dress has been essential for propping up the male heterosexual orientation. He hoped that in the future clothing would be eliminated altogether.

Hollander (1994) builds on Flugel's ideas. She believes that the trouser suit as worn by western men since the eighteenth century contrasts with the skirt by emphasizing the possibility of activity rather than the capacity for reproduction epitomized by the skirt. In my view, this line of reasoning can lead to the conclusion that by wearing trousers, women signal an intent to be active participants in the work of their society. They then repudiate the exclusively reproductive role signaled by the wide skirt. The clothing presents not only the contours of the body, but also functions for which the wearer intends it to be used.

Clothing has been of importance to women not only in the wearing, but also as the object of quest in shopping. Winestine (1985) described a woman with a shopping fetish that she traced to a childhood seduction. For Winestine's patient, the seduction had resulted in a feeling of helplessness that she attempted to overcome by experiencing power when she shopped in fancy stores and imagined herself the wife of a powerful rich man. Because the patient could not afford the clothes, she enjoyed using credit cards that she then would not pay for, thus cheating the bankers while blaming them because they kept extending credit to her.

Many reasons on many levels of discourse have been adduced to account for the apparently gender specific female interest in clothes. There is the economic view which cites consumerism and the need for someone to consume the products which will keep business going. Advertising to make women believe that they need clothes certainly is part of it, but this does not explain why women are targeted to be the consumers in the first place. Veblen (1899) pointed out that men use women to display their economic success by wearing expensive jewelry and clothing. But this socio-economic explanation does not address the issue of why women are willing and eager to comply, nor why in other times and places, men have worn the fruits of their economic success themselves, as many do today.

Anthropologists and social critics (Simmel, 1904; Bell 1976; Lurie 1981; Dalby, 1993) have studied the cultural meanings of dress and come up with important conclusions about which rules and what status particular kinds of clothing communicate. Dalby has shown that in Japan kimono styles and patterns not only distinguish men from women, but also women of reproductive age from those no longer capable of reproduction. She has also shown that clothing can be exquisitely attuned to seasons, expressing a convention of season which may not correspond to weather. In such uses of clothing the wearer conveys information about her aesthetic sensibility and awareness of social convention without uttering a word.

Why do women need new and differently styled clothes? What purpose does women's clothing serve that makes the garment industry the largest in the world, larger even than the "defense" establishment worldwide? Bell states: "Nor is it easy to know what effect fine clothes have upon a woman when they are worn by a man, or whether women's clothes have an erotic effect upon those who wear them or upon other women" (1967 p. 48). Do women use clothing as a fetish (Apter, 1991; Gamman & Makinen 1995)? When do we consider clothing a source of pleasure, what makes it a fetish, and as a fetish, should it be thought of as a paraphilia or a perversion?

When clothes are specifically intended for sexual pleasure, they can be fetishes (Steele, 1996). But women's fetishes do not necessarily represent the same fantasies as fetishes men may use. Though both sexes may use black, metals, rubber, leather or other special clothing, the male use of the fetish as a guarantor of the integrity of the penis may not be echoed in the female use of the same objects. De Lauretis (1994) cites Freud's remark that half of all women are clothes fetishists and Apter's (1991) description of women's interest in clothes as a fetish. While Apter believes that this fetish stands for all the losses a female must necessarily endure, De Lauretis believes that the fetish clothing stands for the erotic female body as a whole. According to De Lauretis, the image of her own female body as erotic becomes problematic for the oedipal girl when the mother refuses to leave the father's bed for the little girl's.

This paper considers some psychoanalytic evidence regarding the role that interest in fashion plays in female psychology. It briefly outlines fashion as a way of conceiving the erotic female body: as a covering for the intimacy of the body and as a metaphor for the interior portion of the female genitalia. It also describes shopping for clothing as an activity particularly related to the female interest in clothing.

FASHION AS COVERING FOR THE EROTIC FEMALE BODY

Caper (1994) made dynamic use of one patient's attitude about clothing. His patient had a dream in which she was "looking at some silk blouses on a rack." In the dream, her sister told her that cheaper blouses were just as good since they didn't show because they were worn under jackets and the good ones were almost as expensive as the suit itself. The patient had complained the previous day about a suit she had been given by her mother. In his comment that she would prefer a sexier one, the analyst had hit upon something that changed the patient's view of herself. It countered the patient's unconscious fantasy that he had been trying to desexualize her. By allowing her to want what she believed others did not want for her, the interpretation also helped her to feel entitled to have her own ideas about other aspects of her life. Clothing was the relevant metaphor for that particular patient. For her, clothing was clearly connected with the female genital issues of sexiness, desirability and assertion of the positive value of female sexuality.

The use of clothing to heighten female experience of the body as erotic is celebrated in advertising and fashion magazines devoted to women's concerns about being sexually attractive.

While Donne's teasing poem expresses a man's cheerful impatience with his lover's coyness in covering herself when he wants her nude for lovemaking, the poem also tells of his honest lack of understanding of why she should cover herself any more that a man would. Why is it that we women cover ourselves?

One answer comes from a little girl who heard a song for children intended to teach them about sexual difference. The song says that "Boys are fancy on the outside; girls are fancy on the inside". The little girl was indignant. "No," she said, "That's not true. When I get dressed up, I'm fancy all over." To the male listener, this may sound like compensation for, or defensiveness about, penis envy. To this female listener, it sounds like an expression of whole- body narcissism and pleasure. From the little girl's point of view, her whole body is a source of pleasure and an expression of beauty. By adorning herself, she is expressing her satisfaction with her body, calling attention to it and renewing it by calling attention to different aspects of it. Her erotic pleasure culminates in a shudder of the entire body.

It is only from the male point of view that the penis is paramount. The male emphasis on the penis seems to her reductionistic. Who cares that much about a body part she can only see and not feel? The boy's experience of his penis as the source of erotic pleasure makes him treasure it and pity the girl or fantasize that a girl must be consumed with envy of it. From my point of view, and that of the little girl, this is not such an issue. A woman in analysis feels misunderstood when she is told that her basic motivation is penis envy because that is not her experience; this interpretation is a male fantasy of what his experience would be if he were deprived of his penis.

For women the female body is the erotic object (De Lauretis, 1994). A grown woman experiences male envy and fear of her vulva as well as devaluation of her feminine fullness. Clothing serves as a barrier, allowing her to remove a bit at a time, testing whether the lover will be further attracted or repelled by her femaleness. Thus the removal of the clothing in stages is an important part of courtship.

THE EROTIC EXCHANGE

A woman in analysis described her pleasure in exchanging clothes with friends. She was delighted that her old clothes were new to her friends and theirs were new to her. They all put the things they no longer wanted in a pile and then each tried on the things that she liked. The fun of admiring each other in the new outfits they assembled was the part of their experience she liked best. Other women have described shopping with a friend or a group of friends as a social activity in which they most enjoyed being told what was becoming to them. Giving this kind of judgment was sometimes seen as depleting, sometimes as affirming, but getting it was always pleasurable. The difference between sharing clothes and shopping for them in stores was important. Sharing avoided the aggressive power displays which are part of deciding whether to use one's financial resources to buy the clothing.

When financial resources are not available, not sufficient or conflictual, shoplifting can become the source of the feeling of power. As in the case cited by Winestine, the shopper may feel power in cheating the shopkeeper just as she feels belittled by not being able to buy limitless qualities of what is for sale. As a colleague pointed out to me (Mandlin, 1995) women who shoplift may feel entitled to do so to make up for the emotional supplies of which they believe themselves to have been unfairly deprived. Such women may feel that they deserve protection, attention and affection that they never got and may restore some sense of fairness by taking. Such women, like the shoplifter cited by Winestine, attempt to provoke authorities into setting limits in the hope of obtaining the protection from their own impulses that they have not experienced sufficiently.

EROTIC SHOPPING

The following case example illustrates several of these aspects of how clothing and shopping for it function as salient to female psychology:

The patient, Patty, a tall, long-limbed blonde 30-year-old saleswoman in a high-fashion optometrist's shop, had been in analysis for several years. One of her most puzzling symptoms was her need to "improve" her looks constantly. She spent hours each morning on makeup, on selecting clothing and on doing her hair. While she was beautiful, she was convinced that she was "a dog." Having handsome boyfriends made her frantic because she believed that they were always looking for a woman more beautiful than she was. Clothing and make-up were disguises for her sense of herself as ugly and worthless.

She had been very agitated in the past week. After a disastrous love affair with what she called "a poor, dirty, low-class man," she had an abortion. She recalled an abortion she had concealed from her mother when she was 16 years old. When her mother found out, she slapped Patty and called her a whore. Patty was horrified, became docile, and stopped going to night-clubs. She followed her mother's advice on most things, spent much of her leisure time with her mother or with both parents, and called her mother every day, sometimes several times in the course of a single day.

Shopping was their shared passion. Patty described these outings as teasing glimpses of a world of luxury. The shopping trips would consist of the mother's asking Patty whether she "needed" something to wear. Patty would think of something. They would go to a boutique, Mother would try on clothes, Patty would try on clothes, and each would criticize the way the other looked in her outfits. Patty complained that her mother would insist on buying only the highest-priced designer clothing while restricting Patty to lower-priced items. A remark of her mother's that Patty found chilling and believed to be true was: "Well, you will never find a man who can give you as much as I can." Unfortunately,

Patty believed her. This statement touched on her own fantasy of being her mother's beloved. The fantasy had been nourished by her belief, echoed by her mother's statements, that Mother had held her marriage together for her daughter's sake, that she loved her daughter as much as she hated her husband and that her husband, Patty's father, was a detestable man who contributed nothing to the family. This belief was so strong that Patty had difficulty remembering that it was her father who earned all the money in the family. Patty knew and did not know this alternatingly over the seven years of her treatment.

Her mother doled out money to her grudgingly. She treated Patty as her husband treated her and with a similar result. Patty took money from her mother's purse or from her bank account whenever she was desperate for cash or wanted luxury items she could not afford on her own allowance (when she was not working) or earnings (when she had them). Money became the focal point of her guilt and her anxiety.

Several months before the abortion, Patty had moved her lover into her apartment. Her mother still paid the rent. With regard to her choice of men, she said that she was now aware that all the lower-class, immigrant, and married men she chose were chosen in the image of her father. I reminded her of a family living in her parents' neighborhood who had allowed their unmarried daughter to bring her baby to live with them. She had suspected that the baby was actually the result of the girl's incest with her father. By having the abortion, she had renounced having an incestuous baby. After all of this work, I was feeling quite pleased with her strides towards mature self-awareness. She then came in for her next session with a piece of startling news. Although she had been able to control her shopping lately, she had just bought clothes equal in price to a month's salary for her. She'd had so little time, she had not even tried anything on. In this context, we talked about the experience of shopping.

Her conflict over disapproval of her father was complicated by her sense that without her father she was destined to remain her mother's ""girl' forever. This reactivated her need to shop. She even felt an impulse to buy another one of a particular item her mother had bought for her years before. She was pleased that she had not been buying illicitly this time, but was also aware that she had been able to stop herself from buying something she already had. This was something she had never been able to do before.

The shopping spree that had at first seemed to me to be a regression or a negative therapeutic reaction now took on new meaning as an attempt to make some kind of restitution and to see herself as belonging to what she saw as my world. This shopping spree defended her from sadness and potential depression at her abortion. It also served to placate her self-condemnation about the fantasy incest and the disloyalty to her mother, as well as guilt about ending the potential life of her fetus. It also gave her a feeling of power, overcoming her self-induced helplessness. Because she had chosen to get pregnant with a man who could not support a child, and because she had not developed a career for herself which would enable her to support one, she had virtually ensured that she would feel helpless and have to rely on her mother's support. Thus, either having a baby or not having one would leave her feeling helpless. Only the shopping spree actually brought all of these issues to the fore. Her shopping was a clue to the dynamics of her abortion.

Similarly, Patty's attitude towards her clothing reflected her attitude towards her body. Early in the treatment, she would buy many cheap pieces of clothing, be interested in them only for a few days, and then want more. She frequently borrowed her mother's clothes and those of her friends. She seemed to be searching for another body. She was, I now think in retrospect, expressing with her clothes a restless disappointment with her own body and a wish to change her body back and forth, now thinner and more childish, now fuller and more womanly. Her more recent behavior has expressed her stage in the menstrual cycle, from times when she thinks of herself and dresses as what she thinks of as "fat" and uninterestingly matronly to times when she feels and presents herself as lean and interesting. Her attempt early in the analysis to be very thin was fought against vigorously by her mother. Part of the mother-daughter drama was the wardrobe changes to match her changing bodily shape. As she lost and gained weight, she complained that nothing fit her. She used this complaint to justify buying new clothes constantly. In this, she identified with her mother. But while her mother would change wardrobes only once a season, Patty changed constantly. In order to do this, she spent much of her time on weekends shopping. Shopping became her hobby, her passion, and her constant companion.

She was ashamed of the erotic aspect of buying clothing even as she punished herself for the erotic pleasure she took in it by depriving herself of the other things she could have bought with that money. As she understood her shopping, it was "a release."

She expressed it in highly charged language, more fully realized than any of her sexual encounters with men. "I choose the store. I like the ones where they let you sit there and they show you the stuff. I can hardly afford those. They are too expensive. But I get someone to help me in the other kind. I like them to want me to want it. I like to leave them with it. I like it best when it is just a little too expensive and I can't get it."

Earlier in her treatment she would go on shopping trips with both parents. A sadomasochistic pattern extending back to her childhood was repeated on these trips. As she described it: "When it's my birthday or something, they won't get me a present. But my Mom says I can have a new thing, whatever it is I want. So I go to a store and I find something. Then I go call my Mom and ask her. She won't let me have it. But she says: 'Okay. We'll go for a walk on Saturday.' My Dad comes on these trips with me sometimes. I hate it when she says: 'Yes' and he says: 'No.' I hate when they both do it. She says 'Yes'; he says 'No.' He can't stand it, but he's the one who says he wants to get me a present. They make me beg for it."

For this woman, the erotic interaction around buying clothes was part of a sadomasochistic character disorder of the sort Arlow (1971) described as a perverse character. In the earlier stages, it had been more in her character. In the analysis, it became dystonic and she became more aware of how it replaced all other forms of excitement and pleasure for her. She mourned giving it up even as she understood it as precluding pleasure in her erotic experiences with lovers.

FASHION SEASONS

Mary, a very successful career woman patient reports: "I went to the doctor yesterday. He told me I had started menopause. Not what I wanted to hear. Why does this have to happen now? Anyway, my first thought was to go and spend a thousand dollars on clothes. That kind of a spree would cheer me up. You don't have to worry. I won't actually do it. I would have four years ago. But now I just feel the impulse." This woman is always afraid of losing her mother and father, both of whom have had life-threatening chronic illnesses since their daughter was 8 years old. Now in her fifties, she is still living in dread of her parents' dying, even though they are now in their eighties and have seen her through the decades of her childhood, adolescence and young adulthood. She stands at the brink of a transition into the last decades of her own life, still as frightened of their death and of her own as she was when a little girl. Knowing that she is no longer dependent on them is something that she is only attaining now.

Both she and her parents enjoyed an anniversary card she sent them recently, showing a little girl saying "This card is a miracle. I paid for it with my own money." She has needed loans from them all her life. Often these loans went to pay for clothes she bought on her sprees. Although she has earned a lot of money in her life and complains that her closets are crammed with beautiful clothes she never wears, she has shopped for comfort at every hint that she could be getting more successful, more responsible, or more secure in her relationships. I connected shopping for clothing with a fantasy she had talked of years earlier of having a rich and powerful father who would always be there to protect her. Thus, she was a dependent little girl in order to protect the fantasy from the encroachments of the passage of time.

She denied the passage of time by focusing on her spring wardrobe, her need for new clothes for summer, and her feeling of anticipation for each new season. She kept herself very busy emptying her closets of the clothes of the last season, cleaning and relining her drawers, ironing, shortening, lengthening, taking in, and letting out. It was crucial to her to have the exact new item featured in the latest fashion magazine. When all of her concern with seasons was interpreted as a wish to avoid the passage of linear time, she railed at me. But she was able to cut back significantly on the amount of time she spent in preparing her seasonal wardrobe, a gain which allowed her to spend more time in productive work in her career.

REFUSAL AS AESTHETIC

Elinor had a passion for shopping which usually eventuated in her buying nothing. Her weekend hobby was shopping for clothing and jewelry, which she would return during the following week. She constantly yearned for clothes, felt satisfied when she was buying them and hated them when she "felt trapped" into keeping them because she had bought them. Old clothes, "antique" clothes, were more acceptable. She enjoyed knowing that the antique dealers she bought them from would not accept returns.

Months after this patient had experienced some relief from her continual need to shop, one of her uncles died. At the funeral, the uncle's daughter thanked her for coming. The patient felt terribly sad. She reflected that she did not think that the death of her relative would make much difference to her own life. She then realized that the death of her own father had made little difference to her cousin. Her mourning for this relative was minimal, but she began shopping in a way she called an addiction. The pattern was so severe that she would get to know the salespeople in stores and would feel embarrassed for causing them so much trouble with her constant demands on their time and energy, both to sell her things and to issue credits to her for returning them. Sometimes she would give the clothes away to relatives or friends rather than take them back to the store where she had bought them. Elinor wore the same winter coat for a decade while trying to find a substitute. She could not find anything that she felt comfortable in.

Her shopping pattern had been set when she was a little girl. She recalled being taken to a large city near her hometown to buy new clothes for each new season. She and her mother would choose many things, but she would return most of them. In her analysis it became clear what both she and Mother had been doing and undoing.

23

What needed to be undone was related to the early death of Elinor's mother's father. She was undoing what she feared, her own mother's early death. Her fear of the loss of her mother was concretely embodied in the buy-and-return cycle. It provided comforting proof that anything could be undone, nothing was final, nothing was irreversible, not even death.

When she had been in analysis for several years, she allowed herself more. Clothing now had to do with pleasure rather than seasonal fashion in the service of the denial of death. One day she came in and said: "I bought a coat. It cost several hundred dollars. It's soft and classic. My kind of thing. It is amazing that I did it. And I'm keeping it. You probably don't believe it, but it was between two coats and this was the one I had wanted for a long time. I didn't need it. There were these two coats when it came down to it. The saleswoman said that the other coat was stunning. It would be great. She said people will stop you on the street in that one. It's more different. Has more style. But I knew I wanted the other one. When I brought it home, my husband said it was elegant, just like me, but I think it's classic, simple."

A: Your husband finds it elegant because he thinks it's essentially you—the elegance of renunciation.
P: No. That's saying too much. I was worried. What if I leave it in a taxi and lose X number of hundred dollars?
A: X number?
P: Preciousness. I feel childish and humiliated—small. You would think of a shopping spree as spending $5,000 in a day. I think of hundreds.
A: You can't see yourself as having more than I do. The older person has to have more. Like with your mother having all the dresses in her closet and you borrowing.
P: I have my own taste. I don't care about labels. I'm not stupid enough to be interested in that. I don't care about that.

The next day she came in and said: I had this disturbing dream. *I was leaving my apartment, but there was something wrong with the lock. I could not lock the door. So I went back in and checked the apartment as I frequently do in real life. I looked under one bed, then I looked under another. Finally, I looked under the other bed. A hand and arm pulled me in. I woke myself up.*

"It has to do with the coat I bought yesterday. It has something about being single. Before Bobby moved in with me, I never worried about such things. Now when he goes on a business trip, I have to keep a light on at night. The thing is that I don't know how to understand it. Why should I feel vulnerable now? It has something to do with the voice I heard last Saturday. Both Bobby and I woke up and we both heard it, it wasn't just me. A woman was screaming. She was saying: ""Stop it. Stop." I thought she was getting killed. I remember in our last apartment there was a woman who would scream every Sunday morning. I'd be home alone while Bobby was at church. She'd moan and scream. I hated hearing it. I can't figure out what was so bad about it."

A: The dream and the fears are about being sexual. And how it is like being killed.
P: No. It is not like that. It is something else. Well, the thing is, it is something about being married.
A: Like being married makes you more vulnerable, but that seems not to make sense, after all a husband can protect you.

Later in that same session I suggested that she was afraid that I would pull her into my sphere from under the couch. The saleslady who wanted to sell her the wrong coat was like me in that I wanted to make her into someone she did not want to be.

She asserted that she believed I wanted her to be what I wanted, not what she wanted. For her, wearing clothes a woman would like was being attractive to a woman, something she fought against wanting.

The question of whether women dress for men or for other women may be answered differently for different women. For some women, competition is important, for others seduction is paramount, for still others the change of costume is a change of persona. For this patient, it was clearly related to the issue of object choice. It would seem almost obvious that this would be true for all women. To the extent that it is a sublimated expression of object choice, dress is part of culture. Yet no matter how far it is from overt sexual stimulation, dress is selection of that which touches the skin and therefore that which is closest to the body. Thus, it excites skin eroticism and lends itself to fetishistic use.

For another patient, Lola, torn or defaced clothing had great erotic meaning. She reported this dream: *I am in a room with my mother. I am wearing torn and ripped jeans and embarrassing people. My mother wants me to change. I decided to leave so I started packing. I was sweeping up the floor and I found little lumps of shit. It could be dog shit or human shit. It didn't matter which it was, I needed to sweep it up anyway. I did it frantically.*

She recalled that she had actually had a similar conversation with her mother about a torn sweater she wore when she was visiting her parents' home and recalled that her mother had shamed her into changing it. She then recalled seeing one of her lesbian friends dressed as a 'drag king'. Saying that she thought her friend looked wonderful, the patient wondered whether she herself was aroused by the hyper-masculine style regardless of whether it was affected by a biological male or a biological female. She recalled going to a party with a woman friend who had just broken up with a man. The patient worried that her friend might compete with her for a lover. Then she said "My new motto is sex, I want to have some." For the rest of that session she talked about the themes of competition for lovers, sexually attractive clothes and cleaning. These different themes reminded me of a story she had recently told me about coming home from college to find that her parents had moved their old bed into her room. She was indignant that the mattress cover still had her father's semen stains on it. Her mother had said that she shouldn't get so upset, by her age she should be aware that her parents had sex. I reminded her of this story and said that her mother had seemed to her to be parading her father's sexual emissions as a trophy to show her daughter that the mother was the winner in the oedipal war. The semen stains had been represented in the dream by the shit and by the torn clothing. In the dream she was embarrassing her mother while in the life event her mother had embarrassed her. For this woman, the clothing was a metaphor for sexual excitement in the drag king anecdote, and a symbol of shame in the ripped jeans.

DISCUSSION

Elinor's shopping pattern was one of refusal. Lola refused in a different way, choosing ragged clothing as a refusal of everything her parents could give her. Lola's parents' way of being ascetic contrasted with Patty's pattern of binging by buying more than she could reasonably use. Mary's seasonal shopping and refurbishing was also like a bulimia in that she used an excess in the service of her refusal to accept the reality of her aging.

It would be possible to see Elinor's and Patty's shopping pattern as a bulimia in which the pleasures are of gorging and vomiting. Both women wanted to have more of mothering and of an erotic relationship with the mother than they were able to allow themselves. Both used clothing and shopping for clothing to express fantasies of loving and being loved by Mother. Because shopping for clothes is such a female occupation in our culture, girls experience shopping with Mother as sharing a closeness and acceptable erotic experience. This use of clothing as a female sharing is charmingly depicted by Beckerman (1995) in an elegy to her mother called *Love, Loss and What I Wore*. When there are fantasies about the mother-daughter relationship that cannot be expressed in words, they may be enacted in these "perverse" scenarios.

Why do women develop this symptom? Clothing has an importance for women which goes beyond the meaning it has for most men. As decoration for the body, it calls attention to the features and proportions considered sexually attractive. As seen in the first case, it can serve many functions. Shopping for clothing can be a celebration of the body, as when Patty and her mother displayed themselves to each other in different outfits.

It can defend against sadness and loss, as it did when Patty bought new clothes after her abortion. It can serve as a battleground for conflicting value systems as it did when Patty bought things her parents could afford and when she shopped in discount or "off the truck" bargain places. That kind of shopping expressed her condemnation of her own greed, when she consoled herself that she had spent less than the clothing was worth. It enabled her to indulge in the fantasy of having unlimited power when she bought without thinking of how she would pay for things.

She was able to use shopping as a strip-tease in the dressing rooms she would share with her mother. The erotic aspect of showing herself was further enhanced when her father came along and when salesladies were consulted for their opinions on how she looked in the things she tried on. It became problematic for her when it involved the teasing game of pleading with her parents for things that cost more than they wanted to spend. It became debilitating when she substituted it for genital pleasures. Her statement that "No man will be able to buy this for me" expressed her conflict. She could only allow herself to indulge in this form of erotic pleasure when she gave up men for Mother as Mother had for her.

Patty needed new clothes so often because she believed that her body was ugly. She was able to give up the very frequent shopping when she recognized that new clothes always seemed to her to offer hope of changing but did not ever really change the body beneath. Patty's analysis offers an illustration of the generalization that clothes that conceal the body beneath them also take on the body beneath them, so that patients who hate their own bodies will hate their clothes soon after they buy them.

When is shopping for clothing something worth thinking of as a paraphilia or perversion (Kaplan, 1991)? Perversion is a term reserved for behavior preferred to coitus, usually understood to have a large component of aggression in that it alienates the pervert from potential partners. Paraphilia is defined in the DSM 111 R (1987) as: "Arousal in response to sexual objects and situations that are not part of normal arousal-activity patterns and that in varying degrees may interfere with the capacity for reciprocal, affectionate sexual activity."

But this definition begs the question in that it does not describe what are "normal arousal-activity patterns." Is spanking normal? Is dressing up as a bunny normal? As a fireman? As a devil? Is a velvet glove normal? A whip? Is using one of these props normal? How about candlelight? Mirrors? Nipple rings? It seems that there is such a variety of possible means of arousal that no one could possibly categorize all of them as normal or abnormal.

In practice, I believe, clinicians think of a behavior as a paraphilia worth trying to remove when the patient sees it as a symptom. We call the same behaviors perversions when they entail social opprobrium. For the clinician this variety has serious consequences. When a patient says that she prefers shopping to having a boyfriend, is that to be construed as a perversion? Is it simply a paraphilia or preference? From these cases and many others in my practice, I think it is the driven quality, the need, the constant renewal of a sense of need when there is no rational need that requires the understanding of this as a perversion, or, to put it more usefully, a perverse symptom. The advantage of thinking of it as a symptom is that it becomes a cue for analysis rather than for condemnation. Thus, clothing used for pleasure is not a symptom, used as a paraphilia, it replaces sexual pleasure and is used as a perverse object that defies social convention as well as the human beings who would ordinarily be the objects of sexual desire. If a pair of black boots are worn for their sensual pleasure or to attract a lover, this is part of normal sexuality. If wearing the boots is more important than the other person, it is a paraphilia. If they are worn to harm or spite others and especially to deny their humanity, it is a perversion.

All of the women discussed in this paper used clothing for the "normal" purposes other people use it for. Clothing as costume is part of the embodiment or enactment of fantasy that keeps young children playing by the hour. For adults, fashion can be a fantasy of being a younger person or an older one, being a cowboy or an Arab, trying on in fantasy roles that will never be available in ordinary life. In this sense, dress is a clue to unconscious fantasy (Arlow, 1969) and a part of enactment. For Freud (1907) this kind of fantasy was the kernel of creativity and the center of psychic life. The reality created in such fantasy not only consoled the person, but also provided the basis for change and ongoing development.

As Freud put it in his early remark about all women being clothes fetishists (Rose, 1988), a woman needs clothes to display that she has the female attributes. Here Freud speaks in a modern way about the entire body, not as a metaphor for the penis, but as what is important to a woman. Because the erotic body is paramount to a woman (De Lauretis, 1994), the clothing which can alter, disguise, emphasize and even create body shape is valuable.

29

How does this analytic understanding match up with what has been done on this subject in other fields? Shakespeare took the economic view when he wrote: "Our purses shall be proud, our garments poor,/For 'tis the mind that makes the body rich." But Shakespeare undervalues the use of fashion. For the woman who wants to use clothing to express other values, the cost is not the point. By dressing, a woman can use her mind to alter her body with clothing and cosmetics in ways that allow her to express her mind through her bodily appearance.

While Veblen believed that clothing is mainly used to provide evidence of the earning power of the household, Bell (1967) discussed many ways clothing expresses values. Sumptuary laws show that dress can be used to display wealth. Rare or difficult-to-find materials and workmanship that need many hours of hand labor enhance the perceived value of the clothing. By dressing in archaic or avant-garde fashion, the wearer can make a statement about her place in society and her opinion on whether the good old days are preferable to the future. A woman can use clothing and grooming to display conspicuous leisure, as shown in long fingernails, time-consuming hairdos, frequent changes of clothing and clothing that takes a long time to put on and adjust, and by maintaining an attenuated body.

Artists have been paying attention to the role of fashion and clothing in the human experience. The visual arts have focused on clothing and fashion as expressions of feeling about the body in various ways. Zahm (1995) discusses the fashion of one designer who draws attention to the seasonal and timely aspects of fashion by refusing to change his clothing offerings every season. By recycling other people's designs from the past as well as his own past designs, he draws attention to the artificiality of having new clothes for each season and new clothes that are different from those worn in the corresponding season of past years. In addition, this designer takes the hidden construction elements of clothing and displays them. Thus, he undoes the clothing message that there are secrets contained in the body covering.

The idea of secrets in clothing was carried a step further by Leone & Macdonald (Meyer, 1994). These artists shredded and made into paper their entire shared wardrobe. The wardrobe itself is memorialized in a handmade book documenting the garments that went into the paper. By calling it "foolscap" the artists recycle their clothing, changing it from the choice of images imposed on them by the fashion industry to an entirely self-chosen image, created to express their own needs for paper rather than body coverings. Another take on clothing comes from the artist Annett Messager (Conklin, 1992). She used old dresses as relics, attaching pleas and prayers to them. She was pointing out the function of clothing to mark particular occasions or sequences of the life of the wearer, and the effects on the spectator who may want some of the same. This use of clothing remarks on clothing as body part and relates to the aura of the person who wears the clothing as it attaches to the clothing itself. It seems to me to be parallel to my patient's use of clothing to change her body, and particularly to her hatred of clothing that had already taken on her aura.

Clothes empty of wearers (Felshin, 1993) convey another aspect of the role of clothing in female identity. While they may memorialize particular wearers, empty clothes, especially if they have never been worn, have another function as well. The empty clothes allow the viewer to "try on" or "fit" herself into the clothes. By taking the dimensions of the clothing as ideal, she can measure herself against what is expected or considered desirable.

Artists have shown, in sum, that clothing lends itself to make-believe, to secrets and to emphasis. All of these aspects of clothing are akin to the accessories of paraphilia. Clothes are disguises, but they also reveal the feelings of the wearer.

Clothes lie, but they tell the truth of what the wearer wishes she was. Clothes protect, but they put the fantasies of the wearer right out where the observer can see them and draw his or her conclusions.

Philosophers have taken up the question of why women value dress. Barthes (1993) subjected fashion to a structural analysis similar to that used for linguistic structures. He analyzed the system of description of fashion and compared it with the structures of what was being described. Hanson (1993) alerts the reader to the concerns that philosophy has brought to the subject of dress. She asserts that dress has been devalued by philosophers for being superficial, concerned with change

rather than with the unchanging, unable to withstand or defy the vicissitudes of death, based on the human body rather than the soul and
passive rather than active in that it reduces the wearer to being the
object of the gaze of the artist rather than the active subject. All of this is
true despite Plato's equation of the beautiful with the good. Hanson
concludes that female interest in fashion could expand man's appreciation of embodiment, being in a body and adorning it for pleasure, this
could expand human consciousness and self-knowledge. This paper is
an attempt in that direction.

Rather than ignoring clothing, shopping for clothing and fashion interest as superficial and trivial, I suggest that we attempt to use our
patients' interest in clothing as an important avenue to understanding
their psychology. If clothing is intermediate between the body and the
world, it speaks of what the wearer wants to convey of her body. It tells
the observer something about the wearer's wishes, fears, and moral
judgments. It can express the power of the money spent on it and thus
the power of the wearer or her supporters, parents or spouse. It can
reflect much time and effort spent on selection and acquisition. It can be
costume for a part the wearer is playing in her own life drama. I believe
that seeing it in this way may enable us to see the compromise formation
in degrees of pathology ranging from pleasure through neurotic symptom to paraphilia to perversion.

I am grateful to Janice Lieberman, Lynne Rubin, and all of the members of the RAPS Study Group on Female Psychology of the Association
for Psychoanalytic Medicine for reading and generously contributing to
this paper.

REFERENCES

Apter, E. (1991). *Feminizing the Fetish: Psychoanalysis and Narrative
Obsession in Turn-of-the-Century France.* Ithaca: Cornell Univ. Press.
Arlow, J. (1969). Fantasy, memory and reality testing. *Psychoanal. Q.*, 38:
28-51.
Arlow, J. (1971). Character perversion. In *Currents in Psychoanalysis*, ed.
I. Marcus. New. York: Int. Univ. Press, pp. 317-336.

Barthes, R. (1990). *The Fashion System.* Berkeley: Univ. California Press.

Beckerman, I. (1995). *Love, Loss, and What I Wore.* Chapel Hill: Algonquin.

Bell, Q. (1967). *On Human Finery.* New York: Schocken.

Bergler, E. (1953). *Fashion and the Unconscious.* New York: Brunner.

Bergmann, M. V. (1985). The effect of role reversal on delayed marriage and maternity. *Psychoanal. Study Child,* 40: 197-219.

Caper, R. (1994). What is a clinical fact? *Int. J. Psychoanal..,* 75:903-913.

Conklin, J. (1992). *Annette Messager.* (Exhibition pamphlet) Ames, Iowa.

Dalby, L. (1993). *Kimono.* New Haven: Yale Univ. Press.

Davis, F. (1992). *Fashion, Culture and Identity.* Chicago: Univ. Chicago Press.

DeLauretis, T. (1994). *The Practice of Love: Lesbian Sexuality and Perverse Desire.* Bloomington, IN: Indiana Univ. Press.

Felshin, N. (1993). *Empty Dress: Clothing as Surrogate in Recent Art.* New York: Independent Curators.

Flugel, J. (1930). *The Psychology of Clothes.* London: Hogarth Press.

Freud, S. (1908). Creative writers and daydreaming. *S.E.* 9.

Freud, S. (1927). Fetishism. *S.E.* 21.

Gamman, L. & Makinen, M. (1994). *Female Fetishism.* New York: New York Univ. Press.

Hanson, K. (1993). Dressing down dressing up. In *Aesthetics in Feminist Perspective,* ed. H. Hein & Korsmeyer. Bloomington, Ind: Indiana Univ. Press.

Hollander, A. (1994). *Sex and Suits.* New York: Knopf.

Kaplan, L. (1991). Women masquerading as women. In *Perversions and Near Perversions in Clinical Practice,* ed G. Fogel & W. Meyers. New Haven: Yale Univ. Press.

Lurie, A. (1981). *The Language of Clothes.* New York: Random House.

Mandlin, H. (1995). Private communication.

Meyer, R. (1994). Leone & Macdonald: *Double Foolscap.* New York: Whitney Museum.

Rose, L. (1988). Freud and fetishism: previously unpublished Minutes of the Vienna Psychoanalytic Society. *Psychoanal. Q.,* 57: 147-160.

Schwaber, E. A. (1977). Understanding unfolding narcissistic transference. *Int. J. Psychoanal..*, 4: 493-502.

Simmel, G. (1904). Fashion. *Int. Q.*, 10.

Steele, V. (1996). *Fetish*. New York: Oxford Univ. Press.

Winestine, M. (1985). Compulsive shopping as a derivative of a childhood seduction. *Psychoanal. Q.*, 54: 70-73.

Veblen, T. (1899). *The Theory of the Leisure Class*. New York: Macmillan.

Zahm, O. (1995). *Before and After Fashion*. Artforum. March 1995.

2. *Intimations of youth and unlimited possibilities*

ANITA WEINREB KATZ

The fashion choices throughout history have been infinitely varied. They show who we are, how we are, and perhaps who and how we want to be. According to Rebecca Arnold, "fashion displays the premise and the threat of the future tempting the consumer with new identities that shift with the seasons" (2001,xiv). Following Arnold, it is clear that fashion allows us to create ourselves; the fashion industry structures our creativity in both limiting and expansive ways.

In line with Arnold's statement that fashion allows us to create ourselves, Richards asserts, "Clothes lie, but they tell the truth of what the wearer wishes she was. Clothes protect but they put the fantasies of the wearer right out where the observer can see them and draw his or her conclusions" (p,190, 1996). I would add that clothes stimulate in the observer his or her own fantasies, which may evoke pleasure or pain in the wearer.

In this chapter, I explore how the clothes we wear and buy may be connected with a desire for the illusion of unlimited possibilities that some of us believed we had when we were children growing up. The magic that fashion creates for the adult person is a version of the powerful magical thinking characteristic of the two-year-old (Fraiberg 1996, 120-121).

Fraiberg explains that for two year olds the world is viewed with primitive mental faculties and is still in large part disordered and incoherent; it is a world in which the child explains what he encounters by

35

means of magical thought. The two-year-old thinks she can't fly to Europe with her parents because she does not know how to fly. Fraiberg explains, "Mercifully the two-year-old, who is a creature of strong desires and urgent demands, is also developing in another direction. He is more and more willing to accept substitutes for his unattainable wishes... If he can't have a horse he can be a horse with a rope tied around his middle."

For adults, there remains a need for illusion. Clothes can certainly contribute to fulfilling this need. And in some ways fashion allows the adult wearer to have pretend wings; the illusion of flying when wings are put on the sleeves of an outfit (Illustration #1). Clothes reinforce the illusion of unlimited possibilities for the wearer (Fraiberg, p.134). The baby doll dress allows the adult woman to enjoy the illusion of being a cute little girl (Illustration #2).

Illustration 2

Illustration 1

Fashion can create the illusion of who we want to be and how we want to be seen. Similarly, a good friend or therapist can facilitate a person to experience the pleasures of his or her illusions. In the Australian movie, *Proof*, Andy encourages his blind friend, Martin to drive a car. Martin says to Andy, "I can't drive, I'm blind." Andy responds with, "It doesn't matter, it's dark outside." Joining Andy's illusion, Martin gets behind the wheel and becomes the driver. When Martin crashes, a policeman asks, "How can you drive? You're blind." Martin answers whimsically, feeling very powerful, "I forgot." For a brief moment Andy allows Martin to forget about his limitations and become who he wants to be. In a similar way, fashion allows us to imagine becoming who we want to be.

One of my analysands recalled that in her childhood buying new clothes was a necessary event because each year she was growing and her body was developing in new ways.

I wondered whether there was any connection between shopping for clothes as an adult and a nostalgic wish to revisit childhood; childhood is a time in life when it seems as if there could be so many new and exciting possibilities. Perhaps for some people there is an unconscious hope that shopping can heal a deep feeling of sadness, longing, regret, and anger. The lingering trauma of often feeling not known or appreciated enough as a child may result later in buying clothes as an act of both self-expression and defiance. Buying expensive clothes may also be connected to an unconscious fantasy of getting the love and acceptance that is longed for as a child.

So when we are children, we grow out of our clothes—our bodies and brains change, and we have new experiences of ourselves and others. Some experiences we look forward to and some we fear. These experiences include new talents, knowledge, achievements, adventures, losses, disappointments, body changes and developments, new friends, and much more. When we are adults, we may buy new clothes in order to feel and look different. Through clothes, we enable ourselves to tap into hidden or unexplored aspects of ourselves with the expectation that a new presentation to the world will result in new, enhancing, and empowering experiences about ourselves. I want to emphasize that buying clothes is not just a means to impress others, but it is also for us.

Clothes can help us feel protected from either real or imagined danger, or they can be an invitation for connection and validation. The power of clothes is not always so benevolent; clothes can also invite attack and harm, either consciously or unconsciously.

THE POWER OF ILLUSION

The need for illusion persists throughout life. It exists in all creative endeavors, such as art, music, and theater. I am suggesting that fashion is another area of illusion.

Actors know the power of fashion to create an illusion. They can alter their identities and inhabit other identities, including a different gender. They do this through their actions, manner of speech, and also by the way they dress, both for themselves and for their audience. Clothes may evoke pleasure or fear, disgust or power, and clothes can function as a way of altering ones identity (Illustration #3, Star Wars).

Illustration 3: Star Wars

So not just for actors, but for everyone, clothing (and shopping for clothing) offers the potential for creating a new experience. This new experience includes becoming someone we want to be and creating a new way for others to see us. We are invited to buy and wear new clothing because it allows us to enjoy the illusion of returning to the unlimited possibilities that some of us believed we had in childhood and adolescence.

Halloween is a very important holiday. It gives us the opportunity to inhabit different personae and identities; it allows us to escape from our everyday life. Putting on a mask and costume may be thrilling for some of us. For one woman, her costume on Halloween transformed her into a powerful queen (Illustration 4). For

Illustration 4

one girl, when she was 15½ she transformed herself into an elegant fashionista (Illustration 5). A girl dressing up as a shoeshine boy on Halloween feels the thrill of stepping into a boy's shoes, or a boy as a princess can feel like a regal girl. What girl doesn't sometimes want to be fierce, or fashionable. (Illustration 6)

Illustration 5

Clearly, fashionable clothes can create illusions as well, such as transforming a girl into a boy, or a boy into a girl. What boy doesn't sometimes want to be a girl, and what girl doesn't sometimes want to be a boy?

In the book *Fashion in Film*, (2011) Diana Diamond writes about Sophia Coppola's film *Marie Antoinette*. She goes into detail about the various elaborate outfits and hairstyles in which the

Illustration 6

queen presents herself to her subjects (Illustration 7). However, when she is not in the public eye and is enjoying playing with her children, she wears a simple flowing gown and unembellished gracefully flowing hairstyle. When she goes to the guillotine, she wears her most elaborate queenly attire and walks proudly to the site of her execution. Her fashion and posture deny the abuses and suffering with which she tyrannized the populace. Her fashion disavows the indignity and

**Illustration 7:
Marie Antoinette**

tragedy of her imminent execution. Instead, Marie Antoinette is putting, front and center, her powerful queenly presence (Diamond, 203-232).

CLINICAL EXAMPLES

Shoes create empowering illusions for some of my male patients. Several brief examples of this will follow.

J is unhappy with his daily life and his unglamorous job. He is terrified of sexual intercourse and is aware that this is related to severe castration anxiety. He golfs almost every weekend. This pleasure, along with a very consuming fantasy life, may explain why he often wears golf shoes in his everyday work life. Perhaps the golf shoes represent a fantasied identity that allows him to feel manlier.

Another patient, a young very anxious professional man, has a huge collection of sneakers (he told me an estimate was at least 100 pairs), and he still buys more. He remembered that when he was eleven all of his close friends were going to sleep away camp for the first time, and he wanted to join them. His parents refused to let him go. He was very angry and cried, feeling trapped and humiliated. To console him they bought him a new pair of sneakers. So it seems that the sneakers began to signify to him that he was not a mama's boy who had to stay close to home, but that he was a strong masculine sporty guy who had unlimited possibilities. His anxiety about being a sissy, a mama's boy, frequently

40

returned, and he would then buy a new pair of sneakers, which allows him to revisit the illusion of the unlimited possibilities that he had hoped growing up would offer. The sneakers represented a fetish to defend against his castration anxiety.

Richards sees this kind of passionate wish and behavior as both aggressive and sexual, and may take on the quality that we tend to identify as "perverse" (1996, p118).

CLOTHES AS A NEW EXPERIENCE

The new experience can include being given special attention by the shop owner. This may fulfill a mothering longing that is less conflictual than the mothering that was received when growing up, especially when early mothering (and/or fathering) was less than good.

As adults, many people try to regain or achieve for the first time the freedom to be both separate and connected, to be both ruthless and loving, to re-experience (or experience for the first time) a wonderful feeling of looking forward to new experiences that getting older (growing up) promises to offer, but unfortunately too often disappoints. When in early childhood there is an unreliable connection to mother and/or father, the young child feels emotionally deprived and often confused. He or she may later overly rely on clothes to fill the void.

According to Bion, all of thinking involves emotional experiences that include a realization related to retrieving a lost experience (Bion 1962). Fashion choices, I think, are often based on the desire to recall and relive a past experience. Diana found a dress that looked a lot like the dress she enjoyed wearing when she was a teenager; it was a dress that made her feel pretty and grown up. When she was in her 50s she saw a dress in a store that very much reminded her of this dress, and she bought it. Paradoxically, this revisiting of the fashion she had worn in her teens now made her feel young and freer to fashion her life and future in new ways.

Schapperelli felt that clothing fashioned above the waist "is more spiritual, more intellectual,while the waist down is more basic, more grounded. It's about sex. It's about making love; it's about life" (Bolton 2012)

It is my impression that the desire for transformation is very power-ful in childhood, and for some people, this desire is powerful throughout life. Some people experience joy and power when trying on and buying a new piece of clothing. Flugel states, "For external reasons, the mother is associated with clothes from a very early age. It is she who usually dresses and undresses the child ... and it is the mother who tends to show her love by manifesting an anxiety lest her children be inade-quately clothed" (2007, 134).

Puck, the owner of Koos, a small couture store on Madison Ave, NYC, hints of the unlimited opportunities and promises of youth that her clothes offer. In some ways, Puck takes on a maternal role when she invites a person into her store to try on a jacket or a dress. She states, "It's [trying on new clothes] magical both in the joyous sense of the word, but also in the false sense of the word, believing you can have it all and that it will last; the clothing becomes the created link—the magical object to becoming transformed" (Personal Communication, December, 2015). The magic of unlimited opportunities happens in the store. Until you own the piece, it's full of desire and longing. Once it's paid for and brought home—even though still liked and enjoyed, the high is gone.

Although fashion is one significant way of returning to the unlimited possibilities of childhood, painting, for instance, is another avenue for exploring these possibilities. Hilda O'Connell, a fine artist in New York City has changed her style of painting in significant ways throughout her career. O'Connell moved from representational painting, to field painting, to a more complex form of non-representational painting. She also enjoys exhibiting her work. Her way of being seen and accessing the unlimited possibilities of childhood is through fashioning her paintings, and not through her clothing. In fact, she emphasizes that there is not one piece of her clothing that does not have some paint on it, including her shoes (Personal Communication, October, 2015).

My reflections on Puck and Hilda O'Connell relate to my clinical work with some patients. For example, Eve, in her psychoanalytic work with me, often spoke about shopping for clothes. She both enjoyed clothes and shopping, but also was concerned about spending too much time and money on clothes. Trying on clothes in shops and buying clothes was a magical adventure. When she looked at herself in the mirror in the store, she felt transformed. She told me this experience was like a new discovery of herself. A part of her that had been previously hidden suddenly emerged. But sadly the glow was often short-lived. Her experience of being and emerging in a new and powerful way was momentary. That was what drove her to buy more clothes:the search for unlimited possibilities.

During her baby's first year of life Eve experienced a striking change in her relationship to clothes. She was no longer interested in shopping. Although she still cared about looking nice, there was a shift in her passions and energy. She told me that when she went out, she liked wearing her navy blue jumpsuit. It was comfortable and attractive, and that was all that mattered. Buying clothes wasn't on her mind. Her creative energies and search for fulfillment were directed elsewhere. She was busy being a mother, a wife, and part time teacher. When she looked at her baby she felt transformed. At the time, and for several years afterwards, she did not engage in buying clothes. She did not need to have this experience for fulfillment.

FOREVER ALIVE THROUGH FASHION

In the film *Fabulous Fashionistas* (a documentary by Sue Bourne) women of all ages, including their sevent,ies.eighties, and nineties experience the illusion of unlimited possibilities through the fashion statements they create (Illustration 8). These women challenge the stereotype that older women are ugly and not vibrantly involved in life.

Bourne documents six women's relationship to clothes, and explores the quality of their lives, their interests, passions and activities. These women range in age from seventy to ninety-one. One way that they are challenging the stereotype of aging women is through their fabulous fashions. Fashion is an empowering form of self invention and self-esteem.

The fashion designer Prada also challenges conventional ideas about beauty. She states that if she has done anything it is to make ugly appealing: "In fact, most of my work is concerned with destroying or at least deconstructing conventional ideas of beauty....of the generic appeal of

Ill₁   D)

the beautiful glamorous clichés of beauty that I want to tear apart. An important aspect of my work is exploring what beauty means today" (Bolton 2012, p. 58).

The idea for one of Prada's (Bolton 2012) shows came from reflections on the state of poor people in places like Africa. The show remarked on the fact that while these people have nothing, they have their bodies. So, acts like dancing and dressing become extremely important even if dressing means simply wearing plastic and other recycled items. Dressing is a primitive instinct for everyone (p. 154), Through our ways of adorning our bodies we create opportunities to experience unlimited possibilities.

THE FABULOUS FASHIONISTAS

Each fabulous fashionista is youthful and lives as though she has unlimited possibilities. Each fashions a unique style consisting of clothes, hats, jewelry, hair and make-up. All are physically active, with ongoing careers and hobbies, and all are dedicated to exercise and living well. Many have suffered serious losses—spouse, children—but after mourning, they continue to live vital and creative lives. I will illustrate three of them.

Sue, now in her seventies, has reinvented herself as an "outside artist and curator." She wears some of her art and says that her distinctive look releases her from the tyranny of fashion. Does she mean that she has created her own fashion statement, her own unique look? She feels she does not submit to what the current fashion designers promote to the public. Paradoxically, she is both a rebel and a conformist. That is, she enjoys creating her own fashion statement, so in that sense she wants to be seen and to make a mark in the world. She draws a lot of attention to herself when she walks down the street. She enjoys the attention, and has remarked that this was good as long as she kept short of looking like a clown. Since she has bad feet, she only wears clogs, but even the clogs are colorful; red to match the frequently worn red-patterned garments that are her signature.

Bridget only shops in thrift shops and delights in finding clothing items for a few dollars and putting them together to create a unique outfit. She says, "when I was younger no one noticed how I dressed; now they do." I wonder if being noticed and appreciated now is more important to these women than when they were younger. Perhaps older women are more easily passed over, unseen, and unengaged with, unless they stand out in some significant way.

Gillian, who is 87 years old, but looks 30 years younger, says, "when I'm older I'll do other things. But so far, I haven't gotten old. I like life, I love my job. I was a bellydancer, a director, and choreographer." She likes to wear mini-skirts and doesn't care what people may think. When she was fifty-two she married a man twenty-seven years younger. They have been married for thirty-four years and still going strong. She says, "when I get up in the morning my whole body hurts. When I get on the floor and exercise forty minutes, I feel alive. As you get older, it's tough to get going. You must pit yourself against the aging process and not let it in."

For all these women, it is creating a look that matters. Sometimes they create new looks, and sometimes they return to old looks (such as Gillian's attachment to mini-skirts).

Clearly, all of these women are fully engaged in life and fashion. They admit the reality of the aches and pains in their bodies, which they work on diligently with exercise. These women live fully, not only through their passion for fashion, but also their passion for life. Being fashionable can then be enjoyable, fun, and transformative, but not a compulsive addiction. Throughout life fashion is an enlivening experience that offers intimations of childhood and unlimited possibilities.

REFERENCES:

Arnold, R. (2001). Fashion, Desire and Anxiety: Image and Morality in the 20th Century. New Brunswick, NJ: Rutgers University Press.

Bion, W. (1994). Learning from Experience. New York, NY: Rowman & Littlefield.

Bolton, A & Koda, H. (2012). Schiaparelli & Prada: Impossible Conversations. New York, NY: Metropolitan Museum of Art.

Bourne, Sue (2013). DVD. *Fabulous Fashionistas.* London: Wellpark Productions. Distributed by Zodiac Rights: www.wellparkproductions.com /filmography/fashion.html.

Diamond, D. (2011). Sofia Coppola's Marie Antoinette: costumes, girl power, and feminism. In

A. Munich (Ed.), Fashion in Film (203-231). Bloomington, IN: Indiana University Press.

Flugel, J. (2007). Protection. In M. Barnard (Ed.), Fashion Theory: A Reader (pp. 126-142). New York, NY: Routledge.

Fraiberg, S. (1996). The Magic Years: Understanding and Handling the Problems of Early Childhood. New York, NY: Fireside.

Freud, S. (1927). Fetishism (J. Strachey, Trans.). In The Complete Psychological Works of

Sigmund Freud (Vol. XXI, pp. 147-157). London: Hogarth and the Institute of Psychoanalysis.

Fromm, E. (1994). Escape from Freedom. New York, NY: Holt Paperbacks.

House, L. (Producer), & Moorhouse, J. (Director). (1991). Proof (Motion picture). Australia: Roadshow Entertainment.

Katz, A. (2000). Psychic reality and psychic change: A therapeutic journey. Psychoanalytic Review, 87, 81-100.

Mckee, G. (Producer), Bourne, S. (Producer & Director). (2013). Fabulous Fashionistas (Motion picture). England: Zodiak Rights.

Richards, A. (1996). Ladies of fashion: pleasure, perversion, or paraphilia. International Journal of Psychoanalysis, 77, 337.

Richards, A. (2000). Clothes and the couch. In A. L. Benson (Ed.), I Shop Therefore I Am: Compulsive Buying and the Search for the Self (pp. 311-339). New York, NY: Rowman & Littlefield Publishers.

Wilson, E. (2007). Explaining it away. In M. Barnard (Ed.), Fashion Theory: A Reader (pp. 15-25). New York, NY: Routledge.

3. The Space of Engagement: Fashion and Transformative Communication

VALERIE TATE ANGEL AND CAROLYN TATE ANGEL

I naturally noticed—it was obvious—that I was unusually badly dressed, and even had an eye for others who were well dressed, but for years on end my mind did not succeed in recognizing in my clothes the cause of my miserable appearance. Since even at this time, I was on the way to understanding myself, I was convinced that it was only on me that clothes assumed this appearance, first looking stiff as a board, then hanging in wrinkles...As a result I let my awful clothes affect even my posture, walked around with my back bowed, my shoulders drooping, my hands and arms at awkward angles.
Franz Kafka, 1883–1924 (Tobias 2000, p. 30)

Fashion and psychoanalysis both explore the ways we reveal and conceal ourselves. This chapter will not compare fashion and psychoanalysis; rather, we look at the space of engagement in which we become more attuned to, and aware of, self-experience. Both psychoanalysis and fashion reflect a transformative communication process. Transformative communication is a reflective process and involves a space of engagement with self and other or self and object. M. Merleau-Ponty in his book *Phenomenology of Perception* states that "space is existential: we might as well have said that existence is spatial that is, that through inner necessity it opens on to an 'outside,' so we can speak of a mental space and a world of meanings..."(Merleau-Ponty 1962/1998, p. 293) For Merleau-Ponty, "space is not the setting (real or imagined) in which things are arranged, but the means by which positioning things become possible"(Merleau-Ponty 1962/1998, p. 243). In the consulting room, the past is explored in the intersubjective experience of a profound two-person relationship. It is where we enter into the process of engagement. The unconscious motivations of our behavior become clearer, and maladaptive patterns of behavior change, allowing a new vision of the present. Analyst and patient forge experiential paths to new psychic structures and greater self-cohesion. This lived experience of the analytic process catalyzes a fresh vitality of the self.

In the dressing rooms of our homes or our favorite department stores, we also engage with ourselves intensely, and we try to create and realize our vision of how we want to be in the world. When our idealized self and the image we see in the mirror are in harmony, we feel integrated and good about ourselves. As Bachelard states, "when the image is new the world is new" (Bachelard 1969, p. 48). Ideally, getting dressed can offer us a moment of experience in which we discover the core dimensions of a cohesive self or perhaps an insecure self. The experience in a dressing-room and the analyst's consulting room can provide the self both with an entrance toward self-understanding and potential discovery.

Bachelard's concept of transsubjectivity reflects a unique experience in regard to perception. Bachelard reflects from a phenomenological viewpoint that there is the transsubjectivity of an image. For example, if we are next to an important building we all share the image but each of us sees the image differently. In this chapter, we will explore with the creative fashion director of the iconic fashion store, Barney's New York, the creative process of designing the "windows" which engages the observer to have a singular transsubjective experience.

In the consulting room, a space of engagement unfolds; the patient in the analytic process is more fully coming into being and the analyst begins to know who the patient is becoming (Ogden 2004, p. 864). Both the awareness of transsubjective and intersubjective experience enables one to further understand the self.

The recent book *Women in Clothes* (Heti, Julavits, and Shapton, 2014) queried more than 600 women about their attitudes and feelings about clothing. Fashion matters no matter who you are, said the *Financial Times* in the August 2014 issue (pp. 1-2.).

Attachment to specific styles or articles of clothing is one important aspect of fashion. In *The Language of Clothes*, Alison Lurie writes, "Long before we are near enough to talk with someone either on the street, or at a party, we announce our sex, age and social status through what we are wearing" (Lurie 1981, p. 3). One of the authors recalls that as a young girl, on a trip to Italy, she was given a blue dress on her birthday. This dress became a "favorite" article of clothing that was worn as often as possible. Interviews by social psychologists suggest that people feel that their favorite clothes influence how they express themselves and interact with others (Crane 2002, p.3). Even those of us for whom getting dressed is less about fashion than just about putting on clothes, which is something we all do, we experience an attachment or a feeling of comfort in regard to favorite articles of clothing. The memories about the blue dress, for instance, became a symbol of a cherished childhood experience.

There are also interpersonal aspects to our experience of fashion. When growing up, there was an excited anticipation for the latest issue of *Vogue* to arrive in the mail. Both of us would turn the pages in search of the clothing we could imagine for our wardrobe. Today, when a copy of *Vogue* arrives, there are fond memories of this bonding experience.

HISTORICAL OVERVIEW

For centuries, fashion has been a way of demonstrating class distinctions. It was long assumed that a person would dress as lavishly as he/she could afford, or as the law allowed. In *Dress, Adornment and the Social Order*, E.B. Hurlock explains, "Sumptuary laws specified the type of material and ornaments that could be used by different social classes" (Hurlock 1965, p. 295). There are more subtle issues of self-esteem here, too. The two duplicitous (but psychologically astute) tailors in Hans Christian Anderson's fairytale "The Emperor's New Clothes" capture the Emperor in dreams of rich and kingly fabrics, and tell his courtiers that it is only the unforgivably stupid who will fail to see the beauties of the new robes. The self-esteem of both king and people is therefore on the line as the tailors spin their cloth of lies.

In *The Interpretation of Dreams* Freud uses the same story to explore not the Emperor's clothing, but his lack of it—his exhibition of himself—as wish fulfillment (Freud 1900/1968). Both interpretations are relevant, but in this tale of deceit and gullibility, it takes the innocence of a child to perceive and state the obvious truth, that the Emperor is naked. Rereading this tale, derivatives in regard to feelings of inadequacy and low self esteem are apparent, yet the details about the fine threads and textures in the story are as important as noting the pleasure in thinking about clothing.

By the twentieth century, fashion had begun not only to represent status, but also to symbolize the pleasures of fashionable self-expression. In *Fashion and its Social Agendas*, Diane Crane (2002), analyzes some of the important and striking ways that clothing functions in the social construction of identity in the United States. However, social class is not the only concept that fashion expresses. In *Fashion, Culture and Identity* (1992), Fred Davis acknowledges that while what people wear and how they wear it can reveal their social status, fashion also communicates beliefs. Davis considers clothes a form of political expression: "our masculinity and femininity, our sexual scruples or lack thereof, our work and play, our politics, national identity, and religion" (Davis 1992, p. 70). However, this was not always reflective in fashion. This expansion of fashion's expressiveness began in America during the nineteen-forties. The forties as well as the sixties, as described in the following section, both were pivotal decades revealing the power of fashion's transformative communication as an expression of the self and a reflection of economic, social and political ideals.

Before the Second World War, Europe had dictated fashion. European couturiers decided on the styles that became a season's "look." The demands of the war meant government regulation of the use of materials, as well as the entry of women into the workforce. But the tumult in Europe meant that for the first time America could—had to—originate its own style. American designers such as Claire McCardell had a chance to offer an innovative vision of fashion—the new look for all classes called "American Sportswear." Once the war ended, the European designers were dictating fashion in America once again. The French couturier Christian Dior's "new look" appeared in 1947 and lasted through the fifties. It continues to influence designers today.

Nonetheless, the counter-culture revolution of the sixties consolidated the change that had begun in the forties. Women wanted freedom, going so far as to burn their bras in protest of confining, male-dictated clothing. The 1960s were characterized by political and social upheaval, and the conformity of the fifties was as unacceptable in fashion as it was elsewhere.

Youth was the pivotal issue in sixties fashion. Social and economic development gave young people a unique awareness of themselves as a unified group which could respond to political events and in this process create their own culture. *Vogue* magazine summed up this revolution as a "youthquake" (Steele 1997, p. 49). Social status no longer dictated fashion. Fashion came from the streets. In this new bottom-up model of fashion, styles emerged out of the lower socioeconomic classes and were later adopted by more upwardly mobile groups. In addition, age replaced social status as the determining force in fashion; now it was the teenagers and young adults who were creating styles. By the time the sixties were over, the variety in fashion styles paralleled the change in society and the relationship between different groups. The rise of an alternative fashion dynamic challenged the old regime and resulted in two different approaches to fashion.

TOWARDS FASHION TODAY

We will now introduce how a counter-culture accessory of the sixties has become relevant fifty years later. The Birkenstock sandal has now reached the mainstream. This German sandal company was one of the most popular and comfortable footwear of the counter-culture. Fashion is cyclical and recently the Birkenstock had another revival by the designer Phoebe Philo for Celine. She created a sandal that had a similar feel and on the Paris runways had mass appeal. These Celine sandals were sold out everywhere. What causes women to gravitate towards one style a season? It's an updated version of a classic. It shows social status since it costs ten times more to buy the Celine version then the original Birkenstock. Women can be comfortable and stylish in both sandals. Why buy the more expensive version? What is one trying to say? The contemporary artist, Barbara Kruger, coined the aphorism, "I, shop therefore I am." Kruger worked for a fashion magazine in her early career. In this environment, the clothes one wears make a statement. In regard to the sandal, the shoe can truly make a statement. Flats are a form of comfort, and by buying the Celine sandals one is stating that we embrace comfort while still being fashionable, since we are aware of the latest trends. A woman buys the more expensive Celine sandals to make people aware that she knows what is happening in culture and therefore possibly bolsters her self-esteem. To be considered fashionable is a distinction of social status. For instance, if a person wears a certain look, he/she appears knowledgeable regarding current cultural trends and creates a statement with his/her style.

The fashions of the sixties created a complete upheaval in the fashion industry. There was no longer one style. The counter-culture used fashion to represent and express political sentiments. It is in the sixties that fashion truly evolved into what we see in society today and in the information age of fast paced social media, a new upheaval is taking place.

New York, London, Paris, and Milan are no longer the only fashion capitals of the world. Asian and South American cities have a major influence too. The digitalized fashion world of Instagram and bloggers has globalized and recontextualized the fashion world. The subculture of "street style" has a voice, as does the art of the fashion photographer or blogger. Social media has added a dimension that transforms the immediacy of communication and its impact on fashion. Fashion designers are rethinking how to present their designs, and the traditional leisurely pace of the fashion world has changed. In the digital age, some fashion designers are moving to a see-now/buy-now collection model. No longer do these designers unveil clothes six months before they become available. Their collections are called September and February, to reflect when they can be bought in stores. "The show will become a big marketing and selling tool, not for department stores or glossy magazines, but for direct communication between the brand and the men and women who want to buy it," says Vanessa Friedman, the head fashion critic of the *New York Times* (Friedman 2016). One may wonder what this will mean for the fashion industry, which used to work on a schedule that was always six months ahead. The way a person becomes knowledgeable about fashion is through the particular immediacy of social media. Yet, there is also a built-in vulnerability meter which is triggered by the number of "likes or dislikes" from followers of social media. This new dimension can create another layer of potential anxiety from pressure to have followers on social media. When our self-image and our idealized image are more level, our self-esteem is less vulnerable. A person becomes compelled to "take a selfie" and awaits immediate response perhaps in regard to their appearance or style of dress. This is reflective of how people get to express themselves through fashion while awaiting approval from others.

How a Fashion Story Develops

Many people are not quite aware of how a fashion story develops and now this chapter will focus upon an "inside" view of producing a feature fashion story, which is known as the "well" of the magazine. We will explore how the fashion magazine produces images that tell a story to engage the reader and teach him/her about the fashion of the times.

My father used to ask Carolyn, who worked in fashion, about the stories she was writing for the magazine where she worked. She explained that as a fashion market editor, she did not write, but instead told the stories through clothing. A market editor's job is to select clothing from the latest fashions that have been seen on the runway, as well as in individual market appointments. Market appointments are places where editors go to look closely at clothing and see the pieces up close and in person. Each month, market editors would work with a team of people to choose the top trends for stories to communicate different ideas to readers. In the "well" of the magazine these trends would be articles of clothing on models that would be shot by a photographer for the magazine.

Part of visual culture is being able to synthesize and absorbs many different concepts and explore a theme that emerges to select a trend. What goes into this creative vision is a part of the communication process, which is as self-reflective as is the psychoanalytic process. Both are a process of engagement in which the self becomes as expressive as possible.

A fashion story in the "well "of a magazine is a group of pictures taken by a photographer that tells a story. It is a process that develops in a few different ways with a creative team of people. One way in which a fashion story develops is when stylists, who are the people that select the clothing to be put on the models, decide on a theme for a story. They have seen all of the clothing for the fashion season and decide whether or not it would be interesting to communicate a certain trend or theme to the reader. Clothing from different designers with a similar theme will be selected and shown to the photographer. Next there is collaboration between the photographer and stylist. They decide what model will be wearing the clothes. How will the hair and makeup influence the story? Will the story be on location or at a studio? All of these factors contribute to the final image. The process of creating a fashion story involves many people; there is the photographer, the creative director, the hairdresser, the makeup artist, the set designer, the stylist, and the model. The whole production has to come together through all of these people. The photographer Craig McDean says, "There are tons of conversations that you have to have before you come to the shoot. It's not just one person making all of the decisions. You also have to feel trends and you want to try to be ahead of the trends and you have to interpret them." There are times when photographers will find locations that they want to shoot at or inspiration from films that inspires them as well. The photographer will then give these inspirations to the stylist to continue the conversation. For example, if a photographer wants to do a film noir story, the stylist has to find clothes that work within that genre or theme. The next step in the process happens at the shoot as photographer Craig McDean says, "and then you bring who you are, your essence to it and what you love." All of these factors combine within a shoot. But with all the ideas captured on mood boards and inspirations boards, on the day of the shoot not everything works out as expected, and improvisation is called for. One may have two days to do a shoot and then one may have to find ways around that time frame. There needs to be innovation and flexibility, as preconceived ideas have to be open to change.

One such story for a fashion magazine was created during the Paris Collections, wherein fashion designers display their latest collections in runway shows to buyers and the media. These events influence trends for the current and upcoming seasons. At *W Magazine*, we (Carolyn Angel, senior market editor, and Alex White, fashion director) create a fashion story to show all the trends from the Paris collection. This story is our interpretation of what we have seen on the Paris runways. We call this the "collections" story. At the time, were attending the Fall 2007 fashion shows. After each show, we would go backstage and pick the best look from the collection. We would bring these looks to the studio for the photo shoot where the fashion story was being produced. The photographer for this particular story was Craig McDean. He had ideas about surrealism, and was full of references from Jean Cocteau, Man Ray and other surrealist filmmakers. "So it comes from all of those and then you have to interpret it in a modern way. You have all of the references out at the shoot and you start working on it and you create something throughout the day. My favorite picture from the series was Raquel Zimmerman sitting on a box that looked like dice because it was an idea we came up with on the day; there was no reference" (McDean, personal communication). Ultimately, the team starts with something and it evolves to something else. It's how we go from here to there. "It's not like in the movies where you start with a story board and it's all scripted out. Not like Guy Bourdin who draws the image before he works. It's really about the transformative process," says Craig McDean. The final result for this story, called Topsy Turvy, were different images that told a story to the reader. It was a visual reference of what was happening at the time of these Paris Collections. Ultimately a stylist hopes that what he or she has brought to the shoot is communicated so that someone who looks at the images will go and buy the clothes.

Illustration 13: Topsy-Turvy December 1, 2007 by W magazine
Photography by Craig McDean
Styled by Alex White

A FASHION CREATIVE DIRECTOR SPEAKS

In April 2015, we had the opportunity to interview Dennis Freedman, the fashion creative director of Barney's NYC, to discuss ideas in regard to transformative communication within fashion. One aspect of Dennis' position at Barneys is his responsibility for the famous "windows." Those are the windows (at Barneys NYC Madison Avenue store) where fashion icon Daphne Guinness once got dressed. We watched Guinness' 2011 performance art; she got ready to attend the Metropolitan Museum of Art Costume Institute event celebrating the Alexander McQueen retrospective "Savage Beauty" in an Alexander McQueen gown. As Daphne Guinness created herself for this event, Barneys window became an opening into the world of how we conceal and reveal. We, the public on the street, were participant-observers in this transformation, which was not a person getting dressed but the art of creating a magical and majestic woman going to a fantasy ball. Dennis states the transformation happens when there are very talented people who can transcend an idea, and when it's really great work, it's inspiring. We are all capable of engaging a part of ourselves for this transformation.

Other recent Barneys windows depicted the transformative communication process of fashion. Dennis discussed a set of Prada windows that Bridget Foley of *Women's Wear Daily* called "deep thought" windows because of the relationship between two figures—a man and a woman. Positioned in the window, the figures appear to be aware of each other, but there is no contact between them. In these windows, figures were created to appear real with sensitivity to exquisite detail and reference to German experimental theatre. These windows awaken one to intense experience of the moment. Since there is also music playing another one of our senses is engaged and we feel propelled into the store to find the Prada clothes. One may say that this is very sophisticated advertising and impels behavior in consumers. Yet a person becomes engaged in the moment and lingers at the "Barneys windows" as if gazing at a piece of art. We all see the "window," but each of us has a transsubjective experience, as the images in the "windows" are rendered differently for each of us.

Freedman also discussed the collaborative process between the designer Isabel Marant, and the sculptor Arnold Goron. It was evident that the primitiveness of the windows with large motorized movable figures that move in different ways also reflect the designer's clothing. (See Photo) These windows extend out of the boundary of the window frames and protrude into public space along with sound.

Illustration 14: Isabel Marant

Valerie Angel: Tell me about the collaborative process for the Barneys windows.

Dennis Freedman: Well, it's a collaboration with the designer, Isabel Marant, and she works with Arnold Goron. We took these fairly primitive sculptures made out of foam and paint with simple motors that moved things, which I like because it is low tech, and we created these environments in each window, which had an emotional aspect.

Valerie Angel: What's the emotional part?

Dennis Freedman: We created these appendages and heads and then I wanted them to come out of the window so the head and hands go into the street. I wanted it to break through into the street, which I don't think was ever done.

Valerie Angel: Taking it into the street, the street becomes the space of engagement.

Dennis Freedman: Yeah, the street is the space. We also use sound—always—and there is a soundtrack we made and that is also for the street.

Valerie Angel: The sound I heard was a heartbeat!

Dennis Freedman: Well, there's a heartbeat and then there are these strange voices that were never literal and played off the windows. The Prada windows were also very powerful and psychological.

Valerie Angel: Tell us about those windows.

Dennis Freedman: Miuccia last season was influenced by Pina Bausch and Fassbinder and Joseph Beuys. The window was a kind of twentieth-century experimental theatre. This collaboration was without her, although we usually collaborate with the designer. We made life casts of a man and woman, two strong characters. They were quite complicated to cast because we didn't know how they would be placed in the windows. We would cast an arm and then a body. The material was like a matte plastic and in the windows they were super powerful. The woman was sitting on a mammoth bed of nails, and then there is another figure in this position near her, and then there is a stairway that leads to infinity.

Valerie: It sounds distressing.

Dennis: It was disturbing. It was a man and a woman and they never saw each other, they were always apart and couldn't look at each other. We had two human voices do a soundtrack in German and we picked dialogue from film and you would walk by these windows and hear voices but the two life casts were not talking to each other. It was surreal.

Valerie: There is a real collaboration with the designer, artists, and yourself. This work seemed to expand your creativity. Now, there is a phenomenon of fashion-designer exhibitionss in museums.

Dennis: These windows bring together very talented people who engage in the space to create an environment that reflects the vision of the fashion designer; and some fashion designers now have retrospective exhibitions in museums.

From our interview with Dennis Freedman it is clear that he finds his position as creative directive of Barneys New York inspiring and challenging, and through the "windows" he brings the latest fashion to the public, transforming how clothes are presented.

CONCLUSION

As Virginia Woolf comments, "Clothes change our view of the world and the world's view of us... there is much to support the view" (Finkelstein 1998, p. 10). When we look at certain clothes, we can be reminded of what happened during a certain period. The clothing of the 1940s and 1960s reminds us of the crises of those years, as expressed in our dress. In the forties women were forced to wear certain clothes because of wartime restrictions. The fashion of the sixties revealed our greater freedom of expression, spirit, and individuality.

How we dress is the embodiment of a dialectic between two desires: to dress for ourselves, and to dress to become the object of another's desire. Thus there is a subjective desire and an objective one, and we need to be able to traverse these two areas fluidly if we are to engage to the fullest our sense of vitality. The space of this engagement may be created within our experience of fashion, as well as in the psychoanalytic process; and, like psychoanalysis, it reflects the singularity of each of us. At times we may be puzzled and unable to locate our desire; at other times, we may refuse our desire in a narcissistic attack on the self. As in the Kafka quotation at the beginning of this chapter, sometimes we appear disheveled and unkempt, and in this way perhaps express a disorganized self-state. At other times, we can regulate our affect more effectively, and our appearance communicates our well-being. Artist Barbara Kruger also said, "You want it, You buy it, You forget it." Perhaps this aphorism mocks the act of shopping. Yet our clothing reflects how we treat ourselves and how the world sees us, so the choice is not trivial. Fashion and psychoanalysis are both supported by a process of transformative communication, which in the twenty-first century is critical for the continued growth and vitality of the self.

REFERENCES

Anderson. H.C., (1983). The Emperor's New Clothes. ed., Haugaard, E.K., *Hans Christian Andersen: The Complete Fairy Tales and Stories*. New York: Random House.

Bachelard, G.,(1969).*The Poetics of Space*. Boston: Beacon Press.

Crane D., (2002). *Fashion and its Social Agenda*. Chicago: The University Chicago Press.

Davis, Fred., (1992). *Fashion Culture and Identity*. Chicago: The University of Chicago Press.

Ellison, J., (2014, August 30-31). Why fashion matters – no matter who you are. *Financial Times*. pp. 1-2.

Finkelstein, J., (1998). *Fashion: An Introduction*. New York: NYU University Press.

Friedman, V., (2016) Burberry Announces a See Now/But Now System for New Collection. *The NY Times*.

Freud, S. (1900). *Interpretation of Dreams*. S.E. 4-5. London: Hogarth Press.

Hevi, S., Julavits, H., Shapton, L., (2014). *Women in Clothes*. United Kingdom: Blue Rider Press.

Hurlock, E.B., (1965). Sumptuary Law. In: Roach, M.E., Eicher, J.B. (eds.), Dress Adornment and the Social Order (pp. 295-301). New York: John Wiley & Sons.

Lurie. A., (1981). *The Language of Clothes*. New York: Random House.

Ponty-Merleau-M., (1998) *Phenomenology of Perception*. London: Routledge

Ogden, T.H., (2004). This Art of Psychoanalysis: Dreaming undreamt dreams and interrupted cries. *Int. J. Psycho-anal* 85: 857-877.

Steele, V.,(1997). *Fifty Years of Fashion*. New Haven: Yale University Press.

Tobias, T.,(2000). *Obsessed by Dress*. Boston: Beacon Press.

*We thank Eve Golden for her comments.

4. *Jewelry, A Psychological Perspective*

ELSA BLUM AND HAROLD BLUM

Jewelry, spanning many millennia in time and virtually ubiquitous among cultures, merits consideration of its many layers of meaning. In one way or another, jewelry touches upon virtually all human emotions, expressing or defending against the most profound feelings in culturally acceptable ways. Eliciting a broad gamut of feelings in owners, donors, and viewers alike, and associated with the deepest of human emotions, jewelry frequently represents life's greatest joys and deepest sorrows. While the monetary worth of jewelry lends it survival value, the earliest crafting of jewelry made no contribution to biological survival. This suggests that jewelry serves important psychological functions and piques our desire to understand these psychological meanings.

While it is fascinating to consider the variety of psychological meanings of jewelry, in view of the complexities of human nature, it is naïve to make any interpretations regarding any individual's relationship to his/her jewelry. Emotional meanings are complex, and there is no one-to-one relationship between any aspect of jewelry and an individual. For example, a costly gem may represent extreme narcissism for one person, but for another may reflect a defense against, or in fact concrete insurance against, financial and/or other insecurity, realistic or imagined. The meaning of jewelry for an individual is also affected by gender, sexual orientation, culture and sub-culture. Despite historical changes, individual differences, and cultural and economic influences, many of the underlying meanings of acquiring, giving, receiving, and wearing of jewelry have survived through millennia.

The single word "jewelry" denotes an encompassing assortment of objects, as varied in form as the human mind can conceive, crafted of a vast array of materials taking myriad forms. It shares much with other arts and crafts, and, though this may be a debatable issue, we do not view these categories as dichotomous. We define "crafts" broadly, considered on a continuum with fine arts. We view all as emanating from what appears to be a virtually universal human impulse to create, decorate the utilitarian, and often produce objects with little or no utilitarian function whatsoever. "The arts squander brain power, physical effort, time, and precious resources" (Dutton, 2009, p. 136). Like other visual art forms, jewelry can be figurative, abstract, or somewhere in between. Sharing many elements with other art forms and valued as an art for its aesthetic value, jewelry can nevertheless be differentiated from other varieties of arts and crafts, as well as from clothing. Made to decorate the body and fasten garments, jewelry does not serve any biological function. Unlike clothing, jewelry neither provides warmth nor does it conceal the body. Differing from other visual arts and crafts, the intention of jewelry is for it to be worn and visible to numerous observers. The relatively small scale of most jewelry necessitates its being viewed at close range. Jewelry has significance in terms of its personal meanings for its owner and/or donor; it contains interpersonal implications depending how it is received (as a gift, inherited, or purloined), and cultural connotations in its designation of status and group membership. In this chapter, we will explore jewelry's many emotional and symbolic meanings, both conscious and unconscious.

Considered to date from 90,000 to 100,000 B.C., the oldest discovered jewelry consists of three beads that are perforated shells to be strung. Found far from the sea, the beads had clearly been transported. Other prehistoric beads, previously considered to be the oldest, were probably concurrent with Neanderthal man, homo sapiens, and the development of symbolism (Tait 2008). These beads were found in tombs, apparently intended for use in the afterlife.

Across the ages and in many cultures, jewelry, beginning with simple beads, has been used for trade and valued as a monetary equivalent. Metaphorically "gem" or "jewel" denotes excellence—a gem of a person, performance, or book; a woman characterized as a jewel, "ruby lips," etc. The value of jewelry is extolled in the old song "Diamonds Are a Girl's Best Friend." (Robbin 1949). The themes of diamonds and money permeate the narratives of plays and film. The Bible (Proverbs 31:10) states, "Who can find a virtuous woman? For her price is far above rubies." Similarly, gold, treasured through the ages for its durability, beauty and malleability, also appears in metaphors, symbolizing warmth and beauty (Sarett 1979, p.122). Describing a child as "as good as gold," "a heart of gold," and the "golden rule" suggests that gold signifies virtue. In ancient Rome, only certain classes were permitted to wear gold.

Given its monetary value, jewelry can and has been used to reveal, conceal, transport, or bestow wealth. When the Wolfman returned to Freud from Russia after the overthrow of the Czar, his family had lost their estates and he was no longer a wealthy aristocrat. He represented himself to Freud as impoverished and was referred to Mack-Brunswick for free treatment. For several years Freud also arranged for an annual collection from colleagues for the Wolfman's financial support. His hidden wealth in the form of valuable jewels given to him by his mother was only later revealed in his analysis by Mack-Brunswick. He had concealed his jewelry from Freud and Mack-Brunswick to avoid paying a fee for treatment, fearing both the loss of financial support and of his idealized object, Freud (Freud, S. 1918; Blum, H. 2013). The concealed valuables also aided him in maintaining the fantasy of his former aristo-cratic high status, which bolstered his severely injured narcissism.

While jewelry may signify wealth, status, and prestige, it may also deceive, with the observer assuming that gems worn by a wealthy person are real, or when worn by a person of lower social class, fake. A poignant example is De Maupassant's short story, "The Necklace" (1884). The main character, a beautiful woman of modest means, yearns for the accoutrements and admiration bestowed by wealth. Invited to a special event, she borrows a necklace from an affluent friend. When the neck-lace is lost, she and her husband live in poverty, struggling for ten years to repay the debt incurred by reparation for the loss with an apparently identical diamond necklace. To their chagrin, they learn, only after the debt incurred for the replacement has been paid off, that the original was a fake. Ironically the jewelry itself was desired in order to misrepresent the borrower, a woman of modest means, as a person of greater wealth and higher rank. Paradoxically, Helena Rubenstein reported (Papi & Rhodes 1999, pp. 196-197) that her jewelry was so large and flamboyant that customs officials assumed it must be fake, even though it was not. Thus the fake had been perceived as real, the genuine as fake. In the lyrics of Gilbert in HMS Pinafore, "Things are seldom what they seem, skim milk masquerades as cream." A person can also masquerade as either wealthy and aristocratic, or poor.

The durability of most jewelry has significant psychological meaning. This durability as well as its transportability lends monetary value to jewelry. These characteristics enhance its commercial worth as emphasized in advertising:for example, the De Beers advertisement reads, "Diamonds are forever"; Patek Philippe reads "you never actually own a Patek Philippe. You merely look after it for the next generation." In a transient world, jewelry will endure, perhaps to some degree providing reassurance regarding one's own mortality. While most jewelry is very long-lasting, on the other hand, some objects, which share many characteristics with jewelry, are in fact ephemeral, for example Hawaiian leis, which symbolize love and are garlands of flowers given for arrivals and departures. They, in a paradoxical way, suggest an abundance that permits the expenditure of time and money on things that will not last; they are a type of conspicuous consumption with its own psychological concomitants. Similarly, daisy chains and other floral garlands resemble jewelry and vice versa.

The monetary equivalent of jewelry, with its concomitant emotional significance, is evident in many cultures: for example, in jewelry that is part of a woman's dowry. The cost of a gift of jewelry may consciously or unconsciously symbolize the wealth of the donor, the expectations of the donor regarding the relationship, and the desire to display both wealth and relationship. Costly jewelry may be coveted also to defend against perceived or actual financial insecurity, concretely and symbolically, realistically and emotionally.

The issues of identity and narcissism are important aspects of the personal meanings of jewelry. Related to a person's self-esteem, narcissism may be enhanced, and low self-esteem compensated for, by the collecting and wearing of jewelry, because jewelry signifies wealth, success, status, taste, and attractiveness. Indicative of wealth and status, jewelry may compensate for earlier narcissistic injuries and feelings of inferiority. The wearer/owner of the jewelry may or may not be aware of these feelings, which may be shared by family. Embedded in these notions is the representation of the response of the viewer to the jewels.

A male patient came to his sessions impeccably and expensively dressed sporting a gold Rolex watch. He had led a deprived childhood as the humiliated son of servants. It was crucial for him to boost his self-esteem, anticipating the admiration and envy of the success he had achieved by all those he encountered. In the context of socially acceptable behavior he redressed earlier injury, gratifying his narcissistic wishes. Prior to psychotherapy the patient was essentially unaware of the deeper meaning of his need for displaying his wealth to compensate for early humiliations and humble background. Wearing gold jewelry symbolized his self-aggrandizement, which defended against self- denigration.

Narcissistic gratification is derived not only from the pride of ownership, feelings of being successful, loved, of high status, etc., but from the fantasies and realities of how one is viewed by others. While the fantasized admiring response of another may indeed be accurate, another scenario is also possible. Perhaps rather than admiration, another person could feel that the owner of the jewelry is too ostentatious, has poor taste, etc. Envy may color perception; hostility and resentment may be masked by expressions of admiration.

In a concrete way, jewelry may confirm identity, as in ID bracelets, Egyptian cartouches, or signet rings. Jewelry also, however, may influence one's internalized sense of identity. The notion of jewelry's contribution to her identity was apparent to Helena Rubenstein. In her autobiography she noted "Although I no longer need the added courage that handsome jewelry once gave me (it was not easy being a hard-working woman in a man's world many years ago) I am aware that the wearing of exotic jewelry has become associated in many people's minds with the 'image' of Helena Rubinstein, a mark of my identity, so to speak. And since I shall always love beautiful things, I feel I might as well enjoy wearing those I have."

The lyrics of the "The Jewel Song" (Barbier, J.,1859) from Gounod's *Faust*, convey a similar notion:

Ah! I laugh to see myself
so beautiful in this mirror,
Ah! I laugh to see myself
so beautiful in this mirror,
Is it you, Marguerite, is that you?
Answer me, answer me,
Respond, respond, respond quickly!
No! No! That is no longer you!
No... no, this is no longer your face;
It is the daughter of a king
It is no longer you,
One must greet her as she passes!
Ah if only he was here!
He would see me thus
Like a lady
He would find me beautiful, Oh
Like a lady,
He would find me beautiful!
Let us complete my metamorphosis,
I am late, but I look forward to try on
this bracelet and necklace!
God! It's like a hand
Which arises on my arm! Ah! Ah
Ah! I laugh to see myself
so beautiful in this mirror!

Marguerite envisions herself as beautiful, as a royal person, as she will be reflected in a mirror, and as she will be viewed by a lover. As part of one's identity, jewelry confirms one's self-image or ego ideal as attractive, wealthy, successful, and famous. Conscious confirmations of self-worth may, however, defend against unconscious feelings, which may be quite the opposite: inferiority, insignificance, being unloved. This defensive aspect of jewelry is evident in other contexts as well.

Issues of narcissism enter into the very selection of jewelry by the owner or donor. Jewelry conveys multiple messages between donor and recipient, wearer and observer; messages regarding taste, value, relationships, and status are communicated both consciously and unconsciously. Choices are endless; jewelry may be uniquely crafted or mass-produced, emblazoned with sparkling gems or incorporating more modest semiprecious elements. The variety of jewelry is endless: vintage or contemporary, precious or base metal, costume or valuable, false or genuine, enduring or crafted of more ephemeral materials. Large and gaudy pieces may neither be for the shrinking violet, nor for the more delicate or the more exhibitionistic person who craves attention. A piece of jewelry by a famous designer may be especially treasured, worn in anticipation that the owner's taste and discrimination will be particularly admired. Identification with previous owners of inherited or antique jewelry may afford the new owner an additional source of narcissistic gratification. Jewelry once owned by the rich and/or famous has particular cache, altering self-perception, conferring increased status through the new owner's identification with the previous owner, and the attribution of higher status by the observer. Its monetary value is enhanced by its provenance; many such items of jewelry are further valued as being in fact one-of-a-kind pieces commissioned for their original owners by famous manufacturers and/or designers. The sense of being unique is likely internalized by the new owner. Jewelry made by famous designers may be particularly valued as "timeless." A rare gem or unique item of jewelry may appeal to its owner's desire to feel special and unique, and to be considered so by others as well. Conscious or unconscious fantasies regarding one's jewelry may embody an owner's self-perception as attractive, fashionable, trendy, daring, or discriminating. A person may choose among his/her items of jewelry according to mood on a particular day, social setting, or kind of impression one wishes to make. Choices demonstrate one's taste, both reflecting and influencing self-perception.

Jewelry's intimate relationship to the body is manifold and complex. Its role as enhancing the body, complementing clothing, and declaring status has implications regarding one's sexual attractiveness. "Jewelry beautifies, within the value system of the local culture, and sometimes renders the wearer socially or sexually desirable" (Metcalf, B. 1989).

Sexual connotations of jewelry with generational overtones are evident in the phrase "family jewels," a metaphor for testicles. Often touching the body itself, jewelry can emphasize particular characteristics:for example, pendants lead the eye to the breasts, earrings to the ear lobes and face. Exhibitionistic wishes may be expressed by wearing large or unusual jewelry, or jewelry that emphasizes erotic parts of the body. It may simultaneously be a compromise, partially expressing, partially defending, against desires to exhibit the body itself. Wearing appropriately valuable jewelry may signify that a potential mate is of desirable social and financial status.

Culture and fashions of the times are critical factors in the relationship of jewelry to the body. Modifying the body itself to wear jewelry has entailed piercing the earlobes, for centuries and across cultures, common and not especially painful. More recently, in some cultures, piercing of the lips, genitals, and nipples to accommodate jewelry, particularly rings, has become common, acceptable, and desirable. Piercings may be intended to enhance sexual pleasure, often considered daring, identified with counter-culture, and expressive of individuality. A seriously disturbed female adolescent patient had multiple piercings; her nipples, lip, and ears. She was Asian and had been adopted at about one year of age by a white family. Her piercings had multiple meanings. These included her identification with counter-culture age mates, as well as unconscious anger at both her biological and adoptive mothers, turned masochistically towards herself. Exhibitionistic features were related to erotic fantasies about her piercings' increasing her sexual attractiveness. The piercings represented both her identification with other rebellious teenagers, as well as her personal conflicts.

While purchasing, owning, giving, and wearing jewelry are related to both conscious and unconscious self-representations, these self-representations are inevitably enmeshed with internalizations of real and fantasized others. They may be viewers of the jewelry, donors, or forebears. The psychological meanings of jewelry include aspects of internalized interpersonal representations in numerous ways. While relationships themselves are conventionally symbolized by jewelry, such as engagement rings and wedding rings, each item may embody a host of fantasies regarding the other and the relationship, whether current or past. Status as a mother or grandparent may be denoted by charms on necklaces or bracelets representing faces of children in profile. One may wonder why some women choose to announce this status to all who see them, while most do not. Could their emphasis on this status unconsciously defend against perceived shortcomings in other areas?

Jewelry's long-lasting quality renders it a frequent component of an inheritance. Internalized representations of the deceased, along with associated affects and memories, become enmeshed in the gift. For the owner of jewelry, realistically contemplating mortality and the relationship with the prospective gift recipient can have emotional significance and be fraught with conflict. From one elderly wealthy patient's perspective, the quality of her relationships with her heirs was critical. Anticipating her death, she was writing her will, painfully aware of her animosity towards one daughter-in-law. Considering the family relationships and how she might be remembered, she opted for an equitable distribution of her jewelry, despite her marked ambivalence towards one of the women. In another case, however, a granddaughter experienced as distant and unloving was deliberately excluded as a recipient of her grandmother's jewelry.

For the recipient, as well as donor, inherited jewelry may also have intense psychological connotations, related to the multiple aspects of a relationship with its many complexities. A legacy of jewelry may serve to counteract negative aspects of the relationship, real or imagined, or may be experienced as too little, perhaps as compared with the inheritance of another recipient. Inherited jewelry may memorialize and represent a loving relationship, providing intergenerational continuity, compensation for loss, and help in bridging the chasm of separation. Inherited jewelry with its special meaning may be particularly treasured by the recipient as a link with the deceased. The intense emotion which may be invested in such an inherited piece of jewelry is beautifully narrated by Alan Kurzweil (2015) in his memoir "Whipping Boy." Having lost his father at age five, the author treasured the Omega watch he had inherited and had brought with him to boarding school. It had been stolen by a classmate and tossed over a balcony into the snow, never to be found.

71

The recounting of his decades long search for his boyhood tormentor permeates the narrative. It attests to his heartbreak and rage over the loss of the watch, virtually his only memento of his deceased father. He ultimately realizes that the watch had been a talisman, representing the time of his intact family and happy life. Thus a piece of jewelry may be a very poignant reminder of a relationship severed by death and may be especially valued, far beyond its monetary worth.

Lockets in particular have concretely represented others (frequently the deceased) and often contain miniature paintings and photographs of the loved other. During the Civil War, soldiers frequently gave lockets containing a bit of their hair to their wives or fiancées before going off to battle. In Victorian England lockets were particularly popular. They symbolized a close relationship with the person whose picture or hair they contained, providing links to ease the pain of separation or to aid mourning by not only keeping this concrete memento, but by wearing it, thus demonstrating to others that the deceased person is remembered. These overt memorials may also serve to modulate survivor guilt. Queen Victoria wore black jewelry when she became a widow, symbolizing her mourning, but permitting her to wear jewelry.

The enduring quality of most jewelry renders it ideal as a gift for commemorating special relationships and important life events, such as weddings and engagements, rites of passage such as graduations, and sixteenth birthdays. Engagement rings and wedding rings communicate the enduring attachment of the wearer to spouse or fiancé(e) and her or his unavailability to others. It is not a symmetrical arrangement, since the man in our culture does not traditionally announce his "engaged" status with a ring. Embodying the circle, a symbol of eternity for the Egyptians, rings were exchanged just as today at a marriage and were given at a betrothal. The jewels are a concrete and visible confirmation of the exclusive relationship. The monetary value, and the permanence of the gifts, symbolize the closeness and anticipated long duration of the relationships, and in some instances financial aspects of the relationships as well. In addition to gifts of wedding rings and engagement rings, symbolizing love and the marital relationship, jewelry is frequently given as external representation of affection on numerous other special occasions, such as birthdays and anniversaries. These also serve to commemorate the occasions themselves, reinforcing memory and re-arousing associated affects.

While a gift of jewelry may, as its manifest purpose, represent love, it may also consciously or unconsciously be used by the donor as a sop to the conscience, evading or assuaging guilt. The gift may also be a bribe to the recipient. Gifts of jewelry to one left at home during a trip are not uncommon and could serve to compensate for the separation. Guilt over the donor's behavior, or even fantasized behavior, while away may also be an aspect of the gift, which may be a bribe to the recipient, conscious or unconscious. A patient whose business trips were marked by a long-term extramarital liaison frequently returned with gifts of jewelry for his wife. These "signs of affection" were means of relieving his guilt, and ensuring the continuation of the marital relationship, which he also desired. Living in "a captain's paradise" with partners in two ports, he also bought gifts, though less expensive, for his mistress. He rationalized this affair and was only partly conscious of the degree of his guilt to-wards his wife. Some buyers of jewelry consider the purchase as a gift to themselves; the "gift" may be a means of compensation for real or imag-ined injury. For example, after an argument, purchasing jewelry may serve affect regulation, containing anger, and restoring damaged self-esteem.

In Freud's famous "Fragments of an Analysis of a Case of Hysteria" he related Dora's father's giving her mother a bracelet, incurring the latter's wrath, since she had wanted pearl earrings (Freud 1905, p. 68). Was the gift due to the husband's guilt over his affair with Frau "K"? Was his wife's anger possibly a displacement from her rage over the affair, which she may have suspected? Freud indicated that such secrets were most difficult to keep, since in the same case report he indicated that betrayal oozes from every pore. Had Dora's mother received uncon-scious messages about the affair from her husband, her daughter, or her husband's lover, her supposed friend? According to Dora, her mother responded that since she didn't want the bracelet, and since it was very expensive, he might as well give it to someone else. She might well have had Frau K in mind. Dora stated that she had enjoyed wearing jewelry but had stopped wearing it when she became ill, suggesting the emotions that may accompany and affect the wearing of jewelry. Dora's reaction appears to have been connected in some way to Herr K's gift to her of a jewel box, generally interpreted as having been an implement of seduction, symbolically representing the female genitals. He wanted a reciprocal gift of her virginity.

Magical powers have been attributed to much jewelry in the past and, to some degree in the present as well. While an individual's magical thinking may be considered pathological, magical thoughts shared by a group are socially acceptable. Amulets have been worn throughout the ages and in numerous cultures to allay human anxieties, to ensure luck and prevent misfortune in an unpredictable and little understood world in which disease and early death were rampant. These magical attributions to amulets and gems could defend against conscious and unconscious fears, both rational and irrational, and could thus serve to stabilize emotions. Magical powers may be inherent in particular figures or images or in the materials themselves. An Egyptian amulet portraying a fish, dating from the second millennium B.C. is thought to have been worn by a child as a protection against drowning. Specific representations conferred special powers, such as the falcon or bull (Tait, H. 2008). For both Greeks and Romans, and in other cultures as well, jewelry, often with particular figures was worn to ward off the "evil eye." These representations of the "evil eye," worn as pendants, were thought to prevent retaliation by the powers that be for their envy and revenge when something good occurred, as in the Yiddish expression "keyn einhora" (without the evil eye). The Romans' engraved rings, used as seals, representing the identity of the owners, also denoted their beliefs. They had magical properties as well, "conferring luck and protection"(Burke 2006, p.190).

In some cultures, such as Egyptian culture, particular stones had specific meanings and beneficial powers. Green feldspar or turquoise was the color of new life and symbolized fertility; lapis lazuli, the color of the heavens; for the Romans, carnelian represented courage. Hindu tradition associates gold with immortality. During the Middle Ages as well, precious stones and engraved gems were thought to possess magical qualities. Particular stones were considered to have special magical powers: for example, jade represented, among other qualities, beauty, grace, and purity; carnelian was associated with power and success and was thought to enhance life.

While amulets and gems warded off evil and magically conferred desired attributes to the wearer, in fiction rings themselves can have magical evil powers, embodying aggressive, hostile, and sadistic wishes. In the Nibelungen CycleRing of Wagner, (1848-1876) who wrote both music and libretto, gold is stolen from the Rhine Maidens and made into a ring with the power to control all in exchange for foregoing love. The wearers of this ring all met their deaths. In Lord of the Rings, the ring has evil powers and must be destroyed (Tolkien, J. 1954) . According to rumor, which was never confirmed, Lucrezia Borgia wore a ring containing a compartment for poison, which she used to poison drinks with lethal consequences.

Jewelry is significant in psychoanalysis in other contexts, as well as in the Dora and Wolfman cases. Rings, as suggested above, have special symbolic significance both historically, in the present, and in the history of psychoanalysis in particular. Freud, himself, wore a Roman ring with a large dark green stone on the fourth finger of his right hand, where, according to Eastern European Jewish custom, one wore a wedding band (Burke 2006). Freud's interest in rings was one aspect of his devotion to antiquities, which for him, among other meanings, symbolized the uncovering of layers in history as in psychoanalysis. In 1913, Freud gave a Roman intaglio to the members of his secret "Committee," which each then had set in gold. These rings signified Freud's affection, group affiliation, devotion to Freud and to psychoanalytic principles. Unlike high school or college class rings, which are all identical, each was individually chosen, with perhaps a special message in the intaglio. Freud's own Roman ring was engraved with a bust of Jupiter, the sovereign god, all-good and all-powerful. For Ferenczi, he chose a carnelian with a Dionysian scene. Burke suggests that the image may have been a message to Ferenczi to be more light-hearted (Burke 2006). On the other hand, it may have had the opposite meaning, to comply with Freud's tenets and check his Dionysian tendencies, perhaps more germane at the time. While the rings given to the secret Committee were not successful in ensuring group loyalty and cohesion, Freud later gave additional rings to indicate affection and special relationships with proponents of psychoanalysis, including Anna Freud and Marie Bonaparte.

All jewelry is the product of the culture in which it was produced and in which it is worn. A great deal of jewelry specifically announces group status, part of the wearer's identity and his/her representation to others. Class rings announce to others an affiliation with a particular group, which may or may not confer high status, depending on the exclusivity and status of the group represented. Pins and pendants, as well, may represent one's inclusion in and identification with a particular group. The icons of many religions are reproduced in jewelry, meant to be displayed. Some of these may have magical implications for the wearers, signify their beliefs, etc. Honor societies, such as Phi Beta Kappa, confer keys which may be worn as pendants, and would convey special narcissistic gratification. Fraternities and sororities use Greek letter pins, often given to a girlfriend, usually as a precursor to formal engagement, thus symbolizing the close attachment of the couple as the pin itself symbolizes attachment to the group. Many less conscious meanings related to an individual's self-representation as a member of a group are also communicated. Narcissistic fantasies may include exaggerated notions of one's status or of viewers' reactions of admiration to inclusion in an exclusive group considered to be of high status. Conversely, a wearer may have unconscious concerns regarding his worthiness or may fear negative consequences of the viewer's envy.

While most of the jewelry sold at present is factory-produced, a large variety of handcrafted jewelry is also widely available. This genre often has its own significance, for both creator and owner, as well as an implicit relationship between them (Hushka, R. 2010). On one end of the spectrum, this jewelry ranges from relatively simple designs, using modest materials and, variable in its individuality, often sold at street fairs. At the other extreme of the spectrum, handcrafted jewelry may use precious materials and be of sufficient originality and craftsmanship to merit display in crafts museums. Art-studio jewelry may resemble contemporary art in its reliance on the emotional impact of its content rather than the more abstract characteristics of color, balance, textural interest, etc. For example, in an article by L. Den Besten. is illustrated by a photograph of a necklace composed of several pairs of scissors, connected to each other, blood-red blades apart (Schobinger 2016). This threatening item, clearly not to everyone's taste, makes a powerful statement, subject to interpretation. This statement is the expression of both the artist and the wearer. Like this piece, much of this genre is highly unconventional, but as art that is meant to be worn; it must be considered jewelry. R. Hushka describes the complex relationship between the creator and the purchaser of this type of jewelry and the communicative aspects of the jewelry for both (Hushka 2010). Its appeal is through emotional and intellectual response to its content rather than to sensual enjoyment.

Jewelry is essentially ubiquitous, spanning time and cultures, multiform in physical attributes, imbued with endless meanings, personal and cultural, conscious and unconscious. It can serve to both defend against and express affects, such as pride, shame, humiliation, love, pleasure, guilt, sadness. Jewelry may also counter anxiety, such as fear of loss and separation, social anxiety, narcissistic denigration, fears, both realistic and imagined, of financial disaster. On the other hand, it often commemorates joyous occasions and symbolizes treasured relationships. Jewelry shares many attributes with what we consider fine art, but its close personal relationship with the body differentiates it. It has been created from time immemorial, valued overtly for its permanence, beauty, and value, but also for its satisfaction of essential psychological needs for individuals, groups, and cultures.

REFERENCES

Barbier, J. (1859). The Jewel Song from Gounod's *Faust*.

Blum, H. (2013). The Wolfman's Rorschach. *International Journal of Psychoanalysis*, 94: 937-944; 967-991.

Burke, J.(2006). *The Sphinx on the Table*. Australia: Random House.

De Maupassant, G. (1884). *The Necklace*. New York: Dover Publications

Den Besten, L. (2016). Bernard Schobinger: Meaning in Every Material. *Metalsmith, vol.36/1;*50-57.

Dubin, L. (1987). *The History of Beads.* New York: Abrams.

Dutton, D. (2009). *The Art Instinct.* New York: Bloomsbury Press.

Freud, S. (1905). Fragment of an Analysis of a Case of Hysteria. *SE 7:*3-122

Freud, S. (1918). From the History of an Infantile Neurosis. *SE 7:* 3-122.

Hushka, R. (2010). "Holding objects: The psychoanalytic mechanisms of wearing jewelry.", *Art Jewelry Forum.*

Kurzweil, A.(2015). *Whipping Boy.* New York: Harper Collins.

Metcalf, B. (1989). On the nature of Jewelry. Retrieved from brucemetcalf.com/page/.essays/nature_jewelry.html.

Papi, S. & Rhodes, A. (1999). *Famous jewelry Collectors.* London: Thames & Hudson.

Robins, L. (1949) Gentlemen Prefer Blondes. [Recorded by masterworks broadway].

Sarett (1979). *The Jewelry in Your Life.* Chicago: N. Hall.

Tait, H. (2008). *Jewelry 7000 Years.* New York: Firefly Books.

Tolkien, J. (1954). *Lord of the Rings.* New York: Mariner Books.

Wagner, R. (1848-1876). Der Ring des Nibelungen.

5. Fashion as Metaphor: Playing in the Transitional Space

CLAIRE STEINBERGER

There is no limit to what a metaphor calls to our attention, because what we see is also shaped by our sensitivities and our experience.

Donald Davidson (1978)

INTRODUCTION

A Personal View

Fashion is in my blood. By dint of my personal background, I was ripe for a therapeutic "fashion narrative," as well as for a couple battling with the psychological challenges of individuation and adult intimacy, navigating the narrow line between fantasy and reality.

The world of fashion permeated my development and informed my feminine and social identity, supporting an over-exaggeration of external forms of (corporal) desirability and perfection. I was on the fashion runway at an early age and dressed up and was watched by a maternal audience from childhood into adolescence. As a teenager, I wrote poetry and short stories, yet turned to beauty contests and the certainty of being seen as a way to support my shaky self-esteem. In this idiosyncratic way, the fashion metaphor strikes a sensitive chord in me. The overly close relationship with my mother and the idealized and seductive style of my father fit well with the experience of glamor, on-stage performance, and mutual eying permeating this therapy. I could identify with my female patient, who described her clothing as "armor" as well as "amour." I remembered a boyfriend telling me, "You walk to be seen."

COUPLE THERAPY

Fashion in the Tri-Personal Field

In this couple's treatment, the tri-personal field functioned as a play space in which the couple expressed—and pulled—their inner selves with the outside world. In a nonverbal way, fashion communicated the couple's internal experience through sensory and bodily action, including skin and skin covering, posture and movement, seating arrangement, facial expression, eye contact and eye movement and vocal tone and intensity. On a sensory and experiential level, the participants were able to see, hear and sense each other (Richards 2013). As the therapy progressed to a more abstract or symbolic plane, thought-filled images and narrations exposed trauma and the outcome of early separation and narcissistic struggles.

As an intuitive witness-participant (Poland 2000), the analyst supported the safety of the therapeutic environment, where the couple began to tell their stories and spontaneously contact and make sense of challenging polarized love and hate feelings and ideas. Ultimately, the couple created their own emotional integration by transforming frightening images into mutual understanding. In this way, fashion's changing sensory and symbolic expressions became the crux of the deepening therapeutic work.

Brief Background

W (the wife) and H (the husband) were a well-educated, bi-ethnic (Euro-Asian) couple in their mid-thirties. They came to therapy because they were unable to let go of their relatively brief (year-and-one-half) marriage. Although H appeared to have made the decision that he no longer wanted to be married, he seemed frightened to be alone and ambivalent and guilty about leaving his angry and accusatory wife.

The Wife

W grew up in an upper middle-class Asian family, and came to the United States with her mother and younger siblings when she was a teenager. She described her home as having a nightmarish atmosphere, in which her father was a "dangerous and insane alcoholic" and her mother was "always very good." Trapped in an early family or parental-child triangulation or threesome, W became her mother's ally and her parent's referee. She remained financially dependent on her father, labeling the clothing she wore when she visited, "my protective armor." In one session, the analyst freely associated to the word "*amour*" (love) while H whispered, "*mort*" (dead). In an intuitive way, the three of us were approaching W's clothing as a special character or thing that held multiple (metaphoric) meanings having to do with self -protection, erotic love, and death.

W was drawn to a glamorous career in the arts, but found it difficult to find and maintain work. She was not able to reflect on her problems in any significant way and had dreams of becoming a writer and playwright.

The Husband

H described his childhood with little emotion or sentimentality. He grew up in Europe with an older sister and younger brother and his parents were divorced when he was three. His mother hooked up with a cult leader who became an intimidating step- father whom H feared and hated. Growing up in a cult environment, H moved more than twenty times during his childhood. He was home-schooled and it was difficult for him to form and maintain friendships.

H described his mother as "soft and in a different world." In his first childhood memory, he remembered being ill and his mother as being "unable to connect to him, leaving him wanting and thirsty." This early experience translated into an exaggerated fear of finding himself—or someone else—with an unrelenting desire for wanting more than he could provide. In the couple therapy, for example, H described his wish to escape from hearing his wife's complaints and the dreaded feeling that he would never be able to satisfy her. He transferred similar experiences into his work world, where his bosses complained that he was remote and hard to reach. We explored the image of his leaving his bosses, "thirsty and wanting more," relating to it to the same feelings that he had experienced with his mother.

THE CONSULT

Fashion in Sensory and Symbolic Forms – Body and Mind

The early aspects of the treatment emphasize the couple's sensory (non-verbal) communications and what they meant for me. In that sense, it conveys what I intuitively and subjectively experienced.

Although the verbal content of the consultation was important, I begin by highlighting the chemistry between the couple and myself relating it to a feeling of being on the same wavelength. This affective fit supported a sense of psychological safety that played a significant role in holding—and moving forward—the treatment (Steinberger 2014). It helped the couple to contact, share, and explore difficult and traumatic experiences.

Fashion: On-Camera Presence

W and H exuded an unusual presence, conveying a sense of wanting to be seen—a kind of mutual exhibitionism. They were the performers and I was the voyeur. Their elegant, yet nonchalant demeanor suggested an underlying purposeful effort. These early impressions were reinforced in future sessions by W's continually changing and lavish wardrobe. She seemed to be wooing her reluctant husband with an array of softly-colored long and short skirts, silky low-necked blouses and carefully culled heels that matched her sensual outfits.

Sitting close to each other on the office couch, W and H created an aura of being special. I became aware of my role as a spectator and of looking at them as if they were on camera—or on a fashion runway. I associated to captivating films, perhaps to *Scenes from a Marriage*? In terms of our shared inner worlds, I connected to an on-stage experience that resonated with my own childhood struggles. I knew about spending lots of time getting dressed and made-up for my boyfriends.

As the Consult progressed, the couple watched and listened to each other in an intense and concentrated way. I also saw W touching her husband's arm, expressing feelings of intimacy as well as aggression—a form of friendly hit—or punch. In future sessions, she appeared riveted to what H was wearing. On one occasion, after carefully scanning H's outfit, she pointed to his multicolored socks and asked, "Are those the socks that I bought for you?" H responded with a look of stoic discomfort and whispered, "No." W's spontaneous question had seductive as well as investigative connotations. Here, fashion—the colorful socks—became an object holding multiple meanings. In this way, W used them to communicate her desire for exclusive intimacy as well as her feelings of rivalry and rage.

The Wife

W was an attractive and seductive woman with a waifish and childlike aura. Although she was somewhat petite, she appeared taller than she was in high stiletto heels. In the Consult, she wore a short light gray low-necked dress, and her arms and legs were conspicuously bare. The silk skirt moved with her body in a sensual and suggestive way, and her long black hair was pulled back in a loose bun that she periodically pulled out and let down. Her evocative style seemed aimed at stimulating an erotic *? really* response from her husband. At times, it could feel as if she were seducing me as well. I examine the meaning of their deeply erotic and sensual communication in the post-consult exploration, linking it to their heightened attraction and intense wishes for union and togetherness.

The Husband

H was a lanky man with blond hair curling below a tilted, dark blue cap. Like his wife, he emanated a youthful, almost childlike demeanor. Although he worked for a conservative business firm, he presented a casual, bohemian appearance. H spoke in soft, seductive tones that were constrained and cautious. As mentioned, he maintained a detached mask-like façade during W's evocative and rebuking attacks. He quietly shared that although he could understand his wife's hurt feelings, he did not feel safe with her.

Marital History – Holding On and Letting Go

The couple shared that they had decided to marry a few months after meeting each other, believing that they had fallen deeply in love. It was W's first serious relationship. Her disappointment with their small local wedding was an early example of W's tendency to feel dissatisfied. In a self-fulfilling interpersonal way, his wife's struggles fit with H's dread of intimacy and the frightening images of a demanding, never- satisfied wife who would always desire more than he could manage. It also meshed with his childhood memories of a dissatisfied, persecuting stepfather and his own needy feelings in relation to his mother.

Although there were few fights during the time they were together, H eventually felt emotionally overwhelmed and unexpectedly moved out of their apartment. At the time of the consult, he was dating another woman. He shared feeling trapped between his wish to escape the relationship and his panic of being left alone. Although W was hurt and enraged by H's betrayal, she was desperate to bring him back. At one point, she (defensively) mocked his other woman by sharing, "she is nowhere as attractive as I am." It reminded me of Shaw's *Pygmalion* the narcissistic and self-aggrandizing myth adapted by Lerner and Loewe's popular musical, *My Fair Lady*.

W's attacks fell on a stone-faced H, who softly responded that he no longer wanted to be married. It seemed however, that W did not hear her husband's words or that H's wishes were not put out in a clear and unambiguous way. As the analyst, I was picking up the couple's feeling of uncertainty—a sense that on some deep level the decision to separate had not *really* happened. In touch with their ambivalence, I had a sense of anxiety, experiencing myself as walking on an emotional tightrope.

Fashion in Three-Way Communications

As the consult continued, I had the sense that I was never out of the couple's sight. I was aware that W was keeping her eye on me and wondered if she was afraid that I would take her husband's side and "throw bombs at her" as she had experienced with their former couple therapist.

Ultimately, the couple's seductive communications seeped into the tri-personal field, where I became aware of my own rapt attention. I associated my concentrated engagement to my own personal narrative, where I was the ever- watched child who lived under her mother's unwavering voyeuristic eye. I also wondered how the couple's strong pull for my attention and for turning me on related to their own childhood stories. Along this line, in a future session, W shared, "We know you find us interesting." They seemed to enjoy the idea of my being enticed by them as well as their fashion statements, where I was captivated by the way they looked and moved and felt.

As the consult terminated, I felt in sync with the couple's desires for an all-consuming closeness and union. When they shared that they had fallen in love because they were both on the "same wavelength and creative and poetic and could read each other," I responded that it seemed as if they had fallen in love out of a sense of feeling intensely close, "like peas in a pod." I associated to John Donne's classic poem, "The Ecstasy" with its merging two-in-one love images. I also associated to my first experience of falling in love and resonated with their "peas in a pod" idealization. At that moment, I saw myself with long dark hair, wearing a striped black and red sweater sitting next to my comely nerdy-looking boyfriend who called us "Beauty and the Beast". It was his humorous way of letting me know that he was fond of me and found me attractive. Today, I think of Woody Allen's untoward appearance and confidently funny self-effacing style. It still makes me smile.

Fashion's Binding Ways: Body and Mind
The couple's strong sensuality came through the bodily communications taking place between them. I had an unwitting sense of emotional understanding and closeness. I also had a somewhat strange feeling of disconnection a sense that I was living in another world. It seemed as if I were dangling between a present here-and-now reality, and some other illusory or unreal space. H had shared the same sense of being in another world by describing an experience in relation to his mother.

As the couple eyed one another intensely, I sensed that they were expressing attraction, as well as caution. It seemed as if I were watching a slow-moving dance, and found myself floating in the interpersonal space and its rhythms (Katz 2010). From my witnessing parental-like perch, I saw myself as a rescuer. I imagined two huddled and whispering children somewhere in the dark—scared, confused and lost. I was *with* them, needing to be present, not too far or too close.

In this way, fashion began to move beyond sensory experience, entering a place where fantasy and imagination represented an-ever emerging world of feeling and thought.

WITNESSING TRAUMA
(Psychic In-sight (on purpose?) and Change)

Visions of Hell – and Heaven

On the clinical runway, photographer and subject are in it together. It's a mutual creation. In this way, the tri-personal field becomes a stage, offering opportunities to creatively try out – and play with – invisible or hidden characters and images in present time (Winnicott, 1971). When forgotten scenes and memories jump on the clinical runway, they can evoke intense feelings – fashion's deep shades of red, orange and black.

In an early session, when I was unable to stop W from attacking H for running away and betraying her, I made a spontaneous decision to have the couple participate in what I called a "memory and imagination" exercise. The unexpected opportunity to freely associate to unsafe and safe psychological experiences uncovered critical episodes from their formative years, including childhood abuse and trauma.

In this unexpected way, childhood trauma entered the therapeutic space, where harrowing memories were captured and reported. When scenes of early parent-child relationships entered the session, they linked the past with the present, conjuring up stark, scary imagery—psychic pictures marked by opposing angelic and evil images (Kalsched, 2016).

The analyst was the quiet witnessing third party who listened nearby.

Memories: Unsafe and Safe Places

W's *unsafe* memory found her watching television while resting on a couch with her mother. When they suddenly heard her father at the door, there was an impending dread as both mother and daughter waited to see how her father would appear – and what would happen. W then associated to another memory where she was helping her mother to escape their home by sneaking out of the bedroom window. She remembered her irate father's pulling her shoeless down the street in search of his runaway wife.

86

W's *safe* memory found her taking refuge in a school far away from home where she compensated by writing and pleasing her teachers. The nuns in her church and at camp became her friends and saviors.

H's *unsafe* memory placed him in a room with his stepfather. He saw himself standing in front of a table with his stepfather's questioning him in front of a group of people. He was being asked a specific question, but was unable to come up with the *right* word. He was not allowed to leave the room and remembers seeing an exit sign in the back of the room. He felt alone and helpless and inwardly angry. He never tried to run away.

H's *safe* memory involved his standing near a tree when he was about twelve years old. He was talking with his teacher, a soft understanding man whom he admired. The scene was serene and bucolic.

Trauma Imagery and Psychic Change

The provocative imagery evoked a picture of two helpless and terrified children who were hiding precariously behind psychic walls and armor. They were unprotected and barely clothed. The polarized projections of cruel monster-like humans were offset by near-illusory all-good saviors. In this regard, one might associate to the frightened and shame-filled expressions of the biblical Adam and Eve couple losing their innocent childhood freedoms.

Perhaps the fig leaf is civilization's first fashion statement – a metaphoric object weaving together childhood's unbridled desires with society's prohibitions.

Ultimately, the mood of the session changed as the couple's painful feelings were diverted to others *outside* the dyad. In a significant and more reflective way, W acknowledged feeling heartbroken and shared, "I know that we both build walls with distance and space." W's benign self-observing stance showed that she was beginning to look at herself and her partner in more nuanced ways – softening oppositional feelings of love and hate. It also signaled a turning point in the treatment, a time when the partners began to experience each other with more understanding and compassion. They were beginning to discover that both of them had trauma-filled histories that interfered with their ability to compromise and to love.

W's increasing capacity to look into herself led to a decrease in her painful rages. At this time, her clothing and makeup seemed to take on a casual, less dramatic appearance. When she intermittently exchanged her high-heeled shoes for comfortable sandals, she appeared more authentic and less seductively manipulating.

Ultimately, the session's highly charged emotional imagery spoke to the source of the couple's dread-filled interpersonal expectations. It also led to an appreciation of how their physical presentations and clothing styles were appropriated and used for their defensive, self-protective purposes. For example, it seemed as if their immature appearance as well as overly- erotic behavior and attire warded off mutual fears of emotional attack and abandonment. In this way, they were protectively transforming feared enemies into all-loving admirers and saviors walling off the evil and rivalrous feelings lurking inside each other and themselves.

As the therapy deepened, fashion took on multiple forms and representations. The couple's verbal disclosures, for example, led to increased understanding of how their sensual attire aimed to disarm a potentially dangerous other masking and armoring the more vulnerable and frightened feelings inside themselves. Along this line, it appeared that the couple's early attraction had responded to their hidden yearnings for an all-admiring significant other who would offer a heightened sense of unfettered idealization and merger (Freud, 1914).

FASHION METAPHORS ON THE RUNWAY

As treatment progressed and trauma erupted on the runway, fashion continued to show up in unusual fantasies and uncanny imagery. In this way, a medley of dreams and narrations let us see and feel what was deeply hidden and disguised inside of the self. Such telling characters and personifications were encountered in an increasingly safe interpersonal space.

Vampires and Dragons from the (Psychic) Underground

When separation struggles appeared in the transitional space, vampires and dragons became the frightening and exciting figures that lured and devoured their victims, never letting go (Gottlieb, 1994). H tells his dream:

> *I had a dream of a vampire. I was in my flat, sleeping with some-one, a partner. A small bed . . . there was fire and smoke. Someone was driving a car with, no lights, it was turning and unsafe. People were inside the burning building . . . Fire and disturbance and a vampire appeared. I managed to push it away. The lights from my eyes got the vampire to go away. I looked ill. A woman came in screaming. I looked in the mirror, I had no reflection. I thought I was turning into a vampire. In the guest room there was a hole with rats. I was terrified.*

H's vampire dream expressed his ambivalent wishes for an incorporative intimacy where boundaries were compromised for the sake of love. He shared, "I feel very drained, like I am drinking my own blood and sucking my own energy away." I asked if he were afraid that the therapy would not be able to protect him from the "sucking" parts of W and of himself, and that he would be burned alive and killed off by the couple's overpowering neediness and engulfment. In the dream image, there was nothing left to see in the mirror. The self disappears. .

I thought of Dorian Gray.

H answered affirmatively, "It might be my duty to give myself up and surrender."

I responded, "And the vampire gets you and keeps you – and never lets you go." I associated to the frightening images of the analyst's office or guest room where H gets stuck with devouring rats.

Love in the Afterworld – A Fable
In W's short original story "The Hunter," she gave voice to fantasies and near-hallucinatory visions of an ever-loving union. Coping with danger-ous feelings aroused by separation anxiety, she expressed wishes for a non- aggressive and seductive love where a doomed earth-bound thorny love is resurrected in an immortal transformation or metamorphosis and afterlife. She read her story:

H appears with a dragon with clipped off wings. He comes upon a rose garden that has lured him because of its sweet and special smell. The woman there has a healing power through her tears, a healing balm. H's wounds from his cats are being healed through the woman. He combs the woman's hair. There are thorns breaking through his heart and she has to prune the thorns from his heart. After a while, he decides he would rather grow thorns than go through a painful healing from the removal of the thorns. They decide to make love and he decides that he really does love her. And that he will stay. But he finds in the morning that she had bled to death from the thorns that were coming out of him. He had killed the one he loved. He was all thorns. They were like dangerous tigers. Then, he walks to a spot in the rose garden and becomes a thorny bush next to her. Eventually, a golden blossom grows where love can bloom again.

In her narrative, W wrote about an unconscious world that holds all the action – violent, painful and redemptive. Characters such as the hunter and the sweet-smelling rose garden led me to visualize animal images and semi-human personifications that merged all-consuming love with destruction and death. I imagined W as a waif-like alluring cat who used her slinky clothes and long black hair to ensnarl and destroy the hunter-spouse. In this way, fashion was taking shape as a sweet-smelling perfume that could entice and intoxicate a bewitched hunter-lover. Considering my role as a witness-participant and third party, I wondered if W experienced me as a rivalrous feline tiger-cat who would try to undermine her marital wishes as her former therapist had done. Perhaps she was hoping to lure me into her garden by enticing me to give up my fangs and be on her side.

W's narration conjured up eerie animal and plant-like personifications that lured and overcame her uncertain lovers. I associated to how fashion takes over and appropriates the animal world, where it devours and destroys it for decorous objects and/or clothing (e.g., leather belts, bags and furs) as well as adapting it for fanciful costumes with animal-like images and patterns. In this way, fashion's malleable objects become cultural artifacts that bind nature's kingdom with human needs and erotic desires.

Now, I imagine my silk Hermès scarf, enticingly pretty with its soft grey-green foliage and bright orange and black tiger face—and eyes.

Fashion as Faux Flowers

As the treatment progressed, fashion continued to show up in the way objects were used to manage feelings and thoughts in a disguised or metaphoric way.

In this example, W communicated her wish to know who I *really* was by spontaneously pointing to the vase of faux flowers in front of her. Staring at me intently, she shared, "I *know* that these flowers are not you. You like fresh flowers." W appeared to be telling me, "Your fashion is not faux flowers. Your fashion is like mine." She wanted me to know that she felt I was special and that she had a special connection to me. In letting me know that she knew who I *really was*, she was sending me a message that she could read me. I remembered the couple's report of being able to "read each other" when they first met (Rappoport 2012).

Ultimately, W's flower communications carried complex meanings that signaled that fashion was beginning to represent her more authentic and loving aspirations – amour. In a meaningful way, fashion was changing from false or mask-like armor to increasingly genuine self – expression.

A One-Eyed Cyclops

We cannot talk about fashion without considering the sexualization of viewing – the libidinalization of the eye.
(Personal Communication, Harriet Podhoretz, March 10, 2015)

As the treatment unfolded, fashion continued to express itself in various self-images that were projected and put into others. In this session, W expressed a breadth of feelings and thoughts about herself and me—her analyst. Pointing to the grainy wooden office panel, W unexpectedly exclaimed:

Oh, there are two one-eyed cyclops! The one above is open and wide-eyed, while the one below has a squinting eye. The first is feminine and has a bright eye and is Afro-American with full lips. The one below is an Asian one with a black beard. The Asian one is older and smaller and can be critical. The female cannot be one sex, as she would not be reproducing. The first cyclops is in her mid-twenties and is of childbearing age and the second – a female cyclops – is in her forties or fifties with a bright open eye. She seems scared – or surprised. The cyclops are of the same tribe. Perhaps a nymph.

In this representation, the panel that furnished my office functioned as a work of art that elicited W's subjectively felt projections. Her free-floating communications used the wooden markings to express her experience of "eying" – of seeing and being seen. In this way, I found out that W perceived me as an ever-changing multifaced character with different features and identifications. She viewed me, for example, as an old familiar figure from the same tribe and imagined both of us with different erotic, gender, reproductive and ethnic features and identifications. W also suggested that infantile, androgynous, homosexual and heterosexual feelings resided within her as well as between herself and me. Seeing was opening up to all sorts of inner self and interpersonal possibilities – a wide range of colors and designs as far as the inner – and outer – eye could see.

As the therapy progressed, the couple continued to share experiences that expressed healthier, more nuanced ways of viewing and understanding each other – of seeing and being seen. They created opportunities of being together as well as being separate – of having more authentic individual as well as couple experiences.

CONCLUSION

After reading this Chapter, Lou Hagood, a psychoanalytic colleague, wrote:

I am drawn to the eyes—fashion, at first, is "being seen". As in the dream, the car has no headlights versus the lights in his eyes. Is this insight? Fashion changes from "as if" or autoerotic – to intersubjective; here, it changes from "being seen" to interacting.

September 15, 2016

In this therapy, fashion entered the tri-personal field in forms that connected to how the couple were contacting – and transforming – the experiences within and between themselves. The therapeutic space supported a special form of playing, where W and H found new ways of being together under the analyst's eye and ear. As the couple expressed and integrated their trauma experiences, they began to perceive each other in increasingly empathic and forgiving ways. This helped them to connect and, ultimately, let go of one another with less pain and dread.

This multileveled focus on fashion showed its early representation in bodily and nonverbal communication. As the therapy deepened, fashion's expressions broadened with unexpected memories, fantasies and imaginings. In effect, the couple gradually moved from overly-alluring and seductive self-protective fashion statements to increasingly in-depth two-eyed authentic perspectives.

A Broad Application

This interpretation of fashion suggests that all therapeutic encounters are transformative opportunities that carry the ebb and flow of fashion elements on both sensory and symbolic levels. As the therapy progresses, the analyst's witnessing role creates a generative holding environment, where spontaneous creations emerge and play. In a metaphoric way, the clinical runway becomes increasingly open to novel communications that link body with mind and self with other supporting multiple possibilities for seeing, listening, and sensing.

This interpretation highlights how therapy functions on an artistic and creative plane. In this context, fashion captures internal and interpersonal experiences that function like a sculpture or painting – beginning with visceral contact and, ultimately, getting in touch with feeling, thought and instinctual energy. Inherent in this view of fashion and psychoanalysis is the idea that spontaneous actions and presentations express the potential of what is inside to be contacted and witnessed and, in so doing, shared.

REFERENCES

Bion, W.R. (1959). Attacks on linking. *International Journal of Psychoanalysis,* 40: 308-315.

Davidson, D. (1978). What metaphors mean. In *Philosophical Perspectives on Metaphor,* M. Johnson (Ed.). Minneapolis: University of Minnesota Press.

Eigen, M. (2012). On Winnicott's clinical innovations in the analysis of adults. *International Journal of Psychoanalysis,* 93:1449-1459.

Ferro, A. (1999). *The bi-personal field: Experiences in child analysis.* New York: Routledge.

Freud, S. (1914). On narcissism: An introduction. *Standard Edition,* 12:159-171.

Goldman, D. (2016). A queer kind of truth: Winnicott and the use of dissociation. In E. F. Howell & Itzkowitz, S. (Eds.). *The dissociative mind in psychoanalysis: Understanding and working with trauma (pp. 85-96).* New York: Relational Perspectives Book Series.

Gottlieb, R. M. (1994). The legend of the European vampire: Object loss and corporal preservation. *Psychoanalytic Study of the Child,* 49:465-480.

Greenberg, J. (2015). Therapeutic action and the analyst's responsibility. *Journal of the American Psychoanalytic Association,* 63:15-32.

Kalsched, D. (2016). Jung and dissociation: complexes, dreams, and the mythopoetic psyche.

In E. F. Howell & Itzkowitz, S. (Eds.). *The dissociative mind in psychoanalysis: Understanding and working with trauma* (pp. 97-106). New York: Relational Perspectives Book Series.

Katz, A. W. (2010). Healing the split between body and mind: Structural and developmental aspects of psychosomatic illness. *Psychoanalytic Inquiry,* 30:430-444.

Kernberg, O.F. (1974). Barriers to falling and remaining in love. *Journal of the American Psychoanalytic Association,* 22:486-511.

Lothane, Z. (2009). Dramatology in life, disorder, and psychoanalytic therapy: A further

contribution to interpersonal psychoanalysis. *International Forum of Psychoanalysis,* 18:135-148.

Poland, W. (2000). The analyst's witnessing and otherness. *Journal of the American Psychoanalytic Association,* 48: 17-34.

Rappoport, E. (2012). Creating the umbilical cord: Relational knowing and the somatic third. *Psychoanalytic Dialogues,* 22:375-388.

Richards, A. R. (2013). The skin I live in. In: *Encounters with Loneliness: Only the Lonely.* A. K. Richards, Spira, L. and Lynch, A. A. (Eds.). New York: International Psychoanalytic Books, pp. 37-49.

Sander, F. M. (Ed.) 2010. *Created in our own images. W. S. Gilbert's Pygmalion and Galatea – An introduction to the art, ethics and science of cloning.* New York: International Psychoanalytic Books.

Searles, H.F. (1976). Transitional phenomena and therapeutic symbiosis. *International*

Journal of Psychoanalytic Psychotherapy, 5:145-204, 5:145-204.

Steinberger, C. B. (2014). Transforming trauma: The relational unconscious and "chemistry" in the treatment of a paraplegic patient. *Journal of the American Psychoanalytic Association,* 62:399-422.

Stern, D.B. (2011). *Partners in Thought: Working with Unformulated Experience, Dissociation,*

and Enactment. New York: Routledge.

Winnicott, D. W. (1969). The use of an object and relating through identifications. *International Journal of Psycho-Analysis,* 50: 711-716.

Winnicott, D. W. (1971). *Playing and reality.* London: Tavistock Publications.

III

Redesigning the Self

1. A Fashion Journey in Psychoanalysis: Looking as Well as Listening

ANITA WEINREB KATZ

"Or can it be that clothes…make clear reference to who we are and wish to be taken as, while alternatively or simultaneously evoking an aura that 'merely suggests' more than it can (or intends to) state precisely?" (Davis, 1992)

Both the analysand's appearance, and the appearance of the analyst and his or her office, as well as his or her words, convey significant meaning in the analytic situation. In this chapter my intent is to focus on the analytic journey of Esther, and how her fashion statements, clothing styles and fit, hair grooming, posture, facial expressions, and makeup are a powerful message to anyone who sees her. That message may be either conscious or unconscious—a defense and a communication. The message is a way of protecting herself from anticipated actions by dangerous, intrusive or noxious people, as well as her way of connecting by hoping for kind concern: empathy, even pity.

The body and its presentation (clothing, hair style and color) may become the venue in which affective experience is most obviously expressed to the world at large. I believe that fashion and other types of creativity are appropriate venues for discourse in psychoanalysis. It facilitates understanding the meaning of our patients' feelings as well as their conscious and unconscious conflicts. I also believe that an important area of discourse in analysis is the patient's reactions to the analyst's appearance and the appearance of his or her office. I am submitting that as analysts what we witness in the patient (her gaze, posture, and attire) as well as what she sees in us – and how we reflect and interpret this – are significant aspects of the analytic journey. Jarl Jorstad (1988) along with many other analysts, hypothesizes that Freud's emphasis on neutrality and his use of the couch was partially a defense against being stared at. However, Freud's many artifacts belied his admonition that neutrality was essential to the analytic work. Hilda Doolittle (H.D.) sought analysis from Freud because she was suffering from writer's block. Her analysis with Freud empowered her to resume writing poetry. Arlene Richards (1992) refers to Freud's giving H.D. a statue at the end of her analysis with him, having helped her overcome her writing block. The small statue was of Athena, the goddess of reason, intelligent activity, arts, and literature. This gift clearly conveyed Freud's respect and appreciation of H.D.'s creativity, and his role in freeing her to continue.

Fashion choices, clothes, hairstyle, facial makeup, and expressions are statements to the world and expressions of the self that reveal and conceal: they can be an expression of love or hatred of the self, or by the self to others. This does not just refer to the patient and how he or she presents, but also to how the analyst fashions herself and her office (Jorstad 1988).

The first boundary between self and other is skin (Anzieu 1989), and the second includes facial expression, posture and sartorial choices. These are not only boundaries but also communications about the self to another.

When I met Esther, she was searching for a way to manage her conflicting desires for autonomy and for connection. She had learned to anticipate that both dependency and assertiveness would result in disaster. Her facial expressions and the way in which she clothed herself regularly became the stage on which she was given attention (critical or concerned) from her mother and aunts.

THE THERAPEUTIC JOURNEY

Esther began what became a long-term analysis at age 25. She was plagued by repetitive struggles with weight gains and losses. She was as uncomfortable in body as in psyche. She felt safest when withdrawn, entranced by the recordings of Broadway musicals, and enjoying singing along. She had a rich fantasy life filled with exciting sex and vindictive power. Long periods of sleep, enlivened by pleasurable dreams as well as nightmares, were her best source of both soothing and escaping the pain of the day. Chronically depressed, she was as wary of help as she was desperate for it. From early childhood she had been aware of wishes to be understood. She hoped that psychoanalysis would help her to feel more comfortable with herself and in relationships.

At the beginning of our work together, and continuing for many years, Esther looked like a waif. Her hair was unkempt, her clothes fit badly, and she slouched. Her expression was so forlorn and forbidding that when some of my other patients encountered her in the waiting room they expressed their compassion and their hope that I could help her. I waited until I thought there was a strong working alliance between us before I told her that some of my other analysands expressed deep concern about her and hoped that I could help her. I thought that this would be a way of conveying to her the power of her woeful self-presentation. I also hoped this would enable us to discuss the non-verbal messages that were communicated through her self-presentation. She was pleased that her facial expressions, posture, and attire captured the attention and compassion of her sometimes-hated analytic siblings. It meant she was being empathically noticed after a life of feeling criticized, abandoned, or required to take care of her caregivers' needs, a conflictual source of pain and power.

We connected an accident when she was 2 1/2 to her belief that it was very dangerous to be spunky. This accident, a catastrophic injury to her face, occurred when her mother left her alone in the kitchen for a few minutes while she took the garbage out. Esther climbed up onto a counter to reach a can of crayons that she was forbidden to use without supervision. She grabbed her prize, but as she ran off with it following her mother down the hallway, she tripped and fell on the can, badly tearing her mouth on its jagged metal rim. She was hospitalized for three weeks, during which time she underwent the first of two surgeries to repair the cosmetic and functional damage to her face.

The final repair had to be postponed until her growth slowed down at puberty. Esther remembers spending the next ten years with an unsightly hanging lip. Even after it was corrected at thirteen, and her appearance was significantly improved, Esther remained very sensitive about the lingering scar.

Esther's mother had never dealt with important aspects of her own history. At age eleven Esther's mother lost her own mother, who was confined to a mental institution until her death. Everything about her grandmother was veiled in secrecy. Esther's mother, understandably, was unable to tolerate her own psychological realities and was limited in her capacity to tolerate her daughter's separate psychological states. She tended to treat her daughter's body as if it were her own, touching Esther's scarred lip and lamenting the damage as though it were an intolerable injury to herself. This laid the groundwork for Esther's seeking concern and attention through her fashion choices and facial expression.

When Esther began to need a bra, her mother gave Esther one of her own, which was much too large for the young girl. Even in Esther's adolescence her mother would get into bed with her to cuddle many mornings. "You are me," she would say, and, indeed, Esther felt that her mother acknowledged only one body between the two of them. To want something for herself– like a body of her own or clothing that she picked out for herself –was usually not acceptable. When she was 12 years old, orange was the rage in her school. She picked an orange blouse, but her mother refused to buy it for her, saying she looked terrible in orange. Being an agent in her own appearance was scary. It was only recently that she recalled this memory, and at the next session she ordered an orange T-shirt from LL Bean.

Esther's father was even less able than her mother to let her be an autonomous person. He never complimented her on her appearance. Even after she was grown, he discouraged separation as much as he could. When she was in her early thirties, she invited her family for a Thanksgiving dinner at her house. Her father objected to any deviation from the family pattern of celebrating Thanksgiving in the same restaurant. Instead of supporting and enjoying her as a capable and lovely woman, he cruelly rejected her. When Esther did not relinquish the idea of hosting Thanksgiving dinner, he became furious, did not attend, and refused to speak to her for many months.

Esther's father never told her that she was a cute little girl or an attractive woman. Searles stressed the importance of the father's finding a comfortable and appropriate way to experience and express his own attraction and desire for his daughter. He sees this as a crucial factor in the daughter's successful resolution of her oedipal issues, and an enriching and enlivening experience for the father as well. He suggests that this works best in the context of a good marital relationship. Searles adds that there is a corresponding truth to the importance of the analyst's finding an appropriate way to experience and recognize the attractiveness and desirability of his female analysands (Searles 1995;Katz 2002, p. 287). I think this is also true of female analysts in relationship to their female and male analysands.

Esther got a lot of negative attention from her mother and aunts on the way she dressed. Her mother did not respect her daughter's ability to choose what she wore, and Esther was humiliated by her mother's asking a stranger on the subway platform for advice on what style dress would be good for her daughter.

Esther often felt singled out by teachers and peers for being "different" and "weird." She remembers herself as klutzy and fat, with orthopedic shoes and disfiguring psoriasis on her legs, arms, and hands. Lonely and depressed, she had few friends, and spent much of her time withdrawn into a life-preserving but isolating fantasy world. Fantasy, rocking, and music soothed her, and created a walled-off inner space that could not be invaded or usurped by her intrusive mother.

Esther at first lacked the capacity to reflect upon her feelings and put them into words. When I tried to do it for her, she felt criticized. She used my interpretations to beat herself and hate me. I commented once that she held on to her money instead of buying pretty clothes and enjoying being attractive because of a fear of being depleted of the inheritance that made her feel secure and loved by her parents. She took this to mean that she was a greedy and bad person, and she harbored that "criticism" for years. Her endless self-criticisms also served, in true sadomasochistic style, to express her anger at me for the narcissistic wound of my interpretation. (Katz 1990). Only after several years of our work together was she able to consider that it was her own belief that she was a shitty person and that the world was filled with other shitty people. Until then, she simultaneously acted out these beliefs and held them at bay with her verbal diarrhea and her dreams of shit. She lived this out graphically through how she fashioned her appearance as messy and unkempt, and my counter-transference was fear of either my couch or myself being dirtied. Recognizing these feelings, I felt ashamed of my fears and judgments of her. As we continued our work, we both came to realize that her presentation was a form of protection against my invading her body and psyche like her mother did.

Her use of evacuation as a technique for dealing with affect took on new poignancy when she brought in a story that her mother had told her. When Esther was a baby, she once smeared herself with feces. Her mother could not bear to touch her shit, and had gotten a neighbor to give Esther the necessary bath. Esther needed to test whether I too was afraid to touch her shit. We explored the possibility that it might be a creative product as well as a disgusting one.

As she became stronger and more separate, Esther allowed herself to spend her money a little more freely, to "enjoy her shit." She bought an apartment and some pretty clothes. She enjoyed showing me her new clothes and was interested in my critiques of her fashion choices. She still felt guilty for having something nice that her mother had wanted but had not allowed herself, but she also felt pleased that she was no longer an anxiety-ridden martyr, and she became able to wear pretty, stylish clothes, prompting my admiration of her appearance. However, it was hard for her to buy anything that was not on sale. This was not just being frugal, but getting something that she felt entitled to and did not get growing up.

Esther was exquisitely aware of my appearance – my clothes, hair style and color, and was also interested in objects in my office; she commented on them, sometimes lovingly stroking them. I believe that these objects functioned for her as transitional objects (Winnicott 1971) both helping her to connect and separate from me, as well as to take part in a Kleinian paranoid/schizoid position in which she was taking me over and becoming the powerful one. (Klein 1975).

When by chance Esther and I encountered each other while walking on the street, I recognized her, but she did not recognize me because of her avoidant gaze. In our next session I brought this up, and she explained that when she walks she focuses on her path, not the person walking toward her. Informed by Salomonsson's exploration of gaze avoidance as a defense (2014), I suggested to her that by warding off eye contact, she warded off destructive impulses. We understood that gaze avoidance was automatic when the other is a stranger, someone who she feared would look at her critically. This expectation defensively stirred up her destructive impulses.

It is my assumption that looking at fashion – both hair and clothing – might be easier for most people and less scary than looking at their faces, let alone looking into their eyes (the mirror of the soul). This may be related to fear of love's being absent, fear of love's being present, fear of engulfment, and/or fear of criticism.

As Esther slowly allowed herself to pursue her own dreams, she began to anticipate a long-desired achievement—a PhD in Italian. This venture into achieving both an autonomous accomplishment and an elegant persona brought up old fears in new ways. Throughout her analysis, Esther had moments in my office of moving into a state of consciousness that was not expressed in words, but physically enacted in screams, contorted bodily positions, and a lopsided grimace of her mouth that recreated the disfigurement resulting from her accident. At those moments, she often turned around from lying on the couch, pointing to her mouth to make sure that I saw the spontaneous reenactment of her early disfigurement.

Now that she was pursuing the doctorate that she had always desired, these moments increased. The possibility of achieving her life-long ambition of being an elegant, scholarly, strong, accomplished woman stirred up the trauma that her spunk as a 2 ½-year-old had brought upon her. During these periods her body and face went into contortions, and when they were over, I would try to put into words what I thought she was experiencing, or re-experiencing. Esther's facial contortions represented a mask created by herself that she was in control of – yet she seemed to feel they were spontaneous and weirdly out of her control. We linked this with her choosing rag-tag clothing and messy hair to underline and show me and others the pain and suffering that was so much part of her life.

Slowly Esther began to develop a sense of safety with me. She even began to have a sense that I liked her, even though she still thought of

herself—and on a deeper level, of me—as a pain in the ass and sometimes even dangerous. During the first half of her analysis, Esther had
frequently expressed a desire to move in with me. She often sat in my
waiting room for over an hour after her session, not wanting to leave the
safety of my office. But this also gave her an opportunity to survey many
of her analytic siblings, and make sure that they saw her. Eventually she
allowed herself the awareness that indeed her face did take on a scowl or
a glower when she feared she would not be liked or accepted, and her
angry facial expressions sometimes made her fears come true.

Esther was grappling with the right to a separate identity – to be able
to be autonomous without being abandoned, demeaned, and criticized.
She thought that this would be like being reborn. When she finally felt
able to communicate this wish to me, her body expressed her pain and
her rage – she banged her head and legs and rocked on the couch,
drooling and gagging and spitting, and screaming and wailing inconsol-
ably. I appreciated the power and pain in these physical enactments, and
explained them to Esther as a communication as well as an evacuation.
On one occasion; however, when she sat up and began to hit herself, I
told her to stop. She did, saying, in a childish voice, "That's not good for
me, is it?" She found my distinction between communicating with her
body and hurting herself useful. Although these physical enactments
and the altered states of consciousness continued for a while, conscious
self-injury stopped. After a while, we became able to talk about these
dramatic experiences, and understand them, as part of a reenactment of
her experiences in the hospital and afterwards at home. (Katz 1990)

Esther's body and its adornments expressed what her mind could not
contain. She rid herself of anger and autonomous cravings through her
illnesses, her endless evacuation dreams, her comportment and clothing,
as well as in her frenzies on my couch. Esther wanted to have some clout
in her life, but she feared the upsurge of the murderous rage she had felt as
a child when her assertive gestures were quashed. She didn't act on her
impulses to slash and stab, but she wore her pain on her sleeve or rather in
her entire waif-like presentation; yet her dream and deep longing was to
be an elegant, Italian-speaking woman.

As she became able to reflect upon the way she presented herself to the world, she saw her neglectful grooming and wretched demeanor as a way of "becoming my own monster, to scare off people so they would leave me alone." At the same time; however, she was saying, "I'm so miserable, please have mercy and take care of me. Be nice to me; don't hurt me." She was beginning to recognize the downside of her appearance, and she gradually became empowered to enjoy presenting herself as an elegant woman. This was a conscious fantasy that she had believed would never come true. But this transformation did not entirely rid her of all the anxiety associated with coming out to the world as a strong, fashionable woman.

Over the years of analysis, however, as I reliably survived the rage she was certain would leave her abandoned or destroyed by me, she began to think about coming out of her "cocoon." It was notable that initially she had identified cocoons exclusively with tent caterpillars – those creatures that do not evolve into beautiful butterflies, but rather forbode the death of trees. After several years of analysis, she experimented with new ways of seeking attention. Her waif-like presentation began to shift, and she slowly metamorphosed into an elegantly dressed and beautifully groomed woman, a beautiful butterfly, who was proud of her toned body. Instead of mainly looking inward, she began to allow herself to look outward. She bought new clothes and brought them in to show me. Before lying down on the couch, she sometimes looked at some of the objects on my desk and on my shelves, picking some of them up and holding them lovingly. She enjoyed the flowers in my office and commented on my clothes.

Fashion became a medium for connecting and separating with me. She made it very clear that although she admired what I wore, there was an underlying current of criticism of my extravagance, naming me her "fashionista analysta." She prided herself on being frugal and controlled regarding money spent on her clothes – in contrast to the shame she felt when she lost control in public places, becoming enraged when she felt her space was invaded by strangers –on the bus, or in the pool. She sometimes yelled at or pushed the offender, shamefully confessing her out-of-control behavior to me.

She reported how her mother would seek advice from strangers on the subway platform about how Esther should dress. It was as though Esther's opinion, as well as her mother's opinion, was worthless. We sensed that her unkempt shabby clothes were her adult self crying for Mommy : look at me; take care of me. This informed us that she still longed for a connection to her mother, and to be seen and empowered by her mother and me. At times she regressed, lying on my rug, crying "Ma-ma, Ma-ma." These regressed actions clued us into how unresponsive her mother had been when she was an infant. This was replicated in her waif-like appearance as an adult—the internalized mother unable to take care of her.

For several years I had a dog in my consulting room during sessions, and Esther greeted us every day with, "Hello, Dr. Katz; hello, Dr. Dog!" This was not entirely a joke. She developed the custom of spending the first ten minutes of the session on the floor playing with Dr. Dog. I don't believe I have ever seen more loving and engaged play between an animal and a person, and Esther enjoyed my interest and pleasure as I watched them. In this way Esther began to show the loving and joyous side of herself that she had sealed off out of fear that to reveal it would forfeit her right to be cared for by me. My enjoyment contained her joyful experience, and helped her to reflect upon herself both as a loving subject and as a beloved object, and to integrate these experiences into her beliefs about herself in relation to others.

Her fear that to be strong and beautiful meant to be uncared for gradually gave way to a realization that she could be empathic and helpful to others without giving up the right to either lovingly take care of herself or be lovingly taken care of by others. She enrolled in a challenging graduate program. She began to see herself as a competent caregiver. Our work on her loving, empathic qualities was an empowering balance, I believe, to the painful work of uncovering her needy wishes – never to have to grow up – and the terror of her murderous rage. Once she could enjoy being the strong, nurturing one, her relationships improved. When she needed care, she learned to elicit it actively instead of by the passive coercion of a waif-like appearance. In spite of her anxiety, she is becoming the sophisticated and elegant renaissance woman she always wanted to be.

Not long before her dissertation was completed, she told me that her mother had knit some beautiful clothes. She showed me three of the dresses that her mother had knit, and indeed they were beautiful in design and also in workmanship This was not the mother that Esther had described in her sessions. We thought that perhaps these were clothes she had knit before her marriage. Now that Esther had lost weight, these dresses fit her beautifully. There were a few holes in a beautiful black knit dress. Upon my encouragement she brought this dress to be fixed and then came into a session wearing it. She was indeed the elegant woman she had been afraid to be during so much of her life. Yet the enduring effects of her early trauma are still experienced in some sessions as deep feelings of sadness. She is at long last mourning the trauma that she had endured throughout her early life.

DISCUSSION

Esther had a highly developed capacity for physical drama, and could capture my attention in engaging ways—for better or for worse. One of those ways was her appearance—how she presented herself to the world and me. Her psychic journey was concretized by her changing physical presentation—her fashion journey: her clothes, hair, and posture.

Esther came to analysis struggling with conflicted desires for autonomy and loving connections. She harbored the fear that to be autonomous, powerful, and beautiful was to risk abandonment or punishment.

Through fashion, Esther enacted her lack of identification with a caring other, and her angry refusal to accept limits. She longed to be understood, cared for, and admired by her mother. But, Esther's mother competed with her for mothering and admiration.

I was dismayed by a recent note by a psychotherapist in the Op Ed section of the NY Times on the "The Dowdy Patient" (AUTHOR 2015). The therapist wrote that after several years of analysis his female patient was ready to leave, feeling better but still looking dowdy, and still without the longed-for relationship to a man. She had originally gotten into treatment hoping for a relationship with a man.

I speculate that her therapist did not explore her appearance with her. I feel that non-verbal communications, including all aspects of a patient's appearance, are important areas to explore. Perhaps if the way she presented herself and what it meant to her had been explored, a different outcome could have been achieved.

As I hope I have elucidated in this chapter, Esther's nonverbal communications to me, including her way of fashioning herself (clothes, hair, and makeup) were important forms of communication to me and rich areas of exploration and growth.

As her enjoyment of autonomy and power in the analytic relationship developed, and psychic space opened up, she could contain and think reflectively about experiences that had previously been handled only through evacuation or through noverbal communications such as her fashion statements. She was conscious of her appearance and the power it gave her to enlist people to be concerned about her, although it often resulted in painful attacks by her aunts. But she was also conscious of the dangers of changing, and presenting herself to the world as a strong, beautiful woman. After all, the spunky 2½ year old ended up disfigured and hospitalized for 3 weeks.

My role throughout much of her analysis was to function as a container (Bion 1962, 1977), holding onto the evacuated material long enough to note it, and then to offer it back in doses small enough to be metabolized and integrated into a comfortable body/mind marriage. We gradually understood the deeper meaning of her fashion choices, which eventually freed her to choose to present herself as beautiful and spunky in how she dressed, looked, and acted.

Among the important beliefs that she began to question was the "badness" (associated with her "shittiness") that she felt kept her subject to abandonment and punishment. This is an important aspect of fashion statements that is not always clearly delineated. When caretaking is unreliable and autonomy is not encouraged – or is even punished – fashion may come to be seen not only as a technique for ensuring care, but also as the punishment for needing it. Both of these fantasies defend against the original equation of "badness" associated with the desire for beauty and autonomous power. The same developmental failures that result in a fragile ego and hinder the development of mindfulness also contribute to an overly harsh super-ego with which the fragile ego cannot compete (Freud 1923).

Esther learned to seek caretaking through waif-like fashion statements. As her sense of herself became stronger, she had more capacity to contemplate the pleasures and dangers of separateness, to mourn the parental failures she had suffered, and to forgive both her parents and herself (Klein 1975). As her body and mind became more harmoniously married to each other, she could perceive in the present and in the future safe avenues for autonomy, beauty, and connectedness.

Because I paid attention to what she wore, and she paid attention to what I wore, she became a more beautiful fashionable woman. So the exchange between us not infrequently was her saying to me, "That's a pretty dress," or "You look nice," or said critically, "How much did you spend on that dress?" since she prided herself on only buying things that are on sale. And my saying to her, "That's a pretty dress," or "Your sweater is beautiful," or "That haircut becomes you," or "your makeup sings as well as you sing" (she has a beautiful voice, and would sometimes sing to me in her session). But also there were times that I said critical things like "You forgot to put on blush," or "That haircut is not so becoming."

The physical contortions and reenactments of the pain of her early experiences of feeling at risk of accident or abandonment was replaced recently by profound and enduring feelings of sadness. She wanted me to witness her sadness while she lay on the couch looking lovely but turning around at times for me to see how very sad she felt. I imagined that she was in mourning and had me witness how much she had suffered. She no longer in her daily life concretely exhibits her suffering through her facial expression, her unkempt hair and unbecoming style of dressing, but is in touch with her deep feelings of loss of past opportunities—especially in friendships and romance, and is strong enough to endure the pain of her sadness and grieve her losses.

CONCLUSION

I have addressed in this chapter how the patient's facial expression, style and fit of her clothing, jewelry and hair, and her posture are powerful means of communication to others, as well as significant indicators of self-esteem and trust of others. I believe that these fashion statements are important communications and need to be addressed in treatment. They also enhance the analyst's understanding of the patient, and when worked with, these fashion statements help to deepen the treatment.

Also, what I found to be transformative was both her opening her psyche to me, as an empathic witness, and opening her eyes to the world. She was coming out of her shell, looking at me and the surrounds of my office. She enjoys my looking at her, even when I am sometimes critical.

When I first started seeing Esther in analysis, her external appearance (facial expressions, posture, clothes, hair) communicated a damaged, unkempt and disrespected self. As an analyst, I felt my job was to both bear witness to Esther's present pain, and to her re-experience of past trauma in her sessions with me. In addition, I was a self-object who looked at her in a caring, empathic way, including addressing her concrete presentation of her conflicts about being a strong, spunky, and sophisticated woman. And although there are significant changes in her life and in her fashion statements, she at times still comes in with a mixed message. Recently she put on a lovely dress for the afternoon at the ballet, but covered it with a wool sweater that was many sizes too big for her. This seemed to me an expression of both her love and hate in the transference and perhaps in the counter-transference. I told Esther that this fashion statement of beautiful well- fitting dress and shlumpy wool sweater was a poignant reminder to me that there was still the residue of pain and despair in her psyche. After I made this interpretation to her, she replied, "Write that down. It's a beautiful, poignant line." I was deeply moved by her ability, in the midst of her pain, to be able to think of me, and my writing project, and connect to me in a generative way.

Recently she told me: "there is something reparative in putting myself together in the morning – putting on make-up – trying to figure things out – what scarf to wear – like I care about it. I used to throw myself together." When I asked her what this meant to her, she replied. "I wanted my family to see it – a rebellion against my mother. If I tried to look good, it was never good enough, so I rebelled by not trying. "Looking good and being seen as engaged and interested in others in the world was poignantly reflected by the reaction of one of my patients. His session was after hers. He came into his session beaming. "She looks so good – like a totally different person." I beamed back with pleasure at hearing this.

REFERENCES

Anzieu, D (1989) The Skin Ego. London: Karnac Books.

Balint, M. (1979). The basic fault. New York:Bruner/Mazel.

Bach, S. (1994). *The Language of Perversion and the Language of Love.* New Jersey: Jason Aronson.

Bion, W.R. (1962). *Learning from Experience.* New York: Basic Books.

Britton, R. (2003). *Sex, Death, and the Superego: Experiences in Psychoanalysis.* London:

Davis, Fred. (1992). *Fashion, Culture, and Identity.* Chicago: The University of Chicago Press.

Freud's, S.(1923). The Ego and the Id. *Standard Edition* 19: 3-63.

Jørstad, J. (1988). Aspects of Transference and Countertransference in Relation to Gaze and Mutual Gaze during Psychoanalysis. *Scand. Psychoanal. Rev.*, 11(2):117-140.

Katz, A. (1990). Paradoxes of Masochism. Psychoanalytic Psychology 7: 225–241.

Katz, A. (1997). Poisoning the Body to Save the Self. Unpublished paper. Presented at the Fourth International Psychoanalytic Conference of the Psychoanalytic Society of the Postdoctoral Program and Psychoanalytic Institutes of Italy. Florence, Italy. August 1-3, 1997.

Katz, A (2002). Fathers Facing Their Daughters' Emerging Sexuality: The return of the oedipal. *Psychoanal Study of Child, 57*: pp. 270-291.

Klein, M. (1975) *Mourning and its Relation to Manic-Depressive States* in Love, Guilt and Reparation and Other Works (1921-1945) pp.344-369. Delacorte Press/Seymour Lawrence.

Kohut, H. (1971). *The Analysis of the Self.* New York: International Universities Press.

Krystal, H. (1988). *Integration and Self-Healing: Affect, Trauma, Alexithymia.* New Jersey: The Analytic Press

McDougall, J. (1989). *Theaters of the Body: A Psychoanalytic Approach to Psychosomatic Illness*. New York: W.W. Norton.

Muller-Braunschweig, H. (1998). The effects of body-related psycho-therapy in psychosomatic illnesses. *Psych Inq. 18*; pp. 424-444.

Ogden, T (2005), *This Art of Psychoanalysis: Dreaming Undreamt Dreams and Interrupted Cries*. London and New York: Routledge.

Ogden, T. (1986). *The Matrix of the Mind*. New Jersey: Jason Aronson.

Richards, A.K. (1992). Hilda Doolittle and Creativity—Freud's Gift. *Psychoanal. St. Child*, 47:391-406.

Salomonsson, B. (2014). Infantile defences in parent-infant psychotherapy: The example of gaze avoidance. *Int. J. Psychoanal,* 97:65-88.

Searle, HF (1995). Collected Papers on Schizophrenia and Related Subjects. New York: International University Press.

2. *First Line of Defense*

KARLO STEEL

In 1969, the United States was in the midst of responding to the Kerner Report issued by the National Advisory Commission on Civil Disorders. The Commission, formed by President Lyndon B. Johnson, was in response to a series of riots that erupted across the country fueled by racial inequality. Along with other forces, the Commission called upon the media to be more inclusive in its representation of black Americans. Against this backdrop of decisive inclusion, I witnessed three minutes of what would become one of my earliest and most powerful memories.

In December of that year, I saw the television debut of The Jackson Five performing "I Want You Back" on The Ed Sullivan Show. Fronted by the astonishingly youthful Michael Jackson, the prepubescent pop star sang and danced his way into the nation's living room. Seeing such blatant talent, with his breezy vocal delivery and effortless dance moves, was incredibly impressive to me. But it was what he wore during that performance which made the biggest impression on me: a dark purple suede vest edged in fringe, multicolored paisley print shirt, fitted khaki pants, chelsea boots, all topped off with a jauntily cocked lavender chapeau. It all seemed so hip, so cool and very, very adult. I yearned to be that stylish and cute. In fact, within those three minutes I felt a kind of mirroring; that this young, black boy was just like me, especially given my penchant for singing and dancing around the house, which was always met with appreciative stares from family and friends. But I also

Michael Jackson 1969

sensed that Jackson's performance was more than just a cute boy being appreciated. His winning talent and stylishly good looks earned him ADORATION. I felt, if I could just be more like him, then I too would be adored. I was just five years old. I developed a very real obsession with Jackson after witnessing his performance. I told everyone at school that I would "be" him. I pestered my father to buy me the latest Jackson Five singles and any magazine that had pictures of him on the cover. Pop magazines *Spec* and *16* were my favorites, since they catered to the teeny bop market. And although my reading skills were remedial, it didn't matter, because I could always look at him. I would study his clothes, his hair, and his smile.

A few years into the Seventies, the popular music landscape began to change. A new English pop phenomena known as glam rock began to make waves on American shores around 1972, and both *Spec* and *16* started covering some of those acts. David Bowie, then in his Ziggy Stardust guise, was one of them. But he wasn't featured very often, quite possibly because he hadn't had a hit in the U. S. yet. Yet in those occasional black and white images I saw of him, printed on cheap paper, I could clearly see he was very different

Bowie 1980

from the Donny Osmond and David Cassidy, whom those magazines usually featured. I found Bowie's androgynous appearance intriguing, perhaps because I was coming to terms with my homosexuality around that time.

I finally saw David Bowie in 1973 on the hip late night television show "The Midnight Special." As I was struggling to stay awake, the clock struck the witching hour and the program began. The perfor-

116

mance, called "The 1980 Floor Show," was set 5 years into the future. His look, impossibly pale, incredibly thin, unbelievably made-up, was like someone from another, far more glamorous planet. I watched -awed as he appeared in a series of glittering and outré costumes that made little concession to his gender. Over the course of two hours, I went from a pre-teen to a young adult. Seeing him made me realize there was much more to life than what I had been told or shown, and it was a life starkly different from mine. I'd seen a future where all things were bright, alluring and permissible. It filled me with fascination and I wondered if one day I could inhabit that same universe. My mind began racing with possibilities... That night's initiation remained my secret for years. I knew my friends or family wouldn't understand my epiphany.

Although I was monumentally awed by "Ziggy," I knew there would be no way I could "be" him in the same way I could "be" Michael Jackson. For starters, the physical differences between myself and "Ziggy" were just too wide. I was a chubby black boy, and no one ever confused me with being a girl (girlish, yes, but never a girl). Despite that, I dropped Michael Jackson like a hot potato and developed an even larger obsession with David Bowie. I bought all his albums and scoured music magazines for any articles about him. I was fascinated with the way he looked: beyond gender, almost post-human, and very much unlike me. He seemed to occupy an aesthetic space that others simply could not. He was my absolute favorite pop star throughout the 70's despite his sartorial turn away from the flamboyance of Ziggy. Following him throughout those ten years opened my eyes to the bands which influenced him (The Velvet Underground, The Stooges) and all the bands that were influenced by him (too many to mention). The latter started to appear around 1978 with the emergence of New Wave and New Romanticism. They were all his sons and daughters, in artfully applied makeup and flashy clothes. I would listen to their records in my bedroom while gazing at the sleeves and flicking through pop magazines. They seemed so slick. But nothing prepared me for that hot summer afternoon in 1981 when, strolling around my favorite record store, I saw Grace Jones on the cover of her newly released Nightclubbing album.

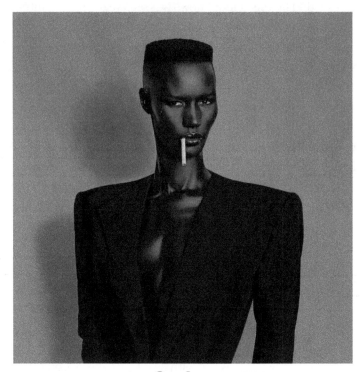

Grace Jones

I can remember what initially caught my eye about that record cover: a severe black silhouette against a dark beige background. I picked it up and suddenly I felt a pounding in my chest. My palms began to sweat and my mouth went dry. I was at once intimidated and excited as I gazed at her startlingly blue/black visage. Her narrow eyes seemed to fix me with a double-dare stare. Her impervious expression, with an unlit cigarette dangling between glossy lips, signaled an aloof, haughty glamour. That angular haircut atop her angular cheekbones and angular jacket (...and angular chest. "Just what sex is she?") revealed an attention to detail of which I was not yet capable, but instantly understood. Her image was powerfully minimalistic; everything was one color: black. Direct and adroit, her pose made her look as though she was carved from expensive black marble. She seemed an elegant and sublime statue, cold and hard to the touch.

Her bulletproof glamour shook me to the core, but with the added realization that, with tremendous effort, I could actually be just like her.

And the fact that she was black was reassuring. Now I had evidence that I could render myself stylishly untouchable and chicly aloof. It would be an escape route from the immense problems that plagued my daily life. I was deeply unhappy during this time, not only with my physical self (pimply and almost fat), but with my entire situation. I was relentlessly picked on in school for being a sissy, I had to endure my parents' inevitable and explosive arguments that occurred almost nightly, and I was occupied with trying to navigate the awful, deathly violence of black 1970's New Orleans. My upbringing was underprivileged, uneducated and unsafe, and I became acutely aware of that at an early age. I wanted escape and I wanted change. I needed a transformation. But in Grace's sly, semi-smile and stony stare, I saw the potential of who and what I could be. And so, I decided to transform. I took up smoking, started dieting, and began speaking with a clipped, indeterminate European accent.

In attempt to get as close as possible to some sort of glamour, which I desperately craved, I decided to enroll in a hairdressing academy after graduating high school. This proved to be a savvy move because it was there that I befriended a girl who would be key to exposing me to night-life and all stylish escapades that followed. Her name was Beth, and she sported that *de rigueur* haircut which every self-respecting 1980's punkette had: a cropped back and sides with massive volume on top streaked with yellow. She looked so cool. I had to get to know her.

Beth took me under her wing despite the fact that I looked like a slightly hip preppy. At first, we went to hardcore punk gigs, which I found exciting. But the aggressively macho and violent types that frequented those gigs unnerved me. Eventually we began to go to new-wave clubs which played electronic dance music. It was there I felt at home. I loved the synthetic sounds and look of the habitués: peroxide, eyeliner, Dr. Martens and lots of black. I became instantly hooked and pestered her to go clubbing as much as possible. But looking like a mall shopper wasn't going to cut it if I wanted to be a clued-in member of *nouveau* disco society. I had to re-invent my look. Luckily, I befriended some of the more extreme poseurs on that scene who taught me a thing or two. So armed with copies of *i-D*, *The Face* and *Blitz* magazines, I began my transformation in earnest.

I cannot overstate the importance those magazines had on my life. I became an avid reader and an obsessive collector (even to this day), combing over every detail. They opened my eyes to style and fashion. It was within those pages where I first saw designers whose work resonated with me: the sci-fi fantasies of Thierry Mugler, the punk-couture of Vivienne Westwood, the austere, deconstructed blackness of Yohji Yamamoto and Comme Des Garçons. I was in awe of all of their work. But above all, it was the great mix master Jean Paul Gaultier whose funky and fresh fabulousness seemed to reflect the new global *demi-monde* of which I was now a part. *i-D* said, "Style is not what you wear but how you wear it" and I took it to heart. I drew immense inspiration from their bold post-modern editorials, frequenting thrift stores, charity shops, dumpsters, anywhere that I could obtain clothing to approximate those looks. In hindsight, my attempts were often hilariously disastrous. I wanted to be as stylishly unconventional as possible but I didn't understand the finer points. But as the decade wore on, and the general trend moved from gender-bending to a more monochromatic uniform-like trendiness, I became better at putting my look together.

The work of stylist Ray Petri (as well as Simon Foxton) was often featured in *i-D* and *The Face*. His work was an interesting combination of high fashion and sportswear often presented on black, Hispanic or mixed race male models. I found his proposals to be strong, sexy, confrontational, and achingly modern. It was through him I became aware that styling was an actual profession. To me, it seemed to be the coolest job on the planet. I began to follow the work of several stylists and secretly hoped to become one. During this time, around 1985, I wore black oversized jackets with white shirts buttoned to the top with a brooch, and a sash across my chest. I finished the look with a stretchy black tube skirt, short white socks and black patent leather derbies: pure Petri. I became known on the club circuit for looking cool. A few years later, I got hired as a shop assistant at the only punk / goth / metal boutique in New Orleans. This was a rather hip position to be in. One day the owner, who was aware of my fashion obsession and intrigued by my trendy take on rock-and-roll clothing, asked me to style the store's segment in a local group fashion show for independent boutiques. I was astonished by her request. It was the first time I was asked to use my fashion skills beyond just selling clothes. I threw myself into the role with gusto. I relished the creative control I was given: selecting the models, hair and makeup, the music, and, best of all, coordinating the looks. At the show, our segment really stood out and was greeted with unexpectedly enthusiastic applause. The owner was so impressed that she asked if I would style some press pictures, and then the next show a few months later. My obsession with fashion and trends was being noticed and, more importantly, being utilized. It was deeply validating.

As the 80s ended so did my time in New Orleans. In 1990 I moved to San Francisco, and it didn't take long for me to immerse myself in the swirling nocturnal activities. But there was a distinct difference between nightclubbing in New Orleans and in San Francisco. In New Orleans the scene was rather small, so there were fewer divisions amongst "alternative" tribes. Punks, new wavers, trendies, goths, queers, freaks–they all hung out together. But in San Francisco clubbing was

Pay Petri

divided along sexual orientation lines, so I found myself striking poses in gay nightclubs. But the truth is that I never felt fully comfortable in those (nearly) all male and highly sexually charged environments. I never styled myself with the goal of getting laid. In fact, my outfits actually inhibited my sex life because most gay men in those clubs wanted to score with a guy who looked as though he just exited a gym or fell off a construction site. Luckily I was able to find a fashion-y clique within that heaving mass of sweaty torsos and tight jeans. But it quickly became clear that I would have to move sexual conquests, in that environment anyway, further down my priority list.

One night out, hanging in the VIP room of a mega gay club, I was approached by another trendy whom I knew from constant clubbing. He asked if I would be interested in styling an editorial in a new magazine he was founding (strangely, I have complete recall of what I was wearing that night: a pair of 1940's wide-legged trousers in a midnight gabardine, a black 1960's *faux* leather bomber jacket, an "Hermès" scarf worn as a cravat, a tuxedo shirt, and vintage black-and-white wingtips), and naturally I jumped at the chance. The magazine was to be called *Surface*, and it would be dedicated to all the fun looks one could encounter at the disco. Once again, I was approached because of the way I looked, not because of my experience. I styled one editorial each in the first three issues and I felt as though I was the next Ray Petri.

Fashion began to cool down from the high octane flamboyance of the 80's and a new pared-down, stripped-back minimalist style emerged called grunge (for lack of a better word), led by photographers David Sims and Corrine Day and stylist Melanie Ward. They really shaped the look of that decade, greatly influencing the leading designers of the day. Like Ray Petri and Simon Foxton before, I followed their work religiously. But these new image makers seemed to ditch the multicultural aspect of the 80's to show (almost) only white people. And brilliant designers like Martin Margiela, Helmut Lang, Ann Demuelemeester and Raf Simons, all of whom I revered, rarely featured black models and almost never any male ones (Lang being the exception). I found their lack of diversity to be disappointing and terribly un-modern, but it didn't stop me from trying to emulate their looks on a retail salary or snapping up their pieces when they made it to markdown in luxury department stores. Also coinciding with this new fashion mood was the musical trend Britpop. Bands like Suede, Pulp and Elastica had a sharp, androgynous retro 70's style which subtly nodded towards my early fascination with David Bowie. I loved the way they looked and I grabbed tickets to see them when they landed in the Bay Area. They were all very skinny and wore it as a badge of honor. So in order to flaunt my Britpop credentials, I chain-smoked my way down to a size 28-inch waist and strutted around town dressed in Levi's bootcut needle-cords, skinny ribbed turtlenecks and 60's C,helsea boots. Smudged eyeliner, chipped black nail varnish and shiny pvc pants were saved for Saturday nights, when I'd haunt nightclubs and gigs as though I was a keyboardist from the latest pop sensation from London.

Justine Frischmann

A friend of mine started a cabaret night where everyone was encouraged to perform. Since this was a perfect way to indulge my pop-star fantasies, I did a few performances of songs by Lou Reed and Alice Cooper with minimal jazz accompaniment. After one particularly good night, I was approached by the host of the club, who asked if I wanted to join his band as keyboardist. That question was music to my ears and I eagerly accepted. But there was just one small problem: I couldn't play keyboards, or any other musical instrument for that matter. "Oh, that's OK. We'll show you what to play," he said. It was a dream come true for someone who idolized pop stars all throughout his life. Now I could actually be one.

That year-and-a-half of pseudo pop life was a gas. I had actually posed my way into pop and I was going to milk it for all it was worth. So, in an attempt to make up for my lack of musical skill, I decided to construct a persona. I dressed to the nines in form-fitted black, piled on the makeup, stood stock still at my synthesizer and stared, scowled and pouted at the audience, all the while chain-smoking with a bored affectation. In my mind I was a cross between Grace Jones, Ralf Hütter and Ron Mael. My friends thought it was hilarious.

Looking the way I did could be polarizing and downright dangerous at times. In the 80's, when I looked more extreme, I had to be very careful of where I was going, how I was going to get there and with whom I was going. Often I would get homophobic remarks and violent behavior towards me by the nearest passersby. And usually the most demonstratively aggressive acts came from other black males. Perhaps they saw a betrayal of what a black man should look like. I also had to be careful around the police too. Once, I was almost carted off to jail after being involved in an auto accident. When the first responder officer saw that I was wearing an American flag as a skirt he became angry and threatened to take me to jail. I was often denied entrance to some of the more "respectable" restaurants, bars, and clubs. And sometimes taxis would whizz right by when they got a closer look at me. The following decade in San Francisco provided a considerable relief because my look was less "in your face" than in the previous decade and its citizens more tolerant. But for the first time I could discern that some people, in certain situations, found me intimidating. Of course, it wasn't only my "fashion stance" which caused people to feel that way; my attitude certainly played a role. But showing up at a bar in a black 1960's blazer with the sleeves hacked off (homemade Raf Simons), no shirt, and skin-tight black leather pants, didn't help. I began to feel like a freak and a lonely one at that. So after returning from a swinging vacation in London in 1999, where my look was greatly appreciated and sex was offered to me nearly every night out, I realized that perhaps San Francisco was too provincial for me and a more international locale was needed. But since moving to London would have been tricky, I decided to try New York as the next best thing, lugging my massive collection of fashion magazines with me.

In 2000, I moved to New York and met the man who would become the most important person in my life, my partner Constantin. After a few months of dating, it became clear to him that I was very frustrated working as a retail sales associate. Although I had been offered opportunities to move into management, I knew that I didn't have the temperament for that role. So I felt stuck. I was thirty-five years old, and my true passion for fashion, styling, trend assessment, and forecasting was not being used. So Constantin generously offered to open our own clothing boutique, with me as the buyer. I accepted without hesitation. After all, it could prove to be the perfect platform for me to utilize my fashion skills. So, after a year of research, negotiations, and buying, we finally opened Atelier New York in autumn 2002. It was not an immediate success, but after two years and word-of-mouth spread, we began to grow.

Atelier ran for 12 years and all throughout I had an abundance of fashion at my disposal, and I really indulged. All those years of dreaming of the perfect designer wardrobe came true. I could embrace almost any look or trend I wanted and be ready for the next one. In the early years of Atelier my look was rough with lots of distressed garments, frayed hems, skinny black pants and big boots, almost all of it in shades of black. But as the decade wore on I became enamored with a softer, more fluid, black and white minimalism. I wore skirts, *kandoras* (traditional Arabic male robe) and lots of gabardine. It was fashion with a capital "F" and I became a bit of a face about town. But after half a decade it began to dawn on me that this way of dressing, which was very elegant, made demands on me which were proving taxing: gabardine is very hot in summer and not very warm in winter, it cannot get very wet, and it requires frequent trips to a good dry cleaner. Also, my appearance was creating an even more regrettable effect on others than I had in San Francisco. Before someone would meet me, they would think I was a cold and arrogant fashion Nazi and feel very intimidated. They felt relief when I wasn't as stern or severe as I appeared. (Again, my attitude and the fact that I was the owner, buyer and creative director for a menswear boutique all added to the picture.) I was told this so often that it became worrisome. I also began to wonder about all the people I didn't meet because of the way I appeared. And then there was the behavior from people who would treat me with a kind of awe and reverence, as though I were a holy man or some precious objet d'art to be put on a pedestal. It made me feel somewhat dehumanized. And finally, (and much more troubling because of the not-so-subtle racism involved) strangers, usually not black, would assume that I worked at the place I was visiting, like a restaurant, the theatre, or clothing stores. For the first time in my life I began to question if I should change my look because it would be better for me on a social level, instead of changing it out of boredom or because I found another look more interesting.

After selling Atelier, I felt the need to reduce–not only to reduce the amount of clothing I owned, but also my appearance. I wanted a somewhat quieter appearance. At first, it felt a bit strange to walk the streets without the usual double-takes, turn-backs, nods, or stares, but eventually I began to revel in the relative anonymity. I started to explore non-black clothing and items intended for work or sports: chefs' jackets, medical scrubs, martial arts uniforms, sanitation jumpsuits, and military fatigues, clothes that aren't considered fashion. Embracing such utilitarian items is the exact opposite of that pristine monastic look of which I was so enamored. And I've rediscovered my passion for vintage clothing, which I used to buy due to lack of funds, but now for the thrill of discovering something unique. I love wearing old pieces that show their age; and by wearing them more I will add to their history. I'm now unconcerned about sitting on the ground or wiping my hands on my pants. Recently, I got caught in a downpour and I took delight in the fact that I didn't have to worry about my clothes.

Writing this chapter wasn't as fun or comfortable an exercise I thought it would be. I had to face some unpleasant truths about myself that I subconsciously knew but never actually addressed. I clung to fashion (or style) as a means of self-protection due to deep insecurity. Fashion is an industry which is founded on insecurity, and that's why it appealed to me. It was, and to a certain degree still is, a tool that helps me to navigate my way through the world. It was a way for me to belong to a group, even if that group was marginalized and unconventional. Growing up poor, black and gay in America posed a few challenges, to put it mildly, so style was my way of showing who I was (artful, a bit strange, perhaps compelling). It was my way of proclaiming "who I am" before others could. But my stylish stance was never passive-aggressive. I have never expected my clothes to do the talking for me. I've ALWAYS had something to say and never had a problem saying it.

Now I have a more cool affinity with fashion. I don't take it as seriously as I used to. In a way, fashion saved my life; but I now feel that I'm in control of it as opposed to vice versa. Maybe this has to do with getting older and feeling more comfortable in my own skin. I no longer feel I have to take a position within the fashion landscape or be boxed in by a concept (black *vs.* color, loose *vs.* fitted, etc). So much of what governed my fashion sense in the past was defined by what I didn't like. I still follow fashion quite closely (it's a part of me and probably always will be) and I can get very excited about certain designers or trends or the work of creative stylists, but I don't feel the urge to incorporate with or annex myself to everything I find interesting. Now I just select what I find interesting, wear it, and let the chips fall where they may. I love my newfound playful approach, subverting and disrupting codes (expensive *vs.* cheap, utilitarian *vs.* rare, "good taste" *vs.* "bad"). Often I find myself amused by wearing unexpected and ironic combinations. It almost feels like those far-off days when I was just discovering fashion for the first time, when it all felt new. But whether I will remain with this approach remains to be seen. After all, fashion is all about change and change is good.

3. Fashioning the Self: Tattoos and tattooing as markers of identity, loss, trauma and transformation

SARA ZAREM AND LINDA MAYERS

"We alter our bodies for reasons of beautification or to be accepted and respected for our physical appearance. Whatever the motive for accentuating the skin, all share common ground, that is, the symbol and its magical power, encapsulating ideas for both display and meditation." (Rush, 2005, p. 75)

T attoos and tattooing have become quite fashionable, but they are more than fashion statements; they are part of our bodies and identity. A recent poll indicated that that 40% of people in Western cultures between the ages of 26 and 40 have at least one tattoo (Pew Research Center for the People and the Press, 2006). Fashion expert Cynthia Nellis (2016) says that fashion is an art form, a method of utilizing clothing, hair and accessories as extensions or disguises of one's personality. Tattooing is a unique form of accessorizing, since it is literally written into the skin and cannot be changed the way one might add or subtract a hairstyle, a pair of earrings, or last year's dress style. Like all fashion statements, tattoos can both reveal and hide aspects of the wearer and this is, perhaps, a major factor in their appeal. Yet fashion, like a work of art, requires the presence of others; fashion is intrinsically social. To dress in order to be seen as glamorous, powerful, and up-to-date requires that the wearer be seen and admired by others. To dress so as to hide aspects of oneself requires the validating presence of another to recognize the performance instead of the real performer. As Kilborne argues, "…fashion is not about fashion *per se*. Nor is it clothes *per se* that make the man. Rather, the wearing of clothes in itself expresses an unstated conviction that we can 'fashion' ourselves and our feelings, that we can make ourselves over…in our imaginations and in the imaginations of those who see us" (Kilborne 2002, p. 110).

However, there are major differences between a sartorial fashion that is ephemeral and disembodied, and one, like tattooing, which "permanently re-inscribes the living body—thinking, breathing, sweating, wrinkling—with a type of agency that is ongoing and inexhaustible… Tattoos invite a level of engagement because they become a permanent addition to the body/self" (Kosut 2006, p. 1042).

This paper will explore the ways in which tattoos are fashionable, especially for women. We consider fashion in two separate overlapping ways: The first is fashion as a phenomenon or object that is currently popular, in style, at a particular cultural moment. The second meaning of fashion is fashion as a fashion statement. In the case of tattoos, these statements are embodied objects that may be worn as body accessories, body decoration, or body armor. Many tattoo wearers consider their inscriptions beautiful and enjoy wearing them as works of art and/or fashion statements that involve aesthetic choices.

We will begin by presenting a general history of the phenomenon of tattooing and speculating on the reasons for its popularity at the current time. Then we review the psychological literature, focusing on the ways in which other psychologists have thought about tattoos and tattooing. Lastly, we weave together the conscious and unconscious elements of choice of image, placement, tattoo artist and observer in our discussion of various case examples. Each example blends these elements in a unique way to configure/construct its own "poetic creation."

A BRIEF HISTORY OF TATTOOS AND TATTOOING

Tattooing is the injection of ink into the skin so as to inscribe an indelible image. It has been around for millennia. There is archaeological evidence of tattooing, including sharp bone needles, charcoal and red ochre, that dates back as far as the late fourth millennium BC, although there is no preserved skin from that time period. From about 2000 BC in Egypt (Rush 2005; Caplan 2000), evidence has been found on mummified bodies. Charles Darwin noted that "Not one great country can be named, from the Polar region in the north to New Zealand in the south, in which the aborigines do not tattoo themselves" (Favazza 1987, 1996, p. 150).

Although it is commonly considered that tattooing was introduced to the West by Captain Cook in the 1800's following his visits to the South Pacific, tattooing was already present in the West before the 19th century. For example, tattoo was used by the Greeks, Romans and Celts to mark criminals and slaves, as well as in Christian iconography brought back on the bodies of pilgrims to the Holy Land as early as the 16th century.

From the mid-19th century to the end of WWII, tattooing gained popularity among soldiers and sailors as a means of expressing devotion and loyalty to their units and country. But as tattoos became more erotic in theme, military authorities discouraged this practice. (We are reminded of the iconographic Norman Rockwell painting of the sailor in the tattoo parlor getting the name of his latest paramour tattooed on his arm, the six names above already having been crossed out). During this period, tattooing was perpetuated as "a folk-art form with an imagery that was traditional and that reflected different elements of popular culture" (Govena 2000, p. 212). Tattoos were also used in carnivals and "freak shows," primarily for shock value.

From the 1900's, tattooing became popular with marginalized groups of men, in gangs, prisons and members of the lower classes to mark their positions as outsiders. These tattoos were limited in scope and design, tending to emphasize group membership rather than individuality (de Mello 2000). Often the tattoos were ascribed magical functions. Interestingly, tattoos also appealed to a number of aristocrats such as Lady Randolph Churchill, Czar Nicolas II of Russia and George V of England (Favazza 1986, 1997). The "forbidden" qualities of tattoos—the exotic and erotic—could be worn discreetly by these carriers of propriety and tradition.

In the 1960's tattooing began to attract the interest of contemporary artists "who created 'body pieces' to explore the ways in which the artist could become both the subject and the work of art" (Govenar 2000, p. 233). By the 1970's, punk rockers and political radicals adopted tattooing as a subversive act and used their images to challenge traditional notions of propriety and the body politic. "The body is a site of symbolic resistance, a source of personal empowerment, and the basis for the creation of a sense of self-identity. By...altering their bodies in symbolically powerful ways, both punks and neo-tribalists may proclaim their discontent [and] challenge dominant ideologies" (Wojcik 1995. P. 35).

More contemporarily, there has been a "tattoo renaissance" that has swept through Europe and the USA (Caplan 2000) as tattoos have emerged from the margins of Western culture. Tattoos are now accepted across social class, ethnicity and gender, and are used to highlight the individuality and uniqueness of their wearers.

In the past, in certain cultures, getting a tattoo was a communal experience. What you had inscribed on your body signaled who you were and where you belonged in the community. Today, tattooing is more commonly a private experience, and the tattoo is a message about one's individual, internal self (Benson 2000).

Tattooing has become popularized by major celebrities from the fashion world (Marc Jacobs) and from popular culture (Angelina Jolie); there is even a Mattel "Tattoo Barbie." (Stein 2011) If you Google "tattoo," you will encounter literally thousands of images of tattooed bodies. It is easy to be overwhelmed by their variety—many of which are breathtakingly beautiful in design and execution. There are online chat rooms to share images, find tattoo artists, and to engage in international tattoo competitions. There are online publications (*Inked*) as well as print magazines (*Tattoo Life*), even two reality TV series (*Miami Ink, New York Ink*), which highlight the work of particular artists (e.g., Ami James) and describe the process in detail. There are current novels (*Girl with the Dragon Tattoo, Electric Michaelangelo, Eve's Tattoo*) in which the heroines wear tattoos whose meaning drives the narrative. A major television network premiered a new police procedural series, *Blindspot*, about a woman covered in tattoos.

As Mifflin so poetically says:

Tattoo Barbie

"[Tattoos are]…both an end and a beginning, a problem and a solution. Written on the skin—the very membrane that separates the self from the world—they're diary entries and public announcements, conversation pieces and countercultural totems, valentines to lovers, memorials to the dead, reminders to the self. They are scars and symptoms, mistakes and corrections" (Mifflin 1997, 2002, p. 147).

TATTOOS AND TATTOOING TODAY

It may be that tattooing has become so fashionable because it speaks so directly to current cultural concerns. Life for 21st century youth across all classes, genders and ethnicities is a life lived online. Adolescents must face the challenges of rapid social change, the growing corporatization of the world with its concomitant anonymity, and the challenges to identity wrought by the infinite possibilities of the Internet. With all manner of information available with a click or two, with social media such as Facebook and Twitter disseminating personal information instantaneously, identities and relationships both real and virtual are now lost and found in cyberspace. With Google at our fingertips, do we need to hold information in memory? How does one create an identity in this New World? Perhaps we can no longer think of adolescents as fashioning a more or less stable identity as much as their contending with shifting, changing, overlapping and contradictory identities.

In the welter of possibilities presented by the Internet, we can be any-thing or no-thing. A conscious choice of a beautiful image to be indelibly injected into the skin may represent a wish to slow or stop the relentless flow of time and these changes wrought by time. As life evolves, one can add to or augment the pictorial narrative, just as one might do with a fashion accessory. Through the act of inking our narra-tive, we symbolically take control of time and its aspects of forgetting and aging. Strenger suggests that various types of body modification, because they attempt to indelibly refashion our biological destiny, might represent "one of the more benign manifestations of the denial of death" (Strenger 2009, p. 169).

As the current political climate attests with the rise of Donald Trump, there are feelings of general disenfranchisement across the working and middle classes, coupled with a real loss of financial power and jobs. With globalization, increased personal surveillance and a heightened sense of anonymity, youth have turned inward to garner a sense of personal control and efficacy. If young people cannot transform the world, they can at least transform their bodies. Focus on community, social change and justice–what used to metaphorically be called the body politic–has lost its symbolic (and/or subversive) stance and become quite literal. This accords quite well with the increasing flatness of our society. Witness the title of Thomas Friedman's bestselling book, *The World is Flat*. Surface and depth have been conflated, with the resulting collapse of inner psychic space. Freud's depth psychology and topographical model of the mind have been replaced by models based on computers and a binary system in which real and virtual reality may be indistinguishable. There is little space for reflection. Are you depressed? No need for introspection or mourning—change your faulty thinking and get medication. Personal interaction in everyday life has been replaced by automation and online services. Gone are most of the bank tellers, cashiers, phone operators, factory workers, teachers and technicians. What real political power is possible today? Is our "choice" at the polls truly a choice? No wonder adolescents and emerging adults choose inscription and body narrative. These paradoxical objects are and are not real choices; they imbue power while they hide powerlessness.

THE MATERIALITY OF TATTOOS

Although tattoos, like fashion, are material/physical, there are also some important differences. In thinking about tattoos and tattooing, we must start from the fact of their being written on the skin. Unlike other art forms, tattoos are embodied and their embodiment unites psyche and soma in a complex interplay of conscious and unconscious meanings. While having an indelible, permanent image may be a wish to transcend one's materiality and mortality, the process of getting an inscription is a painful reminder of the reality that our bodies are fragile and non-transcendent.

While all art may be considered an extension of one's self i.e., the duplication of a thought, or image(s) and belief(s), captured and placed outside the artist, there is a different and paradoxical quality to tattoos:

"Tattooing …is like impregnation. You construct an idea, belief or behavior through analogies in nature and mentally move from the outside (the event in nature, in image, etc.), to inside (one's thoughts), to the outside where assistance, or at least tools are necessary to place the thought or symbol back 'into' or onto the body. This is a coding of the body, a characterization or label, something owned by the tattooed, and it is never separate from the mind and/or culture that thought it up"(Rush 2005, p. 5).

Because tattoos are both in and out of the body, they may serve as evocative objects (Bach 2006), as precursors of internalization or markers along the road to self and object constancy. Referring to one's tattoo can thus evoke thoughts and feelings that are not quite reliably inside one's psyche, but also not entirely outside either.

While tattooing is popular with both men and women, there are some significant differences in the kind of image and its placement between the genders. Female inkings are generally smaller than males' and more likely to be used as accents in one or two areas of the body. Frequent designs include seemingly limitless choices of butterflies, geometric or tribal designs, flowers, stars, fairies, hearts, dragons, swallows, zodiac signs and words or texts. Becoming more popular are abstract designs, copies of

masterpieces (e.g. Van Gogh's *Starry Night*) and even reproducing and transposing one's children's artwork to the parental body. Male tattoos are generally more aggressive in nature, featuring such images as dragons, attacking tigers, swords dripping with blood, and superheroes. They are chosen as "awesome" objects—worn to elicit fear and awe.

Van Gogh *Starry Night*

Today's tattoos are inscribed using a special tattoo gun, which consists of a small set of needles that go in and out of the skin very rapidly, leaving a little ink each time. There is blood, and the tattoo requires time to heal before the image is clearly readable. Getting a tattoo is painful, and pain is often an important part of the process, as it can signify symbolic death and rebirth (Rush 2005). "Pain, like the tattoo itself, is something that cannot be appropriated [by others]…it is yours alone…like the flesh itself pain is conceived of as really 'real,' it speaks its own truth." (Benson 2000, p. 251) The pain of getting a tattoo varies depending on placement, size and whether there are solid patches of ink. Areas with lots of muscle (arm, leg, upper pectoral) and areas with lots of fatty padding (glutes, hip) tend to hurt the least. Sensitive areas (breasts, underarms, face, groin), and hard areas close to the bones (scalp, face, collarbone, ribs, hands, feet) tend to hurt the most. Large designs are more painful than smaller ones; one color tattoos are less painful and less time-consuming that multi-color tattoos. Areas of solid color hurt the most because they require the artist to go over her work several times. Removal of tattoos is difficult and not always successful (Rush 2005). One can add an image and/or augment an existing one as changes in fashion and/or personal narrative dictate.

Choosing the artist to inscribe one's tattoo is another important part of the process. Perhaps as important as the aesthetic collaboration between artist and client is the interpersonal dimension which requires trust in the capacity of the artist to create a physically (clean, sterile) and emotionally safe, holding environment in what may potentially evoke traumatic and/or eroticized feelings. Murphy (2013) points out how the voice of the artist, who may narrate a story about the image he/she is inscribing while she works, can serve as a comforting and soothing word-blanket for the client.

REVIEW OF THE PSYCHOLOGICAL LITERATURE OF TATTOOS AND TATTOOING

Since tattooing is a process that happens on/in the skin, it is important to understand the psychological meaning of the skin and the skin-ego. According to Anzieu (2005), skin has a twofold nature: it is a protective shield and it helps give the body its form and coherence. The unity of the individual thus depends on the skin. Anzieu (2005) advanced the hypothesis of a fantasy of a skin common to mother and child, and on that basis he developed the idea of a skin- ego. He hypothesized that if this connection, through the skin, did not spontaneously and immediately occur, there was a possibility of future psychological problems for the baby. As related to tattoos, one might speculate that from this point of view, a tattoo is an attempt to "love" one's own skin, to give oneself a sense of coherence, to make oneself whole, to make oneself feel beautiful. By getting a tattoo one is, in essence, taking on the role of one's own mother by symbolically giving birth to one's psychological self in a conscious way. The literalness of the scarring and scabbing from the process itself, serves a psychological function of shedding an old skin and getting a better more beautiful skin/self.

When psychologists and mental health professionals became interested in tattoos, their focus was generally on the pathological. This type of body modification was seen as mutilating, perverse, and sadomasochistic, often typifying impulsive acting-out behavior by characterologically impaired individuals (Grumet 1983; Parry 1934; Yamamoto et al. 1963).

Today, however, psychologists who have written about tattoos and tattooing have focused on different aspects: some focus on the particular meaning of the inscription, some on the pain of the process, some on the importance of the recognition and gaze of the Other. McLane (1996), for example, concurs that various forms of body modification may have pathological aspects, but she also considers such processes as potentially healing. Tattoos can function as forms of body confession, "voices on the skin," which both express and manage unbearable psychic pain – where the pain is as important as the image.

Fazavva distinguished between sanctioned and pathological forms of self-mutilation, placing tattoos more in the former than the latter category: "the skin may be thought of a sort of message centre or billboard" (Fazavva 1996, p. 148). The inscriptions constitute corporeal confessions, outer manifestations of inner psychological truths.

Since tattooing has become so ubiquitous, there is less focus on tattoos and tattooing as pathology and more as living art forms. Mutilation has been morphed into beautification (Grogrand 1994; Mifflin 1997). As Benson argues,

"Self mutilation is 'addictive,' beyond the control of the self, something done in secret which merely repeats the original harm without transforming it; body modification, by contrast, is 'done with complete consciousness,' usually considered for some length of time and is often publicly witnessed: inscribed on the skin would be the marks of separation not defeat" (Benson 2000, p. 249).

Karacaoglan, who has worked with patients whose tattoos were obtained during the course of their analysis, considers how "tattooing is a veiled expression of individuality in the form of a fashion statement that may be fashionable because it speaks to psychodynamic issues particularly relevant for adolescents" (Karacaoglan 2012, p. 25). The analyst then goes on to comment about the importance of her role as reader of the inscription, bringing up her unique transference/countertransference matrix as well as the more general issue of the importance of the gaze of the Other.

Stein (2011) is an analyst who herself has a tattoo. While she distances herself from those clinicians who see tattooing as primarily pathological, she is clear that professionals (as well as patients) who have them, nevertheless, flirt with and enjoy their fantasies of rebellion, deviancy and shame, since they do not generally share their inscriptions with other professionals, although they do share them in non-clinical settings.

Murphy (2013) focuses on the positive functions skin marking serves, such as personal biography, coping with loss and memorializing people/events. She also highlights how tattoos and tattooing hold together concrete and symbolic meanings: "It is the potential of tattoos to represent both the material and the dynamic, to resist easy classicization as either, that provides their timeless allure" (Murphy 2013, p. 38).

By far the most extensive work on body modification from an object relations viewpoint has been done by Alessandra Lemma (2010, 2015). She, too, concurs, that tattoos have no unitary function and must always be viewed within a particular cultural context. She delineates five major unconscious functions that she believes skin markings perform:

1. Denial of separation and loss
2. Attempts at separation
3. Attempts at covering up a felt-to-be shameful body
4. Attempt to restore an inner sense of fragmentation (via the constituting look of the other)
5. Expression of grievance against the object/mother (Lemma 2010).

Lemma's approach begins with the importance of the body, and she reminds us of Freud's dictum that "the ego is first and foremost a bodily ego." The way we represent our body in our mind is inevitably object-related and its original source lies in the body's physicality. The first exchanges between a mother and her newborn are primarily tactile and visual – they touch and look at each other. How the baby is responded to by her mother's touch, gaze and understanding all contribute to the development of the body-self and body images (See also Lacan 1953; Kilborne 2002; Winnicott 2005). An implication of this is that the Other's look has a potentially stabilizing or destabilizing influence on one's evolving body: "We never grow out of the search for the (m)other's loving desiring gaze. In more or less compulsive ways we go on searching for it, sometimes using the manipulation of the body to capture it, or to create the illusion that this is possible." (Lemma 2010, p. 40)

INTERVIEWS

The material for our paper is drawn from multiple interviews with people who have skin inscriptions and who were willing to share their experience with us, and from our clinical practices. The tattoo pictures that we have chosen are non-copyrighted images taken from the internet and are close facsimiles of those inscribed on our patients. For reasons of confidentiality we are not showing their personal images. Our interview material resonates well with the themes delineated by Karacaoglan, Stein, Murphy and Lemma.

Merrie

Merrie says that the first thing she did when she turned 18 was get a tattoo. "I did it as a way to assert myself; I knew that my mother wouldn't approve, but now I didn't need her approval. I got an otter tattooed on my back shoulder." "Why an otter," I ask? (SZ) "That's my totem animal. I love them. They go after what they need, they persevere. They are smart and playful. I wanted to always have a reminder about these qualities." "Why your back shoulder?" "Because I wanted to carry these qualities with me, and I didn't want the image to be seen by everyone. I wanted to control who saw it. I want to be a performer, and I thought carefully about having the tattoo placed where I could cover it up, if need be."

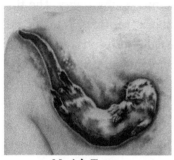
Merie's Tattoo

Merrie's tattoo was not gotten impulsively. Her intention was not to mutilate her body, but to endow it with a beautiful and personally meaningful symbol. Perhaps she needed an indelible reminder of the qualities she desired, as though they might, should she not carry them literally on and in her back, be in danger of disappearing from her psyche. Perhaps, too, Merrie may have been afraid to lose some child-like qualities the otter embodies as she came more fully into adulthood. Like the child who must be ready to give up her teddy bear, Merrie might have been ambivalent about moving on from her childhood. The tattoo allows her body to symbolically separate from her mother and to grow up, while simultaneously freezing time.

Merrie's experience also talks to the issue of body ownership. Having her body tattooed as soon as she is legally able signals, "this is MY body." No longer is she at one with her mother's body. The otter inscription marks a literal and symbolic new body—a body fashioned by Merrie's desire. Like childbirth, the inscription of the otter is borne/born by Merrie as she emerges from the pain of the tattoo by the delivering hands of the artist/midwife. Merrie has given birth to her (new) self. Pain is an important part of this birthing process, as is the tattoo artist's presence. The artist may take on dual roles of midwife and father. The artist becomes s/he who separates the adolescent from the symbiotic tie to the mother and places the new child in the world (Ayran 2006). Lemma might add that Merrie's transition to selfhood with her totem of power, fertility and separation may constitute, much less consciously, "an envious attack on the fantasized powerful maternal body/object" (Lemma 2010, p 33)

Donna

Donna(LM), a tall, large, ungainly, but striking adolescent first came to treatment in her junior year of high school because she was often missing school, complaining of unspecified somatic distress, anxiety and depression. She said she felt dead and empty inside, and as if there were a gaping hole inside her that had to be filled. She had been eating a lot lately which tempo-

Donna

rarily made her feel "full"; but she had gained weight which made her feel even worse about herself and the way she looked. She had started cutting a short time before she came to treatment and said that feeling the pain and seeing the blood oozing out of her wounds was the only way she was able to feel alive.

Donna was the only child of a mother who was totally merged with her, to the point that the boundaries between them were very fuzzy. Her mother was a woman who saw everything through rose-colored glasses, even her daughter's acting out; and her father resented her, particularly her close relationship with her mother, since he felt that she took her mother away from him. He was often verbally cruel. Donna knew that her father didn't like her and was afraid of his temper outbursts, which came often and were unpredictable.

It was during her last year of high school that Donna began to abuse drugs and alcohol. She had stopped cutting by then and claimed that this was now the only way she could feel something and that they helped to calm her down. Again, her parents were aware of this but downplayed the severity of her problem, refusing to send her to a drug rehab program or do an intervention, saying that this would soon blow over.

Donna claimed that she had always felt ugly and hated the way she looked. She felt that these feelings were reinforced by her father's negative reactions to her. Over a short period of time she went from being overweight to being almost wraithlike, although she and her parents insisted that she was eating well and that there was no starvation, binging, or purging going on. About two years into treatment, Donna began to talk about getting a tattoo. She knew that her parents would disapprove, but she didn't care because it was her body and she could do to it and with it whatever she wanted. She even brought several pictures and drawings to sessions to show me what she wanted – large, very colorful images of beautiful, exotic flowers. (The reader will remember that this kind of tattoos is very painful to get because of its high color saturation and size). The topic was dropped and suddenly, several weeks later she came bounding into session, a huge smile on her face (not a usual occurrence), lifted her shirt, and on her back was a gorgeous, large, vibrant tattoo of an iris, which she said she had been hiding from her parents. This was the most animated she had been in a long time. In discussing her experience of getting this tattoo she explained that although the pain was excruciating, she claimed that she had not felt so alive in a long time, and so the pain was almost pleasurable. It seemed that it was with this tattoo, one of several which came later, that she was trying to concretely bring life into her body. She seemed literally to need someone (i.e., the tattoo artist) to give her vitality (rebirth), but also needed these images as a concrete reminder that she was alive. They were a clear and distinct way of separating her body from her mother's because she knew that this was one of the few things that her mother would disapprove of and also a way of feeling beautiful, a way of showing her father he was wrong.

Unfortunately, the tattoos did not fulfill her unconscious needs and fantasies of finally being beautiful and therefore ultimately lovable. The story of Donna did not end well. The reminder/messages of the tattoos did not stick—their emotional infusions were never internalized and soon dissipated. Donna, influenced by her friends, turned to heroin for her momentary hits of aliveness and to escape from her dark reality. While Merrie was able to use her tattoo in a healthy way to continue her growth and development, the outcome of Donna's attempts at dealing with the similar struggles of separation-individuation, and a burgeoning sense of self were, unfortunately, not enough.

Erin

Erin proudly showed me (SZ) a tattoo she had designed as a memorial to her beloved grandmother, who had recently died. Grandmother was a major person in Erin's life and Erin wanted to find a way to have Grandmother with her always. Her tattoo, a specially designed pattern of stars moving across her wrist, simultaneously placed Grandmother in the universe with stars (her death) while keeping her concretely "alive" on earth. Placed on her wrist, the tattoo was easily visible to others and evoked queries about its origin and meaning, provid-

ing a further concrete opportunity to keep Grandmother in mind. Perhaps there was also an unconscious wish to forget certain negative aspects of Grandmother and/or to truncate the grieving process for her. Stars suggested a certain "celebrating" of Grandmother that may have denied other, more negative or nuanced feelings about her. And the physical pain of the process itself may have used the body to concretize the psycho-

Stars tattoo

logical experience. Samuel, in her doctoral dissertation, formally interviewed a group of subjects who had memorial tattoos and concluded that "the ability to relate the loss to others, and to rejoin the outside world, was seen to be facilitated by acquiring [a] memorial tattoo" (Samuel 2010, p. 1).

Recently, some grandchildren of Holocaust survivors are getting their grandparents' numbers tattooed on their own bodies, both to acknowledge their grandparents' experience and to tell the world that they will never forget. "All my generation knows nothing about the Holocaust," said Ms. Sagir, 21, who has a tattoo of her grandfather's number. "You talk with people and they think it's like the Exodus from Egypt, ancient history. I decided to do it to remind my generation: I want to tell them my grandfather's story and the Holocaust story" (Rudoren 2012). The Nazis numbered the Jews to dehumanize them; the grandchildren are using their inscribed tattoos to remind themselves and the world of their grandparents' existence, individuality and humanity. Here again, in the grandchildren's turning passive to active, we can note how the tattoo contains and expresses the oppositions of past and present, forgetting and remembrance, individuality and anonymity, life and death.

Abby

Abby (SZ) had an eighth note inscribed on her hip following a traumatic breakup with a boyfriend that she did not initiate. Twenty-two at the time, Abby acknowledged that her desire to be tattooed was an act of defiance toward this boyfriend, who had vocalized his intense dislike of tattoos. Placed on her hip, a painful place to be inked, allowed Abby, like Erin, to convert potentially unending psychic pain to limited physical discomfort. Abby added, however, that she reveled in the pain. This was not just a separation from the boyfriend that she initiated, but "a spiritual rebirth" through pain of a stronger more self-directed woman. "Why an eighth note?" I ask (SZ) "Because music is important to me. At the time I had the tattoo done, I considered myself a musician and was teaching music." She paused, then added, "I thought an eighth note was pretty. It had a tail and it looked very musical." When the tattoo was finished, she recalled feeling, "Wow! This will be here for the rest of my life." The brevity of the eighth note (relationship) became transformed to the permanence of a musical self no one could take away from her. Perhaps less consciously, the image and its placement also reflect sexual and aggressive themes. If the breakup was hurtful and made Abby feel unloved, the sperm-like image on her hip may be her way of saying, "you were just a sperm anyway." Consciously and unconsciously, passive is transformed into active, the inking itself uniting the opposites of brevity and permanence, loss and remembrance, love and hate. Here not only is passive transformed into active, but once again, the inking itself unites the opposites of brevity and permanence, of loss and remembrance. Paradoxically, the absence of the boyfriend was transformed into an indelible presence.

Breast cancer survivors

Margot Mifflin (1997, 2001) in her book, *Bodies of Subversion: a Secret History of Women and Tattoos*, describes the work of a particular artist, Madame Chinchilla, who tattooed breast cancer survivors. Marcia Rasner, a woman who lost both of her breasts to cancer, decided to have Madame Chinchilla inscribe her chest with a stunning, complex floral garden with roses and butterflies encased in what looks like a halter bra.

The traumatic nature of the loss and her horror at her mutilated body was transformed into a work of art. Rather than covering up from shame, Ms. Rasner can now invite the admiring eyes of others. The need for the Other cannot be over-emphasized, for the sense of wholeness and cohesion that Ms. Rasner hopes to attain can only be brought through recognition by the Other. "The tattoo also gave her the satisfaction of controlling the site of her illness—and spitting in the face of death." (Mifflin 1997, 2001, p. 90). And, as Lemma (2010) might add, the tattoo also served to repair the loss of the internal mother who was unable to protect her child from the disease.

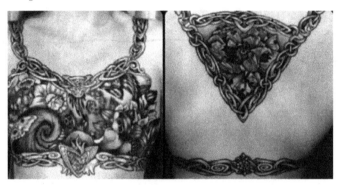

While Mifflin does not mention the relationship that may or may not have developed between Madame Chinchilla and Ms. Rasner, we are struck by the reversal of positions between Madame Chinchilla and the surgeon who performed Ms. Rasner's mastectomies. To have such extensive tattooing on her chest area close to the bone, must have been very painful. Yet, Madame Chinchilla's markings allowed for a reparative rebirth which all could see.

For people traumatized from abuse or neglect at the hands of sadistic or neglectful others, the process of becoming inscribed may offer a more benign reenactment of their trauma (or an aspect of it), a reenactment that may consciously and unconsciously allow for both grievance against the offender and reparation to the self. Particularly for survivors of sexual abuse, surrendering oneself to the penetrations of tattooing needles may transform being done to into doing for oneself.

Serena

Serena (SZ) is a woman in her mid-20's who has 10 tattoos all over her body, ranging from head to foot, some visible for others to see and others inked in more private places. The story of these images is also the narrative of Serena's life; they are embedded in traumatic and transitional points in her life and reflect many of the themes we have detailed: turning passive to active, memorializing loved ones present and past, repairing a loss, celebrating survival.

Unlike our other interviewees or patients, Serena's first tattoo was purchased for her by her father upon her 18th birthday. It was a text that Serena designed and placed on her ankle: "Beautifully scarred." As she explained, Serena struggled since she was 4 or 5 years old with compulsive skin picking. Her body was pocketed with scars and discoloration and she longed to feel "normal." In high school she had an art teacher who, like her, had scars from skin picking. This mentor encouraged Serena to feel proud of herself for her artistic talent, rather than feeling shamed by her different appearance. His support "was huge," and became the inspiration for her choice of text. It is also important to note that Serena and her father had been estranged throughout most of Serena's childhood. His present of the tattoo can perhaps also been seen as the beginning of his (re)presence in her life and a reconciliation of their "scarred" relationship. Now, people could look at her body and seen something beautiful. She controlled the gaze of the Other.

Several years later, she and her father collaborated in getting matching tattoos on their forearms. Thematic content for the inscription was drawn from the trauma of her father's life as a medic during the Vietnam War, with the explicit purpose of transforming the ugliness of his experience into a beautifully fashioned and carefully designed image. Undergoing the ritual process of tattooing together, they were joined in their pain, past and present, connected for life to each other and bearing a striking image for all to see. Here, the tattoo is not done in the service of separation, but (re)connection.

Serena's high-school experience led to her choice of yet another tattoo. Diagnosed with a learning disability, her inability to keep up with grade-level reading was very shaming and a source of terrible anxiety. She did find a series of fantasy novels at the 7th grade level that engaged her. "I taught myself how to read so that I could read these books about a powerful woman who uses magic and symbols to heal and to control death." After having a fierce lion tattooed on her back, Serena chose to inscribe seven symbols from the fantasy series down her spine. "That hurt... It's very anchoring in a weird way. When I try to find my center, I come up from my spine...Most of my tattoos are hidden, are just for me. They serve as reminders or remembrance that this difficult part is over. I won't forget. I control the experience; the experience doesn't control me."

One can speculate that the tattoos down Serena's spine, unlike Donna's, serve as a successful evocative object. The feelings of competence, goodness, lovability and, for Donna, beauty, that may not be psychically integrated can be evoked by looking at and/or thinking about the literal body markings. Unlike Serena's "beautifully scarred" tattoo and the matching tattoo she has with her dad, those down her spine can be thought of as "for me" objects, inscriptions that are markers of an identity to be possessed, not looked at [by Others] (Benson 2000).

Sophia

Sophia (LM), a beautiful young South American, was the babysitter of a young boy I was working with. She brought him to his sessions. After three years she went back to her country to marry her high school

Sophia

sweetheart, something she had been looking forward to for a long time. Suddenly, after a year, she was back, now divorced, as her husband had become a man who was physically and verbally abusive. She wanted to start over and was back to earn money and to go to college, something she was unable to afford at home.

She reappeared on a very hot day, wearing a sleeveless tank top and an array of tattoos, the most striking of which was a large, intricately detailed red bow on the back of her neck. When I asked whether she would mind talking to me about her tattoos she said she would be pleased to and that each one represented a different experience in her life. She was however, most proud of the bow because, she said, it was a constant reminder to her and whoever was looking at it, that despite the fact that her ex-husband had done whatever he could to belittle her and make her feel worthless, she had realized that despite all of that she did, in fact, have worth and that she would be a gift to anyone to whom she decided to commit. She said that the process of getting it had been very painful but that she had felt that to be a reminder of, and warning to her, about how she would feel if she ever got into another abusive relationship She saw it as a concrete manifestation of her healing and the work that she had had to do to make herself feel whole and beautiful again. She felt that this was a gift she had given to herself, an accessory she could wear forever. It is also interesting to note that the bow on a package is originally unopened. It is an invitation to go inside, even though the image is on the outside.

I last saw Sophia on Facebook. She had remarried and moved down South. The picture that she had posted was of her back, inscribed with words from the Song of Solomon 1:2, "Let him kiss me with the kisses of his mouth: for your love is better than wine."

SUMMARY AND CONCLUSIONS

Bow Tattoo

We have tried to show why and how tattoos have become so fashionable. Not only are they popular as interesting accessories but they also carry multiple and complex meanings. They may speak to identity, separation-individuation, recognition, connection and re-connection, early trauma and abuse, a way to manage painful affects and memories, and transformation of enduring psychic pain into limited physical pain. Is it any wonder that they are so popular because at least in fantasy, if not in reality, in this age of increasing uncertainty, they give one a feeling of choice, power and control. As Vale and Juno so eloquently say:

"a tattoo is more than a painting on skin; its meaning and reverberations cannot be comprehended without a knowledge of the history and mythology of its bearer. Thus, it is a true poetic creation, and it is always more than meets the eye. As a tattoo is grounded on living skin, so its essence emotes a poignancy unique to the mortal human condition" (Vale & Juno 1989, p.16).

REFERENCES

Aryan, A. (2006). Body modification. *International Journal of Psychoanalysis, 97,* 849-851.

Bach, S. (2006). *Getting From Here to There.* Hillside, NJ: The Analytic Press.

Benson, S. (2000). Inscriptions of the Self: Reflections on Tattooing and piercing in Contemporary Euro-America in Caplan, J.(Ed.), *Written on the Body: The Tattoos in European and American History.* Princeton, NJ: Princeton University Press.

Brain, R. (1979). *The Decorated Body.* New York: Harper & Row

Caplan, J. ed. (2000). *Written on the Body: The Tattoos in European and American History.* Princeton: Princeton University Press

de Mello, M. (2000). *Bodies of Inscription. A Cultural History of the Modern Tattoo Community.* Durham & London: Duke University Press.

Farrell, K. (2013). If tattoos could talk. *Psychology Today,* Retrieved from https://www.psychologytoday.com/blog/swim-in-denial/201310/if-tattoos-could-talk.

Gell, A. (1993). *Wrapping in Images, Tattooing in Polynesia.* Oxford: Oxford University Press

Favazza, A. (1996). *Bodies Under Siege: Self-Mutilations in Culture and Psychiatry (2nd ed.)* Baltimore: Johns Hopkins University Press

Grognard, C. (1994). *The Tattoo: Graffiti for the Soul.* Australia: Treasure Press.

Grumet, C. (1983). Psychodynamic implications of tattoos. *The American Journal of Orthopsychiatry, 53,* 482-492.

Hewitt, K. (1997). *Mutilating the Body. Identity in Blood and Ink.* Ohio:

Bowling Green University.

Kilborne, B. (2002). *Disappearing Persons. Shame and Appearance.* New York: State University of New York Press.

Karacaoglan, U. (2012). Tattoo and taboo: On the meaning of tattoos in the analytic process. *International Journal of Psychoanalysis,* 93: 5-28.

Kosut, M. (2006). An ironic fad: The commodification and consumption of tattoos. *Journal of Popular Culture,* 39(6): 187-218.

Lacan, J. (1953) Some Reflections on the Ego. International Journal of Psychoanalysis, 34, 11-17.

Lemma, A. (2010). Under the Skin. London and New York: Routledge

Lemma, A. (2015). *Minding the Body: The Body in Psychoanalysis and Beyond.* London and New York: Routledge.

McLane, J. (1996). 'The Voice on the Skin: Self-Mutilation and Merleau Ponty's Theory of Language,' *Hypatia,* 11: 4, 107-118.

Miffin M. (1997, 2013) *Bodies of Subversion. A Secret History of Women and Tattoo.* New York: Juno Books.

Murphy, M. (2013). Tattoos as social networks. *Fort da,* 19(1), 29-38.

Nellis, C. (2016). A definition of fashion. Retrieved from fashion.about.com.

Parry, A. (l934). Tattooing among prostitutes and perverts. Psychoanalytic Quarterly, 3: 476-482.

Pew Research Center for People and the Press (2006). A portrait of "generation next," Retrieved from http://people-press.org/reports/pdf/300.pdf.

Post, R.S. (1968) The relationship of tattoos to personality disorders. *Journal of Criminal Law, Criminology and Police Science,* 59, 516-524.

Rudoren, J. (2012, September 30). Proudly Bearing Elders' Scars, Their Skin says 'Never Forget.' *The New York Times.*

Rush, J.A. (2005). Spiritual Tattoo: A Cultural History of Tattooing, Piercing, Scarification, Branding and Implants. Berkley: Frog Ltd.

Samuel, S. (2010). An examination of the psychological role of tattoos in mourning. Doctoral dissertation. The Chicago School of Professional Psychology

Stein, Ab. (2011). The tattooed therapist: Exposure, disclosure, transference. *Psychoanalysis, Culture & Society,* 16, 113-131.

Strenger, C. (2009). Body modification and the enlightenment project of struggling against death. *Studies in Gender and Sexuality, 10,* 166-171.

Sullivan, N. (2009). The somatechnics of bodily inscription: Tattooing. *Studies in Gender and Sexuality, 20,* 129-141.

Vale, V. & Juno, A. (1989). *Modern Primitives: Tattoo, Piercing, Scarification—An Investigation of Contemporary Adornment & Ritual.* San Francisco: Re/Search.

Winnicott, D.W. (1971). *Playing and Reality.* New York: Routledge Classics.

Wojcik, D. (1995). *Punk and Neo-Tribal Body Art.* Jackson: University of Mississippi Press.

Yamamoto, B.K., Seeman, B.K. & Lester, B.K. (l963). The tattooed man. *Journal of Nervous and Mental Disorders, 136,* 365-367.

4. Female Crossdressing:
Why Would a Woman Dress like a Man?

ADA FRUMMERMAN

F emale crossdressing is a fascinating subject that has received
very little study by psychoanalysts. In this chapter I will both review
the literature that does exist and
discuss interviews with women who
crossdress. Additionally, I will utilize
material gathered from internet postings by crossdressers.

Based on these sources, I have
hypothesized that these women were
given the message that their parents
would have preferred a boy child. In
some instances the parents openly
verbalized regret at not having had a

Colette

son. In others the young girl was dressed by her parents as a boy and or
encouraged to engage in activities that were, for their time,
stereotypically masculine.

Finally, I explore the concept that male clothing functions as what
Joyce McDougall calls a "transitory object." This is an addictive object
that provides momentary relief from anxiety. However, it must be returned to over and over again, because, unlike a transitional object, it

has not been internalized and the soothing function is not independently available.

However, it is first necessary to define the scope of female crossdressing. It is not a simplistic phenomenon. It can range from women who have successfully passed as men for decades to women who wear men's clothing but have no interest in passing. A dramatic example of the former is the well-known jazz musician Billy Tipton who, at the time of death, was discovered to be a woman. Not only had she passed as a man in her profession, but she was married and a stepfather to sons. Another famous example is James Barry (1789-1865) who was a prominent surgeon in the British army from 1813 to 1864. When Barry died in 1865, it was discovered that Barry was a woman.

Along this spectrum are women who crossdress episodically. Some well-known examples are Willa Cather and George Sand. During Cather's adolescence, she went through a period where she cut her hair, wore men's clothing and called herself, William Cather, MD. George Sand was named Aurore at birth and wrote under the name George Sand to promote her career. She crossdressed periodically, and photographs of her show her dressed in both men's and women's clothing.

The women whom I interviewed for this chapter, and women whom I will quote (using sources from Internet postings) fall into the latter category. They are not interested in passing as men and some occasionally wear women's clothing.

EARLY STUDIES

The subject of crossdressing was initially discussed by three sex researchers.

Richard Von Krafft-Ebbing (1840 – 1902)
Krafft-Ebbing was an English physician who wrote the pioneering work Psychopathis Sexualis, an exhaustive catalogue of sexual behavior. He reported on a case of what he called "gynandry". This recounted the story of an individual known as Count Sandor who in 1889, was arrested "on account of deception and forgery" and who, "at the first hearing confessed

that she...was a female, Catholic, single , and worked as an authoress under the name of Count Sandor V."

Count Sandor (born Sarolta) was brought up as a boy, called Sandor and encouraged by her father to ride, drive and hunt. Some (reference Stryker) consider that this individual was a transsexual, i.e. someone who transitions from one gendered social category to another. While it is impossible to determine if this is true, the case presented by Krafft-Ebbing is the first scientific study of an individual who crossdressed.

Krafft-Ebbing believed that any behavior that was not engaged in for the purpose of reproduction was a form of emotional or physical disease (Stryker p. 21). Furthermore, he described, in the case of Sandor an extensive physical examination where he concluded that she exhibited "a congenitally abnormal inversion of the sexual instinct (s26) which expressed itself in anomalies of development of the body."

Havelock Ellis (1859-1939)

The subject of crossdressing was also explored by Havelock Ellis, who was a British physician, writer, and social reformer. Ellis coined the term Eonism in 1920, meaning crossdressing. This term was named after the Chevalier d'Eon de Beaumont, (1728-1810) a French diplomat, spy and soldier who spent the last 33 years of his life dressed as a woman. Ellis considered eonism to be a separate phenomenon from homosexuality. However, he also postulated that in involved some defective endocrine balance: "it would seem probable that Eonism ...involves a much less slighter disturbance in the balance of the play of hormones and chalones, and the path lies open for its modification by suitable gland implantation. It falls short of a disease: it is, simpl variety, though, one may add, an abnormal, in the strict sense a pathological variety (Ellis 2006, P. 110).

Magnus Hirschfeld (1868-1935)

Another pioneer in this field was Magnus Hirschfeld, a German physician and champion of homosexual and transgender rights. Like Ellis, Hirschfeld distinguished crossdressing from homosexuality. "How, in fact, are we to understand this peculiar urge to crossdress. Is it perhaps only a matter of a form of homosexuality? However, more accurate testing revealed that this was not the case, because the main marker of homosexuality, as its root word – homosor "same" – indicates, it the direction of the sex drive toward persons of the same sex…To be sure, some of them had homosexual episodes, which is not unusual for heterosexuals, but they were so transient and superficial that truly inborn homosexuality and only congenital homosexuality…is not a question here" (Stryker 2006).

Hirschfeld went to great lengths to distinguish crossdressing (which he referred to as transvestism) from other psychological phenomena.

He first dispensed with the notion that transvestism and fetishism were identical phenomenon. Transvestites are essentially different from fetishists by the following. Here he quotes Krafft- Ebbing: "The sexual interest of the fetishists are concentrated without exception on a specific part of the body of the women or also on specific pieces of women's clothing" (Hirschfeld 2006, 29) In short, fetishists lack the express urge to put on the form of the beloved object, to identify with it, as it were, to change themselves into it.

He similarly disposes of the idea that masochism and sadism play a role in transvestism. In regards to female transvestism he wrote, men like women and sadism in no way coincides (Hirschfeld 2006, 32) And finally, he states that transvestism is not synonymous with the "illusion of sexual metamorphosis…No matter how much transvestite men feel like women when dressed in women's clothing and women feel like men when dressed in men's clothing, they still remain aware that in reality it is not so." (Hirschfeld 2006, 32)

Hirschfeld introduced a set of categories that could be used to determine where along the continuum of pure masculinity or pure femininity one fell. He called these categories "sexual intermediaries" and argued that it is rare for an individual to be 100% male or 100% female. "Accordingly, a complete womanly and absolute woman would be such a one who not only produces egg cells but also corresponds to the womanly type in every other respect. These kinds of absolute representatives of their sex are, however, first of all only abstractions, invented extremes in reality they have not as yet been observed…" (Hirshfeld, p. 33).

I will describe all four categories despite the fact that only the fourth applies to crossdressing. They are interesting in that they do not subscribe to rigid stereotypical notions of masculinity and femininity. And the discussion is surprisingly relevant today, in that it applies to current controversies about subjects such as surgical intervention for intersex children.

THE SEXUAL INTERMEDIARIES

The sexual organs:
This category applies to individuals who are hermaphrodites or pseudohermaphrodites. A pseudohermaphrodite is an individual whose gender has been misidentified at birth due to being born with ambiguous genitals, e.g. a micro-penis or an enlarged clitoris.

Other physical characteristics:
Men with the soft complexion of women and women with the coarser skin of men: women who have to wear men's and men who have to wear women's gloves and shoe sizes. In short, no matter what part of the body we were to treat, in almost every case we can always perceive many profiles in women, womanly profiles in men.

The sex drive:
This refers to men who are attracted to a manly, or as he puts it an "energetic woman or a woman who is attracted to a "womanly" man which he defines as someone who is passive, dependent and gentle. Homosexuality is included in this category.

Other emotional characteristics:
The fourth category of this continuum included transvestites. "After this general observation of the sexual mixed forms, if we return to the main subject of this work, the erotic drive to cross- dress, it will become clearer to us in many respects and less of rare phenomenon. The important conclusions put in order not only its place as a natural phenomenon, but also its etiology, prognosis and therapy...it appears fitting, too, to give the

new form a new name, a special scientific stamp. The term I use...is taken from the Latin "trans" across and "vestitus" dressed, used also by the Roman classical as transvestism. Both men and women are termed transvestites." Hirshfeld goes on to state that "If one gives it more thought, that it is basically a harmless inclination by which no one is injured, then from a purely medical standpoint, nothing can be said against the actual putting on of clothes of the opposite sex" (Hirshfeld) Hirshfeld's discussion is strikingly similar to the arguments of many feminists, who contend that gender is a continuum. Some totally object to the gender binary and advocate discarding the terms male and female. His stance also is strikingly at odds with that of some psychoanalysts in that it removes the stigma of pathology from transvestism (Hirshfeld, p. 38)

THE PSYCHOANALYSTS

Emil Gutheil and William Stekel

In 1922 Emil Gutheil and Wilhelm Stekel published an "Analysis of a Case of Transvestism." The patient was a thirty-four year old German homosexual woman who dressed in men's clothing. She came for treatment because she had been arrested for crossdressing and was seeking a medical diagnosis, which would prevent further arrests.

This patient's father died when she was two years old and she was sent to live with her grandparents. At age six her mother remarried and she came back to live with her mother and stepfather. The patient reported that her mother was cold and rejecting and that her stepfather repeatedly told her that she was ugly.

Stekel and Gutheil attributed her crossdressing to the "Electra complex which is parapathically (neurotically) expressed in identification with her father." The patient reported, "I had a distinct dislike of 'girl' toys as far back as I can recall...I also recall a winter coat of dark blue cloth which I once had. It had ties (phallic symbol?) instead of buttons (vagina?), and I cherished it very much...I insisted on wearing the coat even in spring and summer."

She goes on to say, "As the years passed, the question of clothing became a serious dilemma (Gutheil & Stekel 1922, p. 282). To go out dressed in airy skirts and hats with ribbons and lace made me feel like a dressed-up mon-key. Following promenades or visits in such clothing, I would be overcome with a deep depression and was glad when I reached home again and could tear the stuff from my body. Every new dress was the signal for a bitter struggle…"

Later on in the analysis she says, "I believe myself to be a handsome male…When I was twelve or thirteen my grandfather was once away from home and I secretly put on his suit. I looked at myself in the mirror and noticed that it quite fitted me and made me look much better (Gutheil & Stekel 1922, p. 302).

Finally, she states that "from earliest childhood I had heard frequently enough that my mother had been irritated by the fact that she had not borne a son. I felt sorry for her, and later I thought that this must be the reason she neglected me. If I had been a boy, everything would have been different" (Gutheil & Stekel 1922, p. 295).

As we shall see, many of her sentiments are very typical of women who crossdress. In particular. they all report a very early dislike of women's clothing and that being forced to wear it was a source of conflict.

Her physical relief at putting on men's clothing is also typical, alt-hough she is one of the few to report sexual associations with wearing men's clothes.

Helene Deutsch

George Sand was the subject of a paper that Deutsch wrote in 1929. Sand, whose given name was Aurore Dupin, was born in 1804. Like some, but not all, of the women whom I will write about, she was in many ways brought up as a boy. Her grandmother who played a significant part in raising her called her my son and "insisted that she be equipped with the virtues of a boy." Aurore's father was a prominent soldier during the Napo-leonic wars and Aurore, at the age of four, was introduced by her mother to one of Napoleon's generals. She was dressed in a uniform like her father's and was introduced to him as "my son."

Deutsch discusses Sand's masculinity complex, which she says results from an unsuccessful striving for a feminine realization of happiness. What does she mean by this and how does it relate to the issue of crossdressing?

In her paper on "The Active Woman: Masculinity Complex," she describes the ideal path towards feminine identifications: "We have learned that in the ego's drive toward adulthood, identifications with the active mother proves a useful instrument.....the activity we see in the little girl as a product of her identification with the active mother acquires a permanent psychologic representation which lends the woman a definite character"(Deutsch 1929, p. 282). Later on she states that "a disturbance in the identification with the mother certainly plays a great part in the development toward femininity…If the mother is excluded from the ego-formation in this period of the girl's life the model is only the father" (Deutsch 1929)

A review of Aurore's early life shows that the destruction of her maternal ideal resulted in the outcome that Deutsch describes. What was the event that resulted in her donning male clothing? According to Deutsch, the rivalry between Aurore's grandmother and mother was decisive. Aurore's mother Sophie was, prior to marriage, a prostitute and was despised by her aristocratic, educated grandmother. As a result of this rivalry, Sophie eventually abandoned the family and went to Paris. The grandmother then revealed Sophie's past to Aurore, hoping to win her complete love. What was the reaction? The twelve-year-old Aurore "refused to study and became like a mischievous, wild, undisciplined boy. She set herself against all things feminine, dressed in mannish garb, and in every way tried to ruin her good reputation as a woman" (Deustch 1929, p. 303). It is interesting to note that Willa Cather's episode of crossdressing also occurred subsequent to an incident, clearly experienced as traumatic, involving her mother. This was the birth of a baby boy. Deutsch states that this behavior was the result of the destruction of the feminine ideal. Aurore could no longer identify with her mother, who up to this point was deeply loved. Aurore's "escape to the masculine" was directly related to disappointment in love. However, she also felt that her upbringing, which was designed to foster identification with her father, was equally important.

It should also be noted that Aurore, who eventually changed her name to further her career as a writer, dressed in both male and female clothing. Deutsch states that this occurred subsequent to additional disappointments in love. Since Sand had many disastrous love affairs with famous men, such as Chopin, this was a frequent occurrence.

159

Fenichel

In 1930 Fenichel published a fifteen-page paper on male crossdressing. He quotes Stekel's opinion that male crossdressing was simply a mask for homosexuality. But he points out that it is necessary to "find out under what conditions this mask in particular is selected." Apparently female crossdressing did not need such an exploration. He devoted one brief paragraph at the end of the paper to female crossdressing, stating it was a "displacement of envy of the penis to envy of masculine appearance." Apparently he felt that penis envy was so paramount in female development that a more extensive dynamic analysis was unnecessary. Apparently he did not wonder why, if this was so paramount, more women did not crossdress!

Hyman Barahal

In 1952, Hyman S. Barahal presented a paper entitled "Female Transvestism and Homosexuality." This fifty-page paper described the analysis of a women who crossdressed and who was analyzed by him while hospitalized.

This patient was born to a seventeen-year-old unmarried woman. Her mother rejected her and she was shuttled from home to home from birth to age 14. From early childhood she had what Barahal termed an "ungovernable" wish to be a boy and insisted on wearing boys' clothes. She also was attracted to girls from an early age. When she was nineteen she married a homosexual man who was about to go overseas with the military. The stated reason for the marriage was to make her eligible for military benefits. However, upon learning that he was scheduled to return home, she panicked and had herself hospitalized. It was in this context that she was analyzed by Barahal.

The analysis revealed the patient's conviction that had she been a boy her mother would have loved her. "My mother always made me feel that she would have been happier if I had been a boy. She made me promise when I was ten years old that, when I grew up, I would take care of her. I told you that I had my hair cut like a boy when I was three years old." (Barahal 1952, p. 395)

There also seems to be an association between feeling protected from danger and crossdressing (which one of my interviewees also expressed).

"There was a red-headed girl about seven years of age who took me and a little boy in the barn and I know that something sexual happened, but I don't remember exactly what, but I was very frightened. Shortly after that I cut my hair and wanted to wear boy's clothes"(Barahal 1952. p. 395-396). In another session she "expresses the strong desire to destroy anyone who wishes to place her in the role of a woman, which to her involves considerable danger"(Barahal 1952, p. 397).

In his analysis of the dynamics behind crossdressing, Barahal seems to be of two minds. He initially states that this woman crossdressed in order to become more lovable in her mother's eyes. "In a compulsively repetitive manner, she started early in life to compete with men for the love of the mother, even to assuming a man's attire"(Barahal 1952, p. 433) However, later on he reverts to a less nuanced position. He explains female crossdressing as a "drive for masculinity." And he states that it does not differ essentially from other similarly motivated disturbances in the sphere of feminine psychology (Barahal 1952, p. 438). This is similar to Fenichel's sweeping analysis, which does not take into account the individual dynamics or the choice of symptom. Clearly all women who experience a drive for masculinity do not crossdress. In addition, he does not offer a definition of masculinity. Rather, he offers an unconvincing example of a woman who competes with her husband as someone who is experiencing a disturbance in her feminine development.

Robert Stoller

In 1967 Stoller published a paper on female (versus male) transvestism. In this paper he declared that while female transexualism exists, there is no such thing as female transvestism. However, the following year in the book *Observing the Erotic Imagination* he takes a different position. Stoller cites three cases. One already discussed here is the case reported by Stekel and Gutheil. All three women experienced sexual excitement when donning men's clothing. And one woman was profoundly disturbed and fantasized that she had "an intraabdominal or intravaginal penis, truly present" (Stoller 1967, p. 150). However, this woman described not only sexual arousal, but other feelings when wearing men's clothing. "My Levi's are just as effective sexually as they were when I was young. I don't rely on them for sex, but do wear them if I'm feeling particularly sad or vulnerable. I discovered that wearing boots further enhanced these feelings of strength: if I'm dressed in Levi's and boots there isn't a man alive who could threaten me on any level at all (Stoller 1967, p. 147).

Stoller, unlike Barahal and Fenichel, does not attribute this behavior to penis envy or striving for masculinity. He speculates, more in the vein of Deutsch, that it is attributable to inadequate parenting. He cites the terrible relationship that these three women had with their mothers (including one whose mother said she would be better off dead) and the absence of a functional father. He finally concludes that the more he has observed, the less he knows. And he makes a crucial distinction: that learning from observation is very different from drawing conclusions from theory.

THE INTERVIEWS

I interviewed three women who offered to discuss why they crossdress. I will present a lengthy section of one interview and, in the discussion I will also present material from some of the other interviews. For purpose of this paper I will refer to them as Ann, Barbara , and Carol. All of these women had relationships with both men and women, but at the time of the interviews identified as lesbians.

Ann is a white Jewish female in her mid 40's working as a maintenance supervisor in a major industry in NYC. She had a younger sister. Her mother had multiple sclerosis. This illness was first diagnosed after her younger sister was born. The patient says that as a young child she was not aware of her mother's illness. It was not until her teens that her mother became bedridden and unable to care for herself. Her father ran a grocery store. She often helped him in the store and found it a source of pleasure. She was brought up primarily in New York City. Her family briefly lived in Florida because the doctors thought it would be better for her mother's health.

INT: Describe how you're dressed and how you usually dressed.

Ann: I'm dressed the way I'm usually dressed. Have on jeans, sweatshirt, T-shirt. I was thinking about my T-shirt this morning . These ribbed little things, what do you call them? Scoop-neck thing, no-sleeves kind of things.

Int: Guido t's?

Ann: I hate the term...my friends usually call them Guido t-shirts. Sweat socks and hiking boots. And that's it.

Int: Earrings?

Ann: Earrings. Three earrings, three posted earring and one in one ear and two in one ear. I have a watch on. No jewelry today. I have a chain.

Int: Is this your usual dress?

Ann: Yeah, except its not the way I dress for work. This is the way I dress almost exclusively outside of work. I don't always wear a sweatshirt: I might wear a shirt – a button-down shirt, a T-shirt, depending on the weather.

Int: How do you dress for work?

Ann: Just sort of a slight variation. More expensive jeans – no, something between dress pants an chinos. Actually, now that its winter I've been wearing light cords. They're bought in Macy's in the men's department. They're wrinkle-free. They're just basic. I have three pairs. They're all the same: green, gray, blue.

Int: Are these regulation colors?

Ann: Actually in my job if we choose to wear a uniform they supply us with uniforms...They come in male and female models.

Int: Which model do you wear?

Ann: I don't wear either. My first week or two as a supervisor I was into wearing this little outfit. But that got old very fast. I ordered both, a man's jacket and a woman's jacket. The woman's jacket was very snug. It didn't have as many pockets as the men's jacket. It was too fitted around the waist and stuff. And the men's jacket I felt the shoulders were too big. I didn't care for it. And almost looked too mannish to me, but mannish in this really straight-world way.

Int: Are there a lot of women in your job?

Ann: It's a traditionally male job. I'm a maintenance supervisor. What I just thought about – how I dressed before I became a supervisor about 2 1/2 years ago – I worked what we called "greens," which meant I wore a green uniform That's not male or female, or I guess it's male but everyone wears the same uniform…And it's funny, as comfortable as those clothes can be I'd still rather always wear my jeans, like, it's all right to wear that shirt, as long as I could wear my jeans. You never get tired of wearing jeans, but you do get tired of wearing green pants all the time– or brown or blue or gray. Somehow you never get tired of wearing jeans.

(The significance of jeans will be described later in the inreview)

Int: Are there other female supervisors and what do they wear?

Ann: There are four of us. My immediate boss, she basically wears dresses. But she's a unit head – I think she's expected to wear dresses…She definitely doesn't wear anything that's uniform-like.

Int: If you moved up, how would you react to being asked to wear dresses?

Ann: I couldn't/wouldn't do it. I think I don't know if I would actually be pressured. I don't know how much in this day and age they can actually tell you about the way you dress. It's possible I might now be picked for a position. I just know that I couldn't do it. I couldn't really change the way I dress.

Int: Do you know why you couldn't ?

Ann: I would just be so physically uncomfortable. I mean I might, like the most I would do would possibly be…Oh God, it feels uncomfortable just even talking about it – like upgrading the type of pants I wear maybe upgrading the kinds of shirt. Maybe I would wear blazers more often. Sort of just, dress up.

Int: Would that be uncomfortable –just even to upgrade?

Ann: It would be something I could live with, but it wouldn't be comfortable.

Int: You said it makes you uncomfortable even talking about it…

Ann: Yeah, it makes me like cringe to try and…certainly that thought of a skirt or something Also, because I work in maintenance, I think the whole thing is so ludicrous. You often have to go places which are dirty…Jt doesn't make a lot of sense for me, you know, to dress up.

Int: When was the last time you wore a dress or skirt?

Ann: I think my sister's wedding in 1970 sometime.

Int: Twenty years ago.

Ann: Yeah, No that's not entirely true. In the early 70's when I worked some temporary job I wore some skirts and blouses, and some jumper-type things. I think that was the last time.

Int: did you have to?

Ann: I don't know that it ever occurred to me that I didn't have to. I think I thought it was expected that I was a woman going to work in an office and I had to dress up.

Int: But when you got home off duty?

Ann: Oh, I threw that stuff in the closet.

EARLY MEMORIES

Ann: I used to fight with my mother all the time on Jewish holidays about having to get dressed. I mean here was my day off from school and my mother would say "here put on this" frilly little thing.

Int: How old were you?

Ann: Anywhere from pre-teen on. I remember having to go to bar mitzvahs and weddings. Having to go out and buy these cute little dresses and having to wear them And I never felt comfortable wearing them.

Int: Why?

Ann: They weren't physically comfortable. They were confining. They were made out of crinoline. They were rough. You couldn't get them dirty, had to be careful about what you were doing. So you basically had to sit in a chair and not move. I have a photograph of my sister and myself sitting at a cousin's bar mitzvah. I had a little blue dress, she had a little pink dress. And she's sitting on my lap. I started very early (giggles). So I remember as far back as then, and I do remember like "No I don't want to wear this."

Int: How did your sister feel?

Ann: I don't think we discussed it. I don't think she minded wearing these clothes. But I always minded. I always felt like– and I can still do this sometimes – nothing felt better than when I had on a pair of jeans and maybe a sweatshirt, and looking down at your sneakers and your jeans, the way your jeans might fall against your sneakers, and I can still do that and get this like, little- boy feeling, and, like that's ecstasy.

Int: Describe the little-boy feeling.

Ann: It's like—it's sort of impish and feeling like you have control, and you're sort of in charge of your life…like you're cute and you're capable.

Int: What is the little-girl feeling that you didn't like?

Ann: Confined. Feeling restricted, physically uncomfortable, unable to be aggressive the way you might want to be. I've always had this feeling that it…it didn't feel like me. There was something odd about it. Something not right

Int. Do you know what "me" felt like?

Ann: Me felt like a little boy, I think.

Int: At the risk of repeating, what does a little boy feel like?

Ann: Okay, at the risk of repeating…I think being able to have fun and freedom. And I guess I always had this sense that little boys were able to do more than little girls were able to do. I didn't want to be held back from being able to do things that felt comfortable and right to me.

Int: Do you have a brother?

166

Ann: No. So my parents didn't really stop me from playing in certain ways, or playing with certain things or certain people, but on the occasion that I was supposed to dress like a little girl they stuck to their guns about it.

Int: Where sense of being a boy was better?

Ann: I don't know that I can answer that. When I was anywhere from 4 or 5 years old, I know that I went through this period of feeling really strongly wanting to be a boy. I don't know how many years it lasted – maybe until I was, you know, pre-teen or something, maybe even some of my teen years. That it was just something – something was, not even wrong, but it felt better to me to be a little boy. I just really don't know where it came from, if it was from my playmates or other parents, or my own parents. I really don't know.

Int: Did you ever wonder if your parents wanted a boy?

Ann: Not that I recall.

Int: Did you want to have a penis?

Ann: At that time I don't think I focused on body parts.

DISCUSSION

How It Started

Ann describes, very specifically, the event, as she recalls it, that is associated with preferring boys' clothing. Carol describes two events relevant to her early preference for boys' clothing. When she was four years old, she was operated on for a heart defect. After the surgery, but while she was still hospitalized, an incident took place when her mother was not present. A nurse took her to a room full of clothing and told her she could pick out anything she wanted to wear. What did she want? Boys' jeans! The hospital did not have any jeans small enough to fit her slight 4-year old frame, so – disappointed to have missed an opportunity to wear clothing her mother would not have allowed - she wound up with a pair of purple corduroy overalls.

Another memory – from her early teens – is related to a country club her parents belonged to that required females to enter using a side entrance. She was particularly incensed that her younger brother was allowed to go in the front door with their father, while she and her mother were relegated to what felt to her like the freight entry. When she pressed for a reason for the club's rule, her mother, a graduate of a prestigious women's college, said "This is just the way it is." What was the reaction of this girl? In the early 50's, women wore slacks with zippers on the side. (This may have generated the wish for blue jeans in the hospital.) In any event, because she associated zippers on the side with the humiliating experience at the club, she refused to wear them and insisted on boys' jeans instead.

How Clothing Feels

The website Bluestocking Blue published other very vivid descriptions of how some woman feel wearing men's clothing. "I am not sure that I feel sexy so much as relieved when I put these clothes on, when I think of myself in every sense as the male I feel I am inside. I can feel euphoric about it, calm, relaxed and I even feel – beautiful?...It's a loving and positive feeling, just feeling like myself. I'm not sure the dressing thing would be sexual for me though. One wonders if this woman who says she feels like a male inside would be thought of as a transsexual man. And Okay, firsties, like the other guys defined, sexy in this context means feeling comfortable and attractive in my own skin. Lemme see...I remember really enjoying the feeling of underwear when I first started wearing it (still do) And I love the way cargo pants hang off my frame. I almost never wear any other kind of pants." All of these women feel more comfortable in men's clothing and I think that the comment "feeling comfortable in my own skin" points to a critical issue. A very primal sense of comfort.

The Difference Between Boys and Girls

This interviewee, Ann, expresses some particularly vivid feelings about the experience of wearing boy's clothing. While many of the interviewees described feeling restricted, almost imprisoned, by women's clothing and all of them emphasize that men's clothing is more comfortable, this interviewee describes, viscerally, the pleasurable feelings associated with wearing boy's clothing. She feels impish, cute, in charge, and capable. Little boys can have more fun than little girls. And she says that she can occasionally recreate this feeling, even decades later.

Her description of looking at how her jeans "broke" against her sneakers is striking, if somewhat puzzling to this writer. But it does locate the event, as she recalls it, when she began to favor boys' clothing over girls'.

Suits

A few of the women felt more powerful wearing men's clothing. Carol, a graduate of an Ivy League Law School and an associate at a prestigious law firm, felt, nevertheless, that she wielded more authority when wearing men's suits: "I think in this outfit I seem more authoritative than I would otherwise, and sometimes more intimidating, which is often desirable and sometimes not, it depends. It's something in my profession that I need to be at times."

One speculates that she had not internalized a sense of power and that donning a man's suit, a powerful symbol, conferred the strength felt she lacked. (In contrast, another interviewee who worked at a prestigious law firm felt that she had to wear women's clothing, that in this environment she had to fit in).

Mothers and Fathers

All women who were interviewed described similar issues with their mothers and fathers regarding their clothing. The resistance to wearing girl's clothing started very early and was a source of intense conflict with her mother. Carol felt that her mother wanted to "make her over in her own image." Was wearing men's clothing a defense against engulfment?

None of them reported significant conflict with their fathers about clothing (with the exception of one interviewee whose father insisted that she wear a bra).

Int: Did you fight with your father about this?

Carol: I wonder whether I'm not remembering things at this point. But my sense is that my father was never really part of any of this discussion. And my father was, you know, outside of this realm. And didn't have anything to say about it.

Fathers and Play

It is of interest that all three women reported that they were allowed to play sports and, in some cases, taught to play by their fathers. They were not told that sports were only for boys (although they did grow up in an era when organized sports such as Little League were restricted to boys.) Two interviewees reported that their father's taught them to play sports. One of the fathers, a former Marine, taught her and her brother how to march and did vigorous Marine Corp drills with them. He was also a wrestling champion and would wrestle with her and her brother.

While it is laudable that these young women, who grew up in the fifties, were not restricted to traditional girls' activities, it is of additional interest that they do not recall that their fathers validated their femininity.

Mothers and Fathers and Bras

It is interesting that Carol did report that when she was an adolescent and did not want to wear a bra, both her father and mother "had a fit at me because they thought it looked obscene, and I thought it looked erotic. This was another fight we had for years."

While none of these interviewees felt consciously that their parents would have preferred having a son, one wonders if the fathers felt more comfortable with girls who were "male"-identified rather than feminine children. Carol's father objected to the fact that without a bra her nipples showed. In other words, when she exhibited obvious feminine qualities he became upset. Was this a defense against the reemergence of unresolved oedipal passions? Katz discusses the reaction of fathers "in the face of their daughters' age-appropriate psychosexual development. …some become disturbed, sometimes extremely so. The emerging bodily and psychological sexuality of a daughter may trigger highly uncharacteristic reactions." Carol's father, who was disengaged during her early struggles about clothing suddenly became highly involved – "he had a fit" – when her body, particularly

170

her breasts, developed. And his insistence that she wear a bra in order to cover up her nipples seemed to be a denial of her emerging sexuality.

Wish to Be a Boy

Ann did express the wish to be a boy. This was not true of everyone. However, this interviewee did not express the wish to have a penis. She said, "I was not interested in body parts."

This sentiment is interesting in that it is reminiscent of the following anecdote… A country minister on a walk discovered a five-year-old boy bathing in a brook with some small girls. After he was scolded what did the candid toddler reply? "I did not know, sir that they were girls. They did not have any clothes on." Apparently for these children the sense of maleness or femaleness is not equated with anatomy.

Pockets

Another interesting point which all three interviewees focused on, with varying degrees of intensity, was the lack of pockets in women's clothing.

Carol: When I was a kid I sometimes got my mother to buy jeans with the flannel lining and the little secret pockets. Men's clothes are full of pockets, which I didn't realize until I started buying them. This goes back to childhood – I couldn't understand why boys' clothes would have pockets and not girls' – and then it was more infuriating that some girl's clothes had phony pockets…It wasn't bad enough that they didn't give you pockets."

This interviewee, who considers herself a radical feminist, views men's clothing as symbolically and practically embodying male privilege. She goes on to say: "I found out that boys didn't need handbags. Men can stow all this stuff in their suits and with expensive suits they will hang right even if you load all this stuff in." And to add to her indignation, women have phony pockets. Women did not have "the real thing."

Since this interviewee was not a radical feminist when she was a child, one has to wonder what the significance of pockets was to a small girl. She refers to " little secret pockets." What was the secret? Pockets were something that boys had and girls did not. Was this a displaced penis envy?

Safety and Shoes

This interviewee, Carol, also expressed, if somewhat indirectly, that women's clothing made her feel vulnerable. Referring to her preference, at a young age, for boys' clothes, she says, "Boys'clothes were always sturdier." (Were young children aware of this?)

Later on she states "I don't want it (clothing) to hamper my movement…if I have to run down the street."

Discussing the issues of shoes, Carol says she wears men's shoes because "I can run in it if I want. If someone steps on my foot they'll be stepping on leather instead of my foot.

And later she says, "The whole thing with women's shoes is that they make you tremendously unstable. I think its ridiculous to put yourself in that position." (While there is much truth to her comments about women's shoes, most women are not concerned with these issues.)

not true

Again, one wonders if she has not internalized a sense of safety and depends on types of clothing – in this case shoes and sturdy clothes – to make her feel secure.

Underwear and Working Out

Carol discussed, in detail, wearing underwear. While she wore women's underpants because they fit her and are comfortable she refused to wear bras, stating that they were constricting and made it hard to breathe. Again, the theme of women's clothing being confining and almost paralyzing emerges. However, when this woman who is an athlete works out, she wears "skintight undershirts that hold everything together and I can breathe." I cannot help but wonder why a bra is more constricting than a skintight undershirt. Again the issue of the meaning of bras arises. *it is!*

Passing as a Man

The women I interviewed did not wish to pass as men. One, however, thought that under certain circumstances it would be helpful. Again, quoting Carol, she says, "No, why would I want to do that? The only time I would want to do that that in actual daily life would be to protect myself from danger so there would be a very practical reason…If I'm walking around late at night anytime and someone decides not to attack me because they think I'm a man, really, that's okay with me." Again, while a woman walking alone at night might feel vulnerable, I think that this interviewee is expressing a preoccupation with a sense of vulnerability and powerlessness which is somewhat assuaged when passing as a man.

Conclusion

Why do women crossdress? I can only offer hypotheses in answer to this question. This is partly due to the fact that the material available is not – save for one example – based on analyses of the women whom I discuss. Furthermore, it is possible that even in-depth analyses would not provide definitive answers – only additional hypotheses. This is because most of the subjects report that their wishes to crossdress arose at a very early age, suggesting that preverbal experiences are key in female crossdressing.

However, certain patterns stand out. The most striking pattern is the report by many of these women that their parents actually dressed and raised them as boys from a young age. Additionally, women who were not raised as boys often reported that they thought that their parents wanted a boy and that they would have been loved, rather than rejected, had they been males.

The women whom I interviewed did not state that their parents directly expressed a wish that they had been boys. Therefore I can only speculate about the dynamics. In two instances, their fathers did not validate their femininity and in some ways reinforced masculine identifications by teaching them sports. These women grew up in an era when sports were primarily a male activity and girls were expected to engage in more "feminine" activities such as playing with dolls. This suggests that their fathers were more at ease relating to them as little boys, since treating them as daughters may have aroused unacceptable sexual impulses.

While these women did report conflict with their mothers, who would have preferred gender- appropriate dress, one wonders if the mothers would, in fact, have preferred having a son. In at least one instance, the daughter's younger brother was very clearly favored by the mother. (This was not covered in the interview but was reported in other contexts.)

The behavior of Willa Cather, born in 1874, seems to reflect a conviction on her part that a boy would have been preferred by her parents. Cather was the first-born child. At an early age she engaged in behavior that was typically male in her era. She dissected small animals and wanted to be a doctor. When a brother was born, and her mother was no longer available to help her comb her long hair, she had her hair cut short, began to dress as a boy, and called herself William Cather MD. Was her mother's unavailability interpreted as a rejection of her femininity? Another literary figure, Radclyffe Hall, wrote the novel *The Well of Loneliness*, which directly addresses the issue. She describes a couple who longed for a son and were devastated by the birth of a daughter. They named her Stephen and raised her as a boy. Both the author and the character adopted male dress. It should also be noted that Hall's father abandoned the family when she was very young. Did she fantasize that this was due to her disappointment at not having a son?

Another intriguing issue is the comment by many of these women that men's clothing was more comfortable, suggesting that there is a self-soothing quality involved. This led me to hypothesize that men's clothing functions as a kind of transitional object that alleviates anxiety and in many cases is empowering. However, since the traditional transitional object loses its meaning and is ultimately discarded, this seems inaccurate. Joyce McDougall coined the term "transitory object," referring to "addictive objects which create no lasting change and must be sought after ceaselessly in the outer world as a symbolic substitute for the mother of infancy" (McDougall, 1985)

Additionally, Winnicott states that, developmentally. a transitional object is the precursor to the child's ability to internalize the mother. My theory is that because these women felt alienated and rejected by their parents, they were unable to adequately internalize a maternal object. By fulfilling the conscious or unconscious wish of the parents (i.e. becoming a boy) they were striving to internalize the parental object and to separate. They attempted to connect with the parents by "giving" them the son they longed for. Ironically these girls seemed, in some cases, to understand their parents better than the parents understood themselves. By wearing men's clothing, they strove to become the longed-for sons.

REFERENCES

Barahal, Hyman S. "Female Transvestism and Homosexuality." Presented at Downstate Interhospital Conference of the New York State Department of Mental Hygiene at the New York State Psychiatric Institute, April 8, 1952.

"Women Who Crossdress." (2012). Retrieved from bluestockingblue .blogspot.com/2012/10/women-who-crossdress.html.com.

Deutsch, Helene. (1944). *The Psychology of Women: A Psychoanalytic Interpretation Volume I.* New York: Grune & Stratton. (Footnote 179-323)

Fenichel, Otto. (1930). "The Psychology of Transvestism." *International Journal of Psychoanalysis.* 11: 211-226.

Flügel, J.C. (1950). *The Psychology of Clothes.* New York: Hogarth Press.

Hirschfeld, Magnus. (2006) "Selections from the Transvestites: The Erotic Drive to Cross-Dress." In: Stryker, S. & Whittle, S. (Eds). *The Transgender Studies Reader* (pps. 28-39). New York: Routledge.

Kraft-Ebing, Richard von. (2006). "Selections from Psychopathis Sexualis with Special Reference to Contrary Sexual Instinct: A Medico-Legal Study." In: Stryker, S. & Whittle, S. (Eds). *The Transgender Studies Reader* (pps. 21-27). New York: Routledge.

MacDougall, Joyce. (1989) *Theaters of the Body: A Psychoanalytic Approach to Psychosomatic Illness.* New York: Norton and Company.

O'Brien, S. (1987) *Willa Cather: The Emerging Voice.* New York: Fawcett Columbine.

Stoller, Robert J. (1985). *Observing the Erotic Imagination.* New Haven: Yale University Press.

Stekel, Wilhelm and Emil Gutheil. *Sexual Aberrations Volume III.* New York: Livewright, 1930. (footnote pps 281-318)

5. Tattoos as Symbolizing Marks: Fashion, Body Rite, Fetish, or Hidden Trauma

INTRODUCTION

Why would anyone want to spend the rest of their life
Seeing death on their arm....

Patricia Cornwell, *Black Notice*, (1999)

Love and Hate Tattoo

As psychoanalysts today, we encounter diverse problems that require different positions in regard to creativity and destructivity in human manifestations. In the last twenty years, and in a context of a certain robotization of the individual in the Western world, we observe how the tangible body is gradually losing these dimensions in the midst of an explosion of digitalized images.

At the same time, body art has developed hugely, in both academic and commercial areas, as an increasingly popular fashion. This has been demonstrated by many surveys in which numerous university students manifested that they had a tattoo, piercing, or scarring. Tattoos allow for a much wider variety of drawings, since through images symbolization becomes more relevant, unlike scarring in which the design is formed only by scars. The word tattoo is derived from the Polynesian word "tatau," which means the feeling of being beaten, and also from another word from the Polynesian, Tohu, father of the night and creator of all the drawings in the world (Salamone, 1994).

I present a clinical case to illustrate a psychoanalytic view of the marked body, in which sexuality and the violence of helplessness could be said to emerge in complex and multidimensional intricacy.

Since prehistoric times, social and sexual places and functions have been defined as means to implore the gods for protection against evil spirits. As a result, tattoos, perforations, paintings, hairdressing, accessories, and clothing are closely interrelated, as in fashion, working together to form diverse images that are far from superficial and structure, as in a kaleidoscope, the body of a given age and culture.

Thus, we may see that tattoos, in the traditional sense, function as a sign of personal identification, fashions shared by certain groups of pertinence, spells or talismans referring to secret societies, amorous fidelity, ornaments, etc. They acquire relevance in adolescence, an extremely vulnerable stage of life, characterized by depression and the vicissitudes of transformation of the original objects of love. Therefore, in many cases, they may also be detected as scars of wounds in the identification structure, diverse in depth and scope, which in some cases reveal a cultural construction of the erotogenic body in its delicate initial balance.

This chapter is the product of clinical investigation into these procedures applied to the bodies of adolescents and young adults, even though they are not limited to these age groups. I consider them to be revealing scars that in my opinion relate to problems concerning the singularity of parental inscriptions in our culture.

Below, I present the clinical case of a patient I shall call Veronica, who, paradoxically, without words but instead through her tattoo, allowed us to begin to narrate a story in the intersubjective space we shared in her sessions. Among folds and convolutions, this story developed gradually, took unexpected directions, and led me, time and again, to reflect on this fashion, this language form, so prevalent in our times.

DEVELOPMENT

In many cases, tattoos are experienced as protective skins, networks to provide support and shelter from intense anxieties, most often suffered but not felt in their full hermeneutic and creative dimension. From my perspective, I try to use their particular language to legitimize the expressive dimension of identity in cultural, social, and individual manifestations.

They form truly crucial points between the somatic and the psychic, and between the individual's biology and history, where the deepest is veiled and also revealed on the skin.

We find that these individuals are often seeking a means to legitimize or express identities they feel are in danger of disintegration, as well as a space for production of subjectivity ciphered on an ontological level, which exhibits auto-poetic space-time segments. That is to say, these adolescents create their own identifying emblems for lack of meaningful referents and of values and ideals transmitted by the culture.

Are tattoos akin to fashion, imposed as relational proposals in social strategy? Fashion, body rite, fetish, or also pure unqualified quantity referring to the terrain of trauma and of "The Disruptive" (Benyakar 2003), of unbound energy? Unqualified quantities? Or, as in the model proposed by Bion (1967): thoughts without a thinker, contents without a container, characters in search of an author? To paraphrase Pirandello (1925), is this skin alteration also directly proportional to the depth of the psychic wound, showing that it is always active?

178

Considering that tattoos aim to exert strong visual attraction, ranging from curiosity and seduction to violence and/or anxiety, I believe that tattoos may be conceptualized as revealing scars, and paraphrasing Dejours (1989), who refers to "symbolizing somatizations," I call them "symbolizing marks" (Catz 2011). That is to say, an inscription and/or deciphering of mourning in a potentially creative space, as in fashion, also indicating tendencies. What is worn, whether clothing, accessories or tattoos, carries a signifying and meaningful mark. It is according to this perspective that I highlight the following verse in a Native American song from South Dakota: "Father, paint the world on my body" (Galeano 2007).

Concerning paternal inscription, we observe that interrupted transmission of the heritage, as well as the freezing of mourning processes, whether in familial, cultural, historical, or social history, destroys the thread of origins supporting the subject's inscription in a personal history that makes it possible to take possession of it and to inherit a name and a culture. "What you have inherited from your fathers, strive to make it your own" (Goethe, quoted by Freud, 1940).

Each tattoo acquires relevance as a testimony, since it deciphers and inscribes this pertinence for the first time. With respect to what I discussed above in relation to parental inscriptions, I believe it is particularly interesting to include the investigations of Garma (1961), who observes that ornamentation on the human body in both forms, clothing and tattoos, was characteristic of the most primitive art.

Ornamentation on the human body was created and inaugurated by prehistoric mothers with the aim of continuing to give their children, magically and after their birth, all the support they were able to give them during their intrauterine life. They made drawings on their infant's body with vegetable dyes to protect them from wild animals, at the same time that they dressed and covered them according to parameters of the social context in which they lived.

This custom must have acquired different aspects at different stages of the growing individual, who no longer needed maternal protection but instead independence. The latter led to the origin of the puberty rites observed in all peoples, both primitive and civilized, where "the marks" of this process may be found in a broad range of creative possibilities.

Psychoanalytic studies of puberty reveal that one of its deepest meanings is to indicate a passing: more precisely, it carries the mark of passage from the mother to the father. For this purpose, one procedure used by primitive groups that worshipped an animal in totemic practices, which extended to skins and tattoos, was learned from the mothers; they covered the infant's body with the skin of the totemic animal or reproduced its image on the child's skin by means of paintings, scars or clothing.

It may be said that from the outset the tattoo has also been a symbolic tool for nonverbal communication between persons of different cultures, forming part of human subjectivity and taking a position as a model of identity that has always been part of the process of communication in different cultures in the world, as well as an artistic expression. It continues to exist and has existed since time immemorial, and is found on mummies tattooed on different parts of the body for objectives generally considered to be therapeutic.

One example is the mummy of the priestess Amunet, servant of the god Hathor, buried in Thebes around 2200 B.C. On her skin, a number of blue scars in straight, parallel lines were found on her abdomen at hip level (Field, 1958). Although they were also used for punishment and discrimination, they were creative and ornamental as well.

In any case, we cannot fail to highlight that the marking of bodies, which produces a painful pressure on the skin, is a paradoxical pressure, since it speaks simultaneously of the need to create a passage and to access understanding of the permanence of this type of language. The wound on the skin expresses a rupture produced in the internal world of the psyche. We also need to consider that in this way, creatively, the tattoo became a language beyond words.

This observation recalls something that Viñar (2007) defines as a traumatic situation: when the metabolism of perpetual self-construction is invaded or overwhelmed by trauma that the psyche is unable to signify or modify. The symbolic production that is the foundation of psychic existence is thereby broken or interrupted and, whether temporarily or permanently, a hole or tear is created that needs mending.

Tattooers usually tell people who go to them for a tattoo that there is no pain greater than the pain they have already felt, and therefore the pain caused by the application of the tattoo is irrelevant.

We could say that marking the body is in some way an act of violence on this body. While we bear in mind that these tattooed images both dress and cathect, they are at the same time always articulated with discourse surrounding fashion and its imperatives.

There are different types of tattoos, which in my opinion exhibit a mute existence transmuted on the skin; in a context of discovery, they possess true ontological eloquence based on their position between socio-cultural determinism and a singular history involving at least three generations.

We could conjecture that, because of parental deficits, the current chain of psychic transmission could in some cases be seriously disturbed, either due to absence of symbolic inscriptions or to the hyper-presence of forebears who expected to be cloned by their descendants; we find this excess in perverted form in fanatical mandates and enslaving nepotisms. In this perspective, tattoos may reveal or camouflage obstacles that are building a rocky road towards adulthood, at the same time manifesting creativity applied to overcoming these obstacles or expressed in the profound meaning expressed in rituals in some cultures.

There are many examples, as in the case of convicts who apply tattoos to avoid psychic collapse and to survive what is often an unspeakable reality. There is the case of "child thieves" for whom tattoos have such a specific meaning that they acquire the dimension of a mute and ciphered language shared by each small group. This is also the case for the tattoos of young Israeli youths with the concentration camp numbers of their grandparents, once imprisoned in Auschwitz, at a time when the living memory of Holocaust survivors is about to disappear with the loss of that generation.

I consider that these individuals express themselves through acts on their body, in constant interaction with their environment, which determines specific features in the constitution of subjectivity. The tattoo thereby acquires relevance as a testimony, a message to be deciphered, beyond but including fashion or ornamentation, where words yield place to images, which are only worth a thousand words if we are willing to search for them.

PRESENTATION OF A CLINICAL CASE

First interviews

Veronica, a woman 35 years old, requested treatment, and when she arrived to her first interview, I met a woman with a neat appearance, impeccably groomed, very pretty and attractive. Her clothing was strikingly fashionable, in line with the dictates of fashion, down to the finest details.

Her appearance suited the demands of her job; she worked at an important multinational company. She traveled constantly, interacting in highly competitive circles with high power of acquisition. She opened this first interview by talking about her family concerns, which actually centered on her original family rather than her nuclear family; she was separated and had an eleven-year-old son.

She took time in particular to tell me about her relationship with her younger sister who, because of addiction to drugs, had fallen into prostitution and had contracted HIV. Her sister usually took refuge in her house, and would appear suddenly and make herself at home, only to disappear for long periods without contacting her. This behavior was a constant source of worry which had finally ended, since after several attempts to commit suicide, her sister had finally succeeded, a situation that threw and pulled Veronica down into what she described as a deep crisis from which she was unable to recover.

As we looked more closely into her history, she placed particular emphasis on the characteristics of her mother, a cold, distant, and selfish person who always placed herself in the position of "The Queen". At her side, her father acted as an attentive and affectionate servant passively dedicated to all the mother's tyrannical demands. As for the children, she and her sister, recently deceased, and their elder brother, had what she called a weak father figure, very vulnerable, though now affectionate towards his grandson Pablo, the patient's son.

She underscored the deep feeling shared by the three siblings of having been abandoned to their luck in childhood, when the only maternal figure consisted in their maternal grandmother, who participated greatly in caring for the children, since the parents, besides paying no attention to them, were always traveling, the household being left in Veronica's care.

In this way, from what I could observe, it could be said that her childhood was marked by the presence-absence of a seductive and neglectful mother and the faded figure of a weak and submissive father. In contrast to this description, Veronica had developed a personality with the predominant traits of a strong character, both authoritarian and obsequious, which allowed her to advance to important positions in the professional sphere.

It was not easy for her to start to talk about her son, since because of her work it was difficult for her to organize his care; her relationship with him could be seen as obsessive care for attention to his material, educational, and social needs, but to the detriment of any affectionate, loving, or tender relationship. At that time she also talked about the attacks of rage and fury her son often expressed towards her, attacking her with some violence and accusing her of leaving him alone and not thinking about him.

She appeared to be the type of woman described as strong and decisive, but with evident difficulties in the emotional area, both with her son and also her ex-husband and the partner she was seeing at the time she began her treatment. She defined her current partner as having a weak character, little power of decision, and being very pleasant like her father; also, as she did with her father, she gave him nicknames and addressed him in diminutives as if he were still a child.

Outstanding aspects of her treatment

I wish to highlight a very significant occurrence in the course of her treatment, when Veronica told me that in our first interview, although she arrived disillusioned by many failed attempts at treatment, she felt that I could help her. To my surprise, she told me that it was because when she spoke to me about her sister's death, she saw that my eyes filled with tears. Throughout the psychotherapeutic process, tears became a recurring term with a multiplicity and multicomplexity of meanings, which opened the way to unexpected perspectives.

A few months after starting her psychotherapeutic treatment, she told me that they are going to say a Mass for her sister, since it coincided with the day that would have been her birthday. As she was telling me everything that had happened around this event, I was able to see for the first time that she had a tattoo on her right arm, a squirrel. She had never mentioned it to me, and when I asked her when she had had it done, we were able to see that it coincided with the date of her sister's death and the tragic circumstances she had to experience. Her son was small but was very anguished and asked why everybody died, since an uncle, Veronica's father's brother, had also died; this uncle had acted as the father of the family and the little boy was very attached to him because of his own father's absences following the separation.

It was to this session that she brought a letter she had written to her mother when she was nine years old but was never able to give to her. With deep emotion, I saw that she took an envelope, its paper yellowing, out of her handbag, from which she extracted a folded piece of paper, with what is obviously a child's handwriting. She started to read it, not without difficulty, reading haltingly, and went along, unraveling a tangled skein of halting words, in which her childish helplessness was manifest, cut through by a scream, muffled by what we could now consider were her tears. She said in her little girl's language that she felt her mother didn't love her, that she never looked at her, that she was never interested in what was happening to her, and that she didn't know how much she suffered because of this.

That she always felt left aside, that she didn't know what to do to get her attention so that she would be loving towards her. The messages were communicated with words heavy with desperation and anxiety.

It was particularly striking to see that the sentences had blank spaces, like erased words, which I thought were due to the consequences of deterioration worked by the passing of time. As she continued to try to read, she told me that these blank spaces were left as she wrote, because her tears fell on the paper at the same time and erased what she had written.

She was never able to give this letter to her mother because she thought and knew that she would never read it, but she did show it to her grandmother, who hugged her with obvious pain and cried with her.

Perhaps she had found in me and in what she called my eyes flooded with tears, a displacement of her grandmother, who was an affective container for her pain, in that first interview when she glimpsed tears in my eyes, concordant with the grief she had not yet been able to find words to express.

And thus, we began to talk about this squirrel she carried on her arm, which actually, as she told me, was not at all what she would have wanted to have done, since she wanted to have a snake tattooed. But she had been a bit shy about having a snake tattoo, and being afraid of what others would say, since it wasn't common at that time to have a tattoo done at her age, she chose a tattoo of a squirrel.

At first, when I asked her about the tattoo, she insisted that she did it because it was the fashion, and she loved to be in fashion in every way, tattoos being an ornament that she decided to wear, according to the dictates of fashion. She tried to minimize the psychic content that might be enclosed in her image, with an air of disdain and lack of interest.

Making an effort, but at the same time quite mobilized by my interpretations about these empty spaces left without words, making room for the possibility that she could have an experience that was outside the range of experiences for Veronica, she tried to give some associations about the motivations that had led her to get a tattoo. These associations led us to possible representations of this tattoo that she had wanted to be the image of a snake and had appeared transformed into a squirrel, which in turn led us to meet the snake symbolically.

At this point she told me that her current partner called her "snake skin", referring to her coldness in relation to certain situations when she was distant and aggressive with him and also with her own son. Even though, as she herself said, she didn't want to repeat the model set by her mother, who she viewed as a lethal mother that let her own mother die of anorexia, which Veronica's dearly beloved grandmother, who covered for her mother, said she didn't have.

In the family, they used to call her mother what they called King Louis XV: "Trois fois moi" or "three times me", always out of touch with her children's needs and monopolizing what Veronica called her vulnerable father, keeping him only for herself, as a servile servant, her squirrel. In relation to her representation of her mother and father, she rapidly identified their respective traits, considering her mother a snake, conniving and selfish, and her father a harmless squirrel whose role in the family was absolutely blurry.

The squirrel appeared as a way to hide the snake or to turn it into what could be called her forsightful and thrifty character, which made her forever fear being swindled by her partner, and whose fate was nearly always "disconnection" from any relationship that might make her feel what she called choked or strangled by others. In this sense, she was conclusive in her relationships, separating from them in a way she called "the three As", that is to say, abrupt, accelerated, and addled.

The squirrel and the snake, in dialectic interplay, allowed us to take a path of representations that made it possible to fathom her jealously guarded, defended, and blocked inner world. She started to call me "The Time Tunnel Doctor." She often said that living and being analyzed was like entering the time tunnel and going through it, but as in the tango, she needed to be well led. She emphasized this aspect, especially when she was starting to resignify many aspects of her life that she apparently knew nothing about, which had remained hidden under what we could call a "false self" characterized by her effectiveness and executive decisiveness in everything she did.

Analytic work progressed following interpretations about what her tattoo revealed and veiled, when she also related the reptile skin to something she had not been able to bring to analysis until then, which was two abortions she had had without her partner's consent: abortions that had provoked break-ups, ill-will, and failed encounters. Later on, she was able to go deeper into the analysis of multiple symbols and complexities in relation to her identification with her dead sister, the working through of her mourning that had been interrupted, and the "false self" she had constructed to over-adapt to a disruptive environment unable to contain her emotions, which had turned her into what has been called a "mental orphan" (Lutenberg, 2013). She discovered the possibility to open up to a potential new mental birth through analysis, in order to undo "mental abortions" she suffered in the course of her traumatic history, as Lutenberg (2013) says; edition in analysis also involved in my opinion a "mental defreeze."

She was able to start to go through in analysis and bring to psychic life, in a dramatic way, the "mental orphanhood" of her siblings as well, the way this situation had affected her sister, and why she had so often felt responsible for her tragic end. In this way, she began to work through her mourning in a dialectic flow that slowly decreased the predominantly persecutory guilt that prevented her from working through this mourning with depressive guilt, relieving her deep pain.

She remembered, not without difficulty, that her sister also had tattoos on her arm, which represented monstrous figures with threatening eyes popping out, which she had started having done in early adolescence. Nobody had paid much attention to them in the family, as if they were somehow desperate cries to which their parents had been deaf and unresponsive. It could be said that her body was the message that, like the letter Veronica brought to session with words washed out by tears, never reached its addressee.

When her sister died, Veronica felt very guilty, as tends to happen to the closest members of the family in any suicide, for not having been able to help her more, for not having been able to prevent her death, even though everybody knew about the systematic abandonment by their parents. For Veronica, the snake represented not only her inner mother but also all the hate she had accumulated inside as a survivor of a historical psychic disaster that had frozen the developmental dynamics of her mind.

This created a catastrophe she had tried to hide with the tattoo of a harmless squirrel, a squirrel that as an image opened the way for us to transcribe with gestures, glances, tears, silences, and words her internal world, paralyzed by what Winnicott (1954) called "a frozen situation of failure."

We may say that the therapeutic process was constituted like Ariadne's thread, allowing her to escape the labyrinth inside which she was locked and that blocked her vitality, after which she was thereby able to continue her journey of progress towards experience.

Her initial allegations that fashion was the only inspiration of her desire and choice of a tattoo gradually opened up a possibility to institute spaces of reflection in regard to fashion and her own purposes. As analysts, we always find that the individual psyche leaves traces of its enigmatic presence, veiling and revealing new horizons of meanings waiting to be discovered.

CONCLUSIONS

We start out with the body scheme which, as a flexible structure, is progressively enriched through time and successive experiences shared by the body and the world. The body is the organic foundation of the entire personality, and fashion covers it, joining it intimately through dress and its undeniable socio-cultural connotation that both dresses and cathects it.

The first body image is of nudity and the consequent feeling of help-lessness. This is resolved with clothing which acts as an envelope, a feature of our body scheme and of our civilization. It is an expression in our own image and in that of others as well. Dress is the silent envelope that marks us, revealing who we are and who we are with.

This is observed more clearly in primitive peoples, where by means of tattoos, dress, and distinctive colors, ceremonies are organized to mark meaningful situations in the lives of individuals or the community; also to denote the place occupied by each in the community, tribe, clan, etc. In our society this stratification persists, signaled by fashion accord-ing to social class. In relation to festivities, commemorations, or mourning, clothing takes part in expected and appropriate behavior, including the fashion of tattoos.

This discussion includes fashion and particularly tattoos that are "Symbolizing Marks" (Catz 2011) of parental mourning processes, scars of vital or necessary and/or accidental mourning. Tattoos appear throughout all ages and cultures, either as fashion or as protective skins or talismans, as a way to feel strong by bearing pain that minimizes other pains suffered.

Tattoos may represent history engraved on the body in order to elim-inate the need to remember it, as a tribute that seeks a piece of eternity, a place where a loss symbolically lies. A difficult passage from repetition to creation is made visible, since behind the photographic definition of the tattoo and the fashion of the tattoo, something may be written in indelible ink, something that asks us not only to discover and re-create it but, in some cases, to inscribe it for the first time.

Deciphering and/or inscription is connected, in the perspective discussed, to complexities concerning the singularities of transgenerational inscriptions in our culture and of different manifestations of intersubjectivity in its traumatic and creative potential; this is a phenomenon that is also subject to innumerable individual variables.

Consequently, I propose the term "Symbolizing Marks" to refer to tattoos as marks that open, by way of the skin and diverse interventions, the way to mental representations necessary to produce psychic conflicts and their possible transformations.

The tattoo is the presence of an absence that requires an act, which in turn, like all human productions, including fashion, is one more expression of human creativity. It could be said that in this space of subjectivity shared by psychoanalysis, art and fashion—as well as the art of ornamentation—a space inhabited by love and cruelty, the vicissitudes of sexuality and death, colors, sounds, words, textures, forms, and images interact to enable endless construction of the ever-changing face of the unconscious.

"The deeper we scrutinize, the more we delve blindly into the underworld of the past and the more undecipherable we find the origins of man, his history and customs, the more they sink into the bottomless abyss, evading our probe, however much we uncoil the rope, ever beyond, into the infinite of the ages."

REFERENCES

Benyakar, M. (2003) *Lo Disruptivo. Amenazas Individuales y Colectivas: El Psiquismo ante Guerras, Terrorismos y Catástrofes Sociales*, Buenos Aires: Biblos. Second Edition, 2006.

Bion, W. (1967). *Second Thoughts*. London: Heinemann.

Calderón Silva, L.G. (2014). El tatuaje como elemento simbólico (graduation thesis). Facultad de Comunicación Social. Universidad Autónoma de Occidente. Cali, Colombia.

Catz, H. (2011). Trauma on the skin. Tattoos: from deadly scars to Symbolizing Marks, Journal-Book published by the Argentine Psychoanalytic Association, 2011, Nº 4.

Cornwell, P. (1999). *Black Notice.* New York: Putnam's Sons. Código Negro, Buenos Aires: Atlántica, 2000.

Dejours, Ch. (1989). *Investigaciones psicoanalíticas sobre el cuerposupresión y subversión en psicosomática.* Buenos Aires: Siglo XXI editors.

Field, H. (1958). *Body Marking in South Western Asia.* Cambridge: The Peabody Museum, quoted by Calderón Silva, L.G. (2014). El tatuaje como elemento simbólico (graduation thesis). Facultad de Comunicación Social. Universidad Autónoma de Occidente. Cali, Colombia.

Freud, S. (1899). Screen Memories. *S.E.* 3.

Freud, S. (1900a). The Interpretation of Dreams, *S.E.* 4.

Freud, S. (1900a). Regression In The Interpretation of Dreams. *S.E.* 5.

Freud, S. (1901). The Psychopathology of Everyday Life. *S.E.* 6.

Freud, S. (1940). An Outline of Psychoanalysis. *S.E.* 23, p. 207.

Galeano, E. (2008). Espejos: Una Historia Casi Universal, Editorial Siglo XXI. Mirrors: Stories of Almost Everyone, Portobello Books, 2011.

Lutenberg, J. (1993). Repetición, reedición-edición. Rev Asoc Psicoan Arg, Special Issue, Nº 2.

Lutenberg, J. (2009), Vacío mental – Turbulencia y Crecimiento Mental. 46th International Psycho-Analytical Congress, Chicago, USA.

Pirandello, L. (1922). *Six Characters in Search of an Author.* New York: E.P. Dutton. Seis Personajes en Busca de un Autor, Madrid: Ediciones Cátedra, 2000.

Salamone, L. (1994). El tatuaje, una mirada encarnada, In La Prensa, suplemento profesional, December 6, 1994, p. 14, quoted by Calderón Silva, L.G. (2014). El tatuaje como elemento simbólico (graduation thesis). Facultad de Comunicación Social. Universidad Autónoma de Occidente. Cali, Colombia.

Winnicott, D. (1958) Collected Papers: Through Pediatrics to Psycho-Analysis. New York: Basic Books.

IV

Culture, Psyche, and Fashion

1. Hairy Situations

CHARLENE HUMBER

T hat hair is an appendage to skin is a biological fact. However, when we think of hair psychologically, we are moved to understand its significance. Styling or not styling hair, how hair is cut, whether it's worn long or short, colored or not, our own or artificial, and how we deal with pubic hair, all have suggestive meanings that will be explored in this chapter. Hair has powerful connotations about how we identify  ourselves as individuals. Our hairstyle is a message we give to others about our personality, though biologically its function is to protect our heads against the hot or the cold weather and to produce both thermal insulation and conditioning. Throughout the centuries, hair has become an important part of our appearance and our intentional expression.

As a self-disclosing, proud African-American woman, it is important for me to show these viewpoints through my own life's lens. From my own personal experience as an African American female, I remember the days of having Vaseline coat the top of my ears and around my forehead, as my maternal grandmother sat me down in the kitchen to do my hair. My seat was right by the kitchen stove as the hot iron was heating up. The thought of my hair being "cooked" did not escape me. Nor did the sizzling sound of my greased, thick, full-bodied hair making crackling noises as it straightened out. It was a painstaking time, trying not to get my hair wet as I bathed, or not to sweat too much during gym class or else the true condition of my hair at birth would be revealed. I would be remiss not to mention the joking statement about how black women "can't get their hair wet!" It was an upkeep that involved constant thoughts of my hair throughout my school day, and long preparations at night. At night the hair curling process involved strips of paper bags, bobby pins and a satin cap. The straightness of my hair gave me a sense of belonging with my white classmates. My hair was manageable and I would comb or brush it in the girl's bathroom as my other classmates would.

Being in between needing my hair "hot combed" and having my natural, coarse hair peering from the roots meant being teased. I remember a not-so-fond memory of having my hair in this "in-between state" and deciding to wear my hair as two braids, split down the middle with a part, one to the left and one to the right. Well, because my hair was a bit past my shoulders in length, the ends of my braids were turned upward. An older neighborhood girl who name-called me "pickaninny" bullied me! At the time, I was only somewhat aware of the term "pickaninny" but, I immediately felt demeaned and disrespected.

In junior high school and high school came the ongoing financial investment of having someone put perm with lye on my hair. Again the Vaseline was used to protect my edges (skin near the hair root) so that my skin wouldn't burn. Again, with the hours of waiting for the perm to straighten my thick full hair, followed by more sitting under the hot dryer for the curls to hold. Am I stating the obvious by comparing "lye" with "lie," the lie I (and so many others) perpetuated to display myself with straightened hair.

In high school, I experimented with having hair extensions braided into my own hair to wear braids. I wore the braids full and long, like Janet Jackson in the 1993 "Poetic Justice" movie. Despite how much the braids pulled my hair so tight that there were small appearing bumps at the front of my hairline, the hair kept my scalp insulated with heat, from the cold weather. Wearing my hair in braids allowed for three months of not needing to fuss daily over my hair. Like every hairstyle, there was the maintenance of greasing the parts, making sure the braids were free from lint, and these hairstyles were limited and painful for my neck.

It wasn't until I went off to a historically black college, Tuskegee University, for undergraduate studies in Psychology, that I felt free to make a decision on how I wore my own hair. I freed myself from all the perms and hot combs and everyday primping over how my hair appeared. I celebrated my full hair with Afros and two-strand twists. I was a "happy nappy"! To this day, I wear my hair natural and as I choose, though I will occasionally have my hair blown out and curled, to sport the straightened look.

I will review briefly the significance of hair in several cultures, with support from psychoanalytical articles and conjectural examples. From folk literature to Greek Western mythology, Medusa's long, curly hair turning into live venomous snakes may speak to the dangerous and mysterious seduction of long hair (Ferenczi 1926) with associations to stories in the public domain, such as the Grimm fairytales, "The Goose Girl" and "Rapunzel." Traditional Freudians would associate Medusa's long hair with a man's penis, and modern analysts might see it as the female vulva. Contemporary women identify Medusa's image with rage and also as the logo for Versace.

In the same way that women and men consciously choose an outfit with their initials engraved on the cuffs of a starched shirt, and designer handbags display repeat initials promoting the handbag's designer, letting the observer know that a certain amount of money has been spent getting "all dolled up," hairstyle is also an extension of how we present who we are or who we wish ourselves to be.

Conventions from Victorian times in England associate wealth and female sexuality with golden, blonde-haired women. Women of a certain age (sometimes, after child-birthing years), or men and women who discover gray hair and use coloring to cover it up, are challenged by the Western stigma of aging, seen as a loss of sex appeal and value as a desirable lover.

In 1913, Freud, under the rubric of "magical thinking," postulated that one's repressed wishes are sublimated in their libido (oral, anal and genital areas) (Freud 1913). Siegel (1971) presented a case study of a man whose fetish was the hair of a women's vagina. He attempted to see behind the hair as if to discover what was hidden underneath or behind the vagina hair. To understand the fantasy of what he could not see with his eyes beyond the hairy vagina, he was left to complete the task with his tongue and mouth, begging the question, where is the woman's hidden penis? He experienced seeing a woman with a hairless vagina as the woman's castration of her imagined penis and this caused him anxiety. For this patient, the pubic hair represented the woman's phallus and recalled to him the pubic hair of his mother.

The hair of a woman symbolized for Freud a "female penis," which in reality she does not have. However, the imagination could still insist that she did have one. The dated Freudian term "castration anxiety" implies the fear that the male could lose his penis, just like the girl has supposedly lost hers. For a child, according to Freud, the ego gets suspended, and the child remains uncertain about the presence or absence of the penis.

The preoccupation with genital differences between males and females also implies the recognition of their individual sexual development. Take for an example, Freud's now-discredited concept of the "female penis" as the absence of a male's penis; this idea underplays the importance of the female's vagina. One can wonder if the purpose of this theory was to have us believe that we should all be the same (Parfitt 2007). Furthermore, the implication of a "female penis" having being castrated implies a devalued existence for the female and a dominant existence for the male, which leads to a belief in male superiority.

Hair can also both express a wish to control and a wish to find relief from control. When a patient feels consumed by powerlessness or destructive feelings, submitting to a "powerful other" can be seen as freeing and providing a sense of security from a feeling of abandonment. (Benjamin 1994). In this case, one can turn to religion or the belief in "the one most high" to provide safety and a sense of security. In A. Richards and L. Spira (2015), a patient in analytic treatment suffering from conflicts receives help in finding

her own solutions, in an effort to come to terms with the unresolved conflicts she has with her caregiver (a child's "powerful other").

Perhaps another way that hair can be linked to sexuality is to look at the role played by the development of hair in the armpits, chest and genital area during puberty, or the "coming of age stage" demonstrating sexual maturity.

In my Supervision with a psychoanalytic psychotherapist, we conversed about a patient she once had in treatment, decades ago. She recalled this male patient sported facial hair by wearing both a mustache and beard and would periodically fondle his beard and comb through his mustache. He would use his hands and fingers to execute these actions. Surely, he could have been simply removing food from his mustache or detangling the hairs in his beard.

Let's take this same example, however, and view it from a psychoanalytic psychotherapist's perspective. Certainly, the interpretations may vary; however, we can agree that the fondling and fingering of the patient's facial hair is in some way serving a purpose for the patient. Let's examine further. This "hair rubbing" action is likely to offer some type of stimulation to the patient. Perhaps even sexual stimulation, thereby correlating it to a form of masturbation. In masturbation we can find a release of both our mental and bodily tensions. Self-masturbation brings pleasure, pleasure that we are also in control of. So, the patient's active interaction with his facial hair, particularly during sessions, could be interpreted as yet another form of masturbation. Without having any background information on this patient let's speculate by adding some imaginary childhood scenarios. What purpose or need could the patient have for "masturbating" in session with the therapist? This patient could have a sexual addiction and therefore have a compulsive desire to engage in sexual activity, particularly sexual intercourse. Possibly, performing this act in session would offer a safer alternative from acting out the sexual compulsion without negative consequences. We might also wonder if the patient was over-exposed to sexual stimulation at an early age or whether sexual abuse existed. The patient's use of fondling his beard and mustache as a form of masturbation gave him a feeling of control over his body and presumably provided some release of sexual tension, through pleasure.

Berg (1936) spoke of the meaning behind cutting the hair, keeping the hair tidy, flattened or scented hair. Berg believed that these hair modifications expressed an underlining desire to control. Control over what or whom is open to question. In Weitz (2001), a women's short haircut was a way of challenging the belief that her attractiveness to men was tied to looking Euro-American, challenging the idea that a woman's worth depends on her attractiveness to men. In essence, according to the culture, a women's haircut should least of all resemble that of a man (Synnott 1987). The hair used in this way was a way to control a woman's individuality and promote the mainstream mindset of acceptable beauty.

Using the prototype of either males or females in high-powered, demanding jobs can be utilized as an example of the need for control. I'll take for granted that we agree with this statement and will expand upon such an individual by adding a few well-compiled variables. This same type of person would also likely demonstrate the need to control, in other areas of their lives. Let's say that the person in our example also likes to control their physique or outward appearance. To maintain control over their body, they may too practice a consistent exercise regimen and let's add that they have an aversion to the bodily odor that can come from sweating in a workout. In which case, it would be more "manageable" to remove the hair from the armpits and genital area, to control the odor that the hair can trap. For a "metro-sexual" male, trimming or removal of unwanted hair is called "manscaping" and for women, "women or ladyscaping," presents a "clean cut" appearance and in intimate settings can also provide a reassurance that acts of oral, anal or vaginal penetration with a partner would be pleasantly received. Some women "vajazzle" their nude vagina with crystals and men may revel in the display of their penis' natural length of endowment, which is another way to control how it is presented. In contrast, the presentation and attraction to the prepubescent genitalia is worth further exploration. All in all, the removal of hair may offer the person some semblance of confidence, while having control over both their odor and bodily presentation. This created example is in no way touches upon a man or woman who loses their hair due to genetics, chronic illness, and stress or hair product mishaps. In these cases, one has no control and may wish to find ways to regain their control over the situation.

Shaving one's hair bald (done as a choice or impulsively in an emotional state) has been attributed to celibacy, loss of the mother, and a need for making reparations and starting anew (Andersen 1980). For example, when Britney Spears shaved her long brunette hair bald in February of 2007, she feared her mom's reaction. Psychoanalyst Bethany Marshall (Marikar 2007) suggested that Britney Spears was "acting out" against the people who were molding and handling her career.

The cutting of one's hair can symbolize a separation from mothering. Klein (1952) states that haircutting can represent restitution of an aggrieved object, or making reparations for it. Cutting off one's hair during a time of mourning represents the object's loss (Andresen 1980). Could this same theory be applied to the freedom of choice? Is there something to make of the choice to simply cutting one's hair in the summer months, for convenience?

Alopecia, the medical term for hair loss when the immune system mistakenly attacks the area of hair growth, begins in the hair follicles (Aldridge 1984). We think of examples of shell-shocked soldiers suffering from alopecia (sometimes with complete baldness) following their traumatic experiences from war battles (Berg 1936). There are profound emotional and psychological effects of the loss of hair that are common amongst men and many women at any age. And let us not forget that the business of hair loss treatments is an approximately $3.5 billion industry.

Cutting off one's hair can also be associated with one's religious faith and beliefs. For example, in the Hindu religion, *brahmacharya* involves practicing celibacy when unmarried and fidelity when married. As the fourth and final stage of life in the Hindu religion (around age 70, for both men and women), *sanyasa* involves a giving up of attachment to material life, when renunciates shave their heads. Tonsure, or the Hindu practice of shaving the head of a monk, also mirrors the Christian religious practice of a shaven head as an expression of celibacy. As with monks, short haircuts are also worn by soldiers and convicts, who are under the discipline of a higher authority (Hallpike 1969).

In Dr. Grinstein's 1963 article, "Profile of a Doll," girls carried images with them of idealized figures such as movie heroines and models in order to repress their earlier conditioning by their own mothers, whom they felt was deficient. The girls' "magical thinking" did not match the world or the changed environment that they were now living in. Unfortunately, this attempt to identify with these unreal, idealized figures leaves residuals of an unfulfilled identity.

Still, today across cultures, for instance in arranged marriages, the promotion of women aspiring to wed a man with wealth not only benefits the bride-to-be, but the mother of the future bride as well. A mother's insistence that a girl remain attractive in hopes of wedding a wealthy man brings with it the possibility of elevating the family status. Psychologically, this can be perceived as a form of prostitution, offering the daughter up to highest bidder. The mother's dilemma is in having to choose between her own needs and those of her child. In psychoanalysis, the mother plays a significant role in the development of her child's internal world, even as she woman contends with remaining a desirable "object" in her own right. The choice is not either/or, but requires the skill of holding the needs and desires of both herself and her child. If the subjectivity of the caregiver is not recognizable by the child, then the child will also struggle with her own self-recognition. Children can successfully develop their own experiences if they had a "good-enough" caregiver who was able to demonstrate to them how to conceive, represent, and symbolize another (Katz 2010).

We often notice people on the street that look so "put together" that we may wish for more time or conveniences or whatever "it" is that allows someone to be able to put time into themselves, creating a "picture-perfect image" of what they want wish the external world to see. In a psychoanalytic setting, the sessions are held with two physical beings in the room, the therapist and the patient. In such a setting, how can either person not take into account how one's hair is worn, the clothes and makeup they choose to wear and not to wear? Many of us have heard of the expression "keeping up with the Joneses." Who or what is it that we are keeping up with, exactly? We carry on this persona or outward appearance because it's easier to mask or "make up!" Masking or making up connotes some type of fantasy: a wish to be someone different from who we really are, to pretend. Have you heard of the expression, "Champagne taste and Kool-Aid money?" As we get older, some of us fight weight gain, to appear more fit or having gray hair, to appear younger than our chronological age. This fantasy, or wish to present someone other than who we are, begs the question of who or what is it that we are trying not to be. One might also wonder about what things are we placing the most value on. An exemplification may be a child who was berated in elementary school for not being bright. This same child, in a fight against being identified as "not being bright," could grow up to pursue two master's degrees as well as a J.D. Take children who were always praised on their looks; as they grow older, so does their determination to keep up their appearance. All in all, we may wish to examine how "put together" our outward appearances are, and how much those appearances line up with our internal struggles.

We are all susceptible to "getting in a rut." These are the times that may not feel up to tending to ourselves or our hair! I'll use us females to provide an example for the times that we may become too busy or mentally distracted to care about our outward appearance. When we are too distracted with other elements in our lives beside our physical appearance or specifically doing our hair, we tend to present as just that, disheveled. Without any intent to judge, we all know a mother who has sacrificed her own self care to always be available, to cater, and tend to the needs of both her children and significant other. Somehow there is never enough time to tend to herself—even when her children have already become adults and created lives for themselves, and her significant other has somehow managed to maintain a professional and social life, in many ways outgrowing her. In other cases, economic reasons may dictate why we may not be able to invest money into getting our hair done. In the biblical reference of Samson and Delilah, Samson gave up the strength found in his hair by falling in love with Delilah. Samson soon revealed his secret to Delilah: of how his strength would leave him, if a razor were to be used on his head. She plotted against him as he slept and had someone cut off seven braids from his head. I use this example as an exaggeration, to help us reflect on the "things" we do in the name of love, even if it leads to our own peril in self-care.

The Weitz (2001) "Woman and Their Hair" study shows how the women acknowledged the cultural power, expectations, and social structures that hair holds and expresses. Women could choose to accept the cultural and social demands of hair beauty, be abstinent about conforming, or weigh in on both sides.

At this juncture, the book has highlighted that verbal communication is not the only form of self-expression. We are not restricted to the use of words; we often communicate by using symbols, which often clearly express what we want to say, instigating emotions in others, and therefore "doing" something (Leach 1958, p. 147). As previously mentioned, a shaven head is often associated with celibacy, and people who wear their hair long are said by some to have a normal sex life (Leach

1958, p. 157). Surely, these interpretations can be both supported and disputed with further investigation. Perhaps it is enough to conclude from Leach's article that we may still find ourselves, if only momentarily, assessing how we currently wear our hair, ready to find our own reasons for how we represent ourselves to the world, and wondering why.

I recently went to get my hair "blown out" and pressed at a Dominican hair salon and hair was the topic of conversation. One "younger than middle-aged" female entered the salon with mid-length hair and requested a perm. After her more than hour-and-a-half process of washing, coloring and drying her hair with the extra-big rollers, she had an additional request for hair extensions at the back of her hair to add length and body to her already existing hair. I felt compelled to strike up a conversation with this mystery woman, and learned that she chooses to experiment with different types of hairstyles as they allow her to be and feel like a different person. She went on to tell me that by having long hair she feels sexier. She also found that her hairstyles serve as a visual distraction from the bottom half of her body. She feels self-conscious about the "baby weight" she still carries from her one-year-old son. Engaged in the conversation, I asked more about how the different hairstyles help her to feel and be a different person. To simplify her response, wearing braids make her feel "bad ass," while long extensions and wigs make her feel more sophisticated and sexually appealing. In the warmer months, she might choose to wear her hair short and this makes her feel carefree. Along with these varied hairstyles, she allows herself to take on all the different personas she associates to them. We both ended up sharing stories of how our hair texture and length has changed since childhood, back when the decisions made about our hair was in the hands of "the decision maker." As we both were women of color, we remembered how our hair was either hot-combed or permed just to be more "manageable" to style.

Weitz's (2001) article speaks about how obtaining power for women is still more accessible by keeping up appearances than it is by having financial independence, political achievement, or career success. Thinking of the power of a woman's hair makes me think of the fairy tale of "Rapunzel," who was able to use her hair to escape the predicament of being locked away.

Baraister (2006) and Bronner (1993) speak of the Jewish history and the transition orthodox Jews made from veiling their hair to wearing wigs during the sixteenth century. Jewish women took up the French fashion and addressed it while still upholding rabbinical law. Most orthodox women began wearing wigs at that time, which they also covered with a veil. The move toward wig-wearing within Jewish law could be seen as a move toward the practices of the dominant (non-Jewish) culture. For within the Jewish women's culture hair was deemed as alarmingly sexual. However, wearing "fake" hair, such as a wig, over ones own hair, lends itself to an opportunity to present a different self. Somehow the practice of wearing someone else's hair, as a wig, while concealing one's own, wasn't technically perceived as only pertaining to hair. It was a way to transform oneself, as if wearing a mask (Baraitser 2006). Psychoanalytically, the wig can be seen as Winnicott's transitional object, the infant's first "me/not-me" possession (Winnicott 1953). It is a way to present a celebration of a "different self," in contrast to the mourning of the "authentic self."

Wearing either a headdress or a hat to cover the hair is an expression of two sides of a conflict. When the hair is hidden, it is a way of expressing fear at its exhibition. However, the headdress itself also has exhibitionistic qualities (Berg, 1936). Around the eighteenth century, British judges and lawyers officially wore white wigs in court. Wigs are made out of human, animal or synthetic fibers, and are sometime also worn in everyday life to disguise hair loss or baldness, or are used as a less intrusive and less expensive alternative to other treatments that restore one's hair. Wigs may be used as a "costume" to portray characters, worn as apparel, or to fulfill religious obligations. In Judaism and Islam, the covering of a woman's hair signifies maturity, modesty, and sexuality, in a patriarchal culture of women belonging to and being treated as the possessions of men (Koppelman 1996).

In contrast, African Americans who wear their hair in an Afro, in twists, and dreadlocks explain that their natural hairstyles are expressions of what distinctly identifies them as individuals and culturally connects them to their heritage. The culture as a whole was not at all accepting of decisions to wear one's hair naturally versus in a perm. This reminds me of a scene in the 1988 Spike Lee movie, *School Daze*, which takes place between the "Wannabees" and the "Jigaboos." It is a great look into the "good hair" versus "bad hair" theory that has plagued the African American culture. The dance scene not only portrayed the hair controversy, but also showed the light skin versus dark skin debate. This discord is certainly not exempt from other "minority" cultures as well. "Good hair" was linked to being light-skinned or passing for white, and in contrast, "bad hair" was paired with being dark-skinned as an "Aunt Jemima"-looking woman. The message, in short, resulted in a deep-seated conflict of choosing between being good (which equaled white, with light-skinned variations) or bad or evil (associated with being black with dark-skinned variations). This message correlates to self-hatred and demoralization. By suggestion, the lighter-skinned African American adopts a white-dominant attitude of prestige and advantage over the darker-skinned African American, who is then left striving for acceptance (Bovell 1943), both of them suffering from an identity crisis and a felt deficiency in their skin complexion.

I live in a community with older adults who have "aged in place," meaning that they live in the same community that they have raised their own families in. I find this to provide a more enriched cultural experience to the neighborhood, as they elect to serve as pseudo-grandparents willing to share their life stories and pass along informational guidance. In various conversations held over the years, I have heard stories about racism, biracial love, and the multilayered issues that come with race relations. Yes, hair struggles have also entered into conversations. For instance, when you're of a mixed race, there are no guarantees as to the type of hair or how it reacts to water! Mainly older adults talk about their hair thinning or falling out due to years of chemical products. Some still wear their hair by coloring it or allowing it to grey naturally. Others sport stylish wigs of different lengths and colors. As some older adults are limited with being on a fixed income, consisting of either just Social Security or with the occasional pension. With these financial constraints and the growing expenses of the "cost of living," both play an important role in "fashion on a budget." Both male and female older adults either choose to care or not care about how they present themselves. For some, what they wear and how they wear their makeup and hair, makes them feel "alive, like sexual beings," or simply having pride in themselves to be "decent and presentable" people.

"Black is Beautiful" was a 1960's cultural movement in the U.S. created by African Americans to dispel the belief that black hair and features were inherently ugly. In 2006, African American women employed at Procter & Gamble birthed a "My Black is Beautiful" campaign to broaden the dialogue and act as a catalyst to help redefine black beauty. Yet, several years ago the projection of the black hair industry, including straightening products, was still estimated to be over $500 billion.

In "Psychological Considerations of Color Conflicts Among Negroes," Dr. Bovell (1943) speaks to the Western profitability of marketing hair products to African Americans, contradicting their native features, and replacing them with straightened hair acceptable to white Westernized sensibilities. Lest we forget, the African American, self-made millionaire, Madam C. J. Walker became wealthy promoting hair-growing shampoo, pomade, strenuous brushing, and applying hot combs to hair. Her pioneering efforts can be correlated to the recent triumph of finally having non-white hair products available in local pharmacy chains, as well as in stores that specialize in selling hair and hair products. From the 1960's on, natural hairstyles for African Americans were once again celebrated, and reinforced their natural beauty.

At the end of the day, good mental health involves realizing that how our hair is worn is our own personal choice, an external expression of who we are and an internal expression of whom we wish to present. Either way, our uniqueness will continue to be displayed in the expression of our hairstyles.

REFERENCES

Aldridge, R.D. (1984). Hair Loss. *British Medical Journal (Clinical Research Edition), 289* (6450), 985-989.

Andresen, J. J. (1980). Rapunzel: The Symbolism of the Cutting of Hair. *Journal of the American Psychoanalytic Association, 18 (28),* 69-88.

Baraitser, L. (2006). Oi Mother, Keep Ye' Hair On! Impossible Transformations of Maternal Subjectivity. *Studies in Gender and Sexuality*, 7, 217-238.

Benjamin J.P. (1994). What Angel Would Hear Me?: The Erotics of Transference. *Psychoanalytic Inquiry*, *14*, 535-557.

Berg, C. (1936). The Unconscious Significance of Hair. *International Journal of Psycho-Analysis*, *17*, 73-88.

Bovell, G.B. (1943). Psychological Considerations of Color Conflicts Among Negroes. *Psychoanalytic Review*, *30*, 447-459.

Bronner L. L. (1993). From Veil to Wig-Jewish Women's Hair Covering. Judaism. *Studies in Gender and Sexuality*, *7*, 217-238.

Ferenczi, S. (1926), On the Symbolism of the Head of the Medusa. In Rickman, J. & Suttie J.I. (Ed. &Trans.).,*Further Contributions to the Theory and Technique of Psycho-Analysis*. London: Hogarth Press.

Freud, S. (1919). Totem and Taboo. *S.E.*,13, 1–161. London: Hogarth Press.

Grinstein, A. (1963). Profile of a "Doll"—a Female Character Type. *Psychoanalytic Review*, *50B*, 161-174.

Hallpike, C. R. (1969). Social Hair, *Man*, New Series, Vol. 4 (2), 256-264.

Opiah, A. (2014, March 25). The Changing Business of Black Hair, a Potentially $500b industry. *The Huffington Post*. Retrieved from http://www.huffingtonpost.com/antonia-opiah/the-changing-business-of-_b_4650819.html

Johansen, T. (2009). *Religion and Spirituality in Psychotherapy: An Individual Psychology Perspective*. New York: Springer.

Katz, A.W. (2010). Healing the split between body and mind: Structural and developmental aspects of psychosomatic illness. *Psychoanalytic Inquiry*, *30*,430-444.

Klein, M. (1952). Some Theoretical Conclusions Regarding the Emotional Life of the Infant. In Roger M.K. (Ed.)., *The Writings of Melanie Klein* Vol. 3 Envy and Gratitude and Other Works 1946-1963. (pp. 61-93). New York: Vintage.

Koppelman, C. (1996). The politics of hair. *Frontiers*, (*17*) 2, 87–88.

Leach, E. R. (1958). Magical Hair. *The Journal of the Royal Anthropological Institute of Great Britain and Ireland*, *88(2)* 147-164.

Lochtefeld, J (2001). Brahmacharya. In *The Illustrated Encyclopedia of Hinduism*, 1:120. New York: Rosen Publishing.

Marikar, Shelia. (2007). *Bald and Broken: Inside Britney's Shaved Head.* Retrieved from abcnews.go.com/Entertainment/Health/story?id =2885048&page=1.

Parfitt, Anthony (2007). Fetishism, Transgenderism, and the Concept of Castration. *Psychoanalytic Psychotherapy 21 (1): 61–89.*

Richards, A. K., & Spira, L. (2015). *Myths of Mighty Women: Their application in psychoanalytic psychotherapy.* London, England: Karnac Books.

Siegel, B. L. (1971). The Role of the Mouth in the Search for the Female Phallus. *Journal of the American Psychoanalytic Association, 19,* 310-331.

Synnott, A. (1987). Shame and Glory: A Sociology of Hair. *British Journal of Sociology,38 (3),* 381-413.

Weitz, R. (2001). Women and their hair: Seeking power through resistance and accommodation. *Gender & Society,15,*667-686.

Winnicott, D.W. (1953). Transitional objects and transitional phenomena—A study of the first not-me possession. *The International Journal Psychoanalysis, 34,* 89-97.

2. Fashion and Style as Culture: How Women Dress and What That Means

ARLENE KRAMER RICHARDS

Beauty

Dressed for war

Dressed as shaman to impress

I became interested in Asian clothing styles at time when I was fascinated with everything Japanese. Then Chinese fashion and Indian clothing appealed to me. The idea that Asian dress could be a way to understand fashion was inspired by Barthes' (1990) research and study of fashion magazines; his aim was to educe a language of fashion. He had not been a reader of fashion magazines, so the language was new to him; his lack of familiarity with the subject allowed him to examine the data and notice things that he would have been unable to see if he had been familiar with it.

By taking one particular example, and by understanding it in a systematic way, he was able to construct a serious scientific framework for understanding the rules of language for writing about fashion. I was more interested in seeing what the rules were for creating, selling, buying, and wearing fashion. By looking at Asian fashions that were relatively new to me, I hoped to learn their language and the messages that my Western patients were conveying.

Study of ethnic clothing styles in other cultures and at other times has shown how wide a variety of signifiers clothes are capable of conveying. Sometimes it is easier to see and appreciate what one sees when one looks with fresh eyes. This is the reason tourism has such fascination for people. And for this reason, I have been fascinated by fashion in China. In this chapter I make use of historical information primarily from a comprehensive study of the evolution of Chinese fashion (Finnane A. 2008).

In her history of Chinese fashion from the 19th through the 21st centuries, Finnane shows how fashion in a whole country follows the clothes worn in a particular city: Shanghai. This pattern of following Shanghai fashion remains in place during the nineteenth, twentieth and twenty-first centuries. This dress was not simply copied from Western styles, but rather developed, as discretionary income allowed the use of fabrics formerly restricted to the court or official dress worn by the rising middle class. Changes in technology such as the sewing machine allowed the evolution of more fitted dress, which was similar to the dress being adopted in the West. Machine-sewn seams are stronger and more lasting than hand-sewn ones. They can endure more stress and can be sewn much more quickly. They lend themselves to rapid change, because they are faster to make and because garments made by machine are cheaper to replace.

A show of Chinese dress and its influence on Western fashion at the Metropolitan Museum of Art in New York in 2014 inspired me to think of how and when the Western clothing influenced the Chinese as well. The mutuality of interaction spurred me to think of how each culture was exotic to the other and how exoticism excites, attracts, and influences fashion.

Chinese dress had a long history before Western influence became significant. The characteristic 19th-century Chinese costume of loose pants topped by loose, wide-sleeved shirts and long vests, as well as pleated skirts for rich women, had evolved over centuries in response to climate, economic issues and cultural patterns.

Much of the documented style was very similar for men and women. Poor people wore outfits that looked to westerners like pajamas; their outfits looked quite different from those of the rulers and officials who constituted the upper classes. Han Chinese had been conquered by Manchu people from Manchuria in the North. The Manchu ruled China from the 16th century until the early 20th Century. While they were a tiny minority of China's people, they were the ruling class. Their influence was enormous (Bai Shouyi 2010).

The social class and gender differentiation in dress evolved in a complex way. The short jacket that constituted the upper part of a Han woman's dress was gradually replaced by a longer jacket that made an overdress redundant. Since the overdress resembled a man's tunic, the sexual differentiation in clothes became both more visible and more valued. Manchu dress featured tighter, shorter sleeves with horseshoe-shaped cuffs. Again, Manchu women wore vests cut shorter on the left than on the right and Han women adopted a similar asymmetric cut, but in jackets rather than vests. Thus Han women's dress contrasted with Han men's and also with Manchu women's, but incorporated elements of each. Since men were more valued than women and Manchu more than Han, the incorporated elements were from higher-status groups to lesser, a pattern seen in fashion to this day.

What is not so much emphasized in current Western fashion is the material from which clothes are constructed. The Asian customs of cut and loose fit were relatively stable, thus putting fabric and decorative embroidery and trim in the foreground of dress. In addition, hairdos and hair pieces were defining features of Chinese fashion. The modern Western look includes hairstyles that signal age, social class and ethnicity, as well as taste. For example, all of the women surrounding Donald Trump in his television ads and appearances sported long, straight, blond hair. In Charlene Humber's chapter in this book, she describes some of the meanings of hairstyle in detail. In the picture above, a Manchu woman wears a hairstyle and long gown typical of her class, while the Han woman wears a wide-sleeved jacket and a swept-back Han hairstyle.

In the 19th century, long, loose clothing style was gradually replaced by Western styles as China became influenced by the Western dress of missionaries, diplomats, business people, and tourists. Media access speeded up the process. But this Westernization of fashion was interrupted by the 1920's return to a more Chinese form of dress, the qipao. With the foundation of the Republic of China, Chinese clothing signaled a nationalistic turn. In Shanghai women no longer wanted to look like Westerners; now they wanted to look like Manchu Chinese. Qi is a Manchu word for "banner people," a term both Manchu and Han people used to refer to the Manchu. The qipao was an adaptation of Manchu men's clothing. If men were more powerful than women and Manchu more powerful than Han, then the Han women's appropriation of Manchu men's dress was two steps up the power ladder.

Once established as Chinese women's dress, the qipao lost the boxy look of the Manchu man's dress. It was cut closer to the body, so tight that slits had to be established up the sides so that the wearer could move. Then the leg exposure of the slits became controversial and the woman had to add pants or a pleated panel to cover the legs under the slit.

Beijing style went in another direction. The sleeve and pant styles worn in Beijing were cut shorter to expose the lower leg and the wrist. This style was opposed by rich conservative families in which women were still expected to wear long, heavy, silk clothes even in summer. In general, Beijing was politically correct; Shanghai was expressive.

With the Revolution in 1949, unification led to clothing that looked like uniforms. The influence of political identification resulted in Russian military style that eventually led to the ubiquitous straight-cut jacket and pants. Urban women wore double-breasted Lenin jackets while men wore the single-breasted four-pocket Mao suit. Gender differentiation persisted. By then, the last thing anyone wanted was to look rich. Women were publicly humiliated during the ensuing Cultural Revolution for wearing jewelry, skirts, any Western styles, and especially high heels. The class markers of clothing reversed meaning. Looking poor was safe; displaying discretionary income was bad and dangerous.

Current Chinese fashion reverses values again. Glitz is now gorgeous. This reaction to the past is a seesaw that propels change. It makes what is new beautiful. While it serves an economic purpose in that people need to buy new clothes to be in fashion, it also serves as a class marker in that the latest fashion is always expensive and gets copied in cheaper versions in succeeding seasons. Thus, wearing the newest fashion shows that the wearer or her husband or family can afford to spend money to buy things that are neither necessary nor durable. Now it is patriotic in some circles to be and look rich.

But the passion for exhibiting wealth has its dangers. To look rich is to invite robbery. The posh look can also backfire when the political compass veers left again, a clue to the wise not to look too rich. The patient who comes to ask for a fee reduction dressed in cashmere and fur communicates a lack of understanding of the contradiction between dressing rich and talking poor; a lack of awareness about the feeling of envy her rich clothing evokes in others. The contradiction between what her clothing says and what her words attempt to convey expresses her conflict. She is the wife of a rich man kept on a luxurious but short leash. She has a giant clothes allowance, but very little spending money. The analyst who sees her can only imagine the pain of her conflict.

The contradiction enhances the male's power by showing that he is the successful person and his wife is a powerless mannequin on which he displays his wealth. When her dress is in the latest fashion, it signals her man's ability to provide newer clothes to replace her costumes frequently.

As Veblen (2011) puts it: "In addition to showing that the wearer can afford to consume freely and uneconomically, it can also be shown in the same stroke that he or she is not under the necessity of earning a livelihood; the evidence of social worth is enhanced in a very considerable degree. Our dress, therefore, should not only be expensive, but it should also make plain to all observers that that the wearer is not engaged in any kind of productive labor" (p. 126). And further, "As the community advances in wealth and culture, the ability to pay is put in evidence by means which require a progressively nicer discrimination in the beholder" (p. 127). That is, the daughter of a mother who wears fur and satin may express her greater refinement by choosing cotton and wool, yet still choose the finest cotton and the most delicate embroidery to express her wish to be recognized as a rich lady.

As an American woman who had spent her junior year of college in Florence told me: " There I learned that you need to get the best fabric you can afford and have it made to your measurements. The style should be classic. That is real elegance." Only beholders who can recognize the best fabric and the best tailoring will know that these clothes signify educated taste and true refinement. In addition, those clothes allow the wearer to be independent of changing fashion and therefore of the man who can provide a constant stream of new money to replace last season's fashion with a new one. That level of affluence and sophistication was reached in China before the Revolution, was preserved in Hong Kong and Shanghai, and is now seen again in those cities.

In China, as in the West, male styles of dress were derived from sporting, military or official dress. And women's styles were influenced by "sing song" girls, professional entertainers who gave pleasure by singing, dancing, and sex. In addition to the horseshoe-shaped sleeve hem, the split skirt and the long overjacket of the Manchu people who had ridden into China—and taken over with their horse culture—maintained an influence exceeded only by the high collar. The Manchu dress allowed for both freedom to ride horseback and warmth to provide comfort in their Northern climate. The S-shaped opening that fastened from the center of the collar to the armpit and down the side allowed the garment to protect the body by having two layers in front so as to prevent exposure of the body in windy conditions. The relative invariance of cut was offset by the emphasis

214

on patterned fabric, contrasting pattern, and color in the edging and was supplemented by jewelry.

While Veblen understood fashionable women's clothing as a way to display the wealth of the husband or father who supported that woman, dress could convey an opposite message. The shamans in Mongol culture would wear jackets embellished with squares of fabric to recall the patches of ragged clothing that were necessary for monks or shamans who were poor by ascetic choice. Those religious figures who became rich had garments of fine brocade and embroidery, but continued the memory of asceticism by wearing patchwork clothing made by cutting up luxurious fabrics and sewing the pieces together. Some even used a single fabric, cut it into squares, doubled them over, and sewed them into the body of the garment as if they were fringe. Ascetic values could thus be expressed even with rich materials.

In general, sharp distinctions between men's and women's dress had not been part of Chinese culture in the peasant class and they were only important in the upper and administrative classes. With the changes in the position of these classes in the twentieth century, the distinctions between male and female faced new challenges. Military wear became more important for both men and women during China's half-century of continuous war, persisted during the next quarter century of Communist rule, and then into the late 20th century as a marker separating Chinese dress from that of the West, as well as that of other Asian nations.

FASHION AND BODY MODIFICATION

Victorian ladies in England, France and Germany used corsets to shrink their waists so that they emphasized the hips; they also used bustling over the gluteal area in order to emphasize their fertility in order to attract men. In "Gone With the Wind" the heroine's maid pulls the strings of the young lady's corset tighter while her maid admonishes her to eat something before the party so that she will appear not to be hungry. Both the corsetry and the refusal to eat in public are used to showcase the woman's ethereal beauty that attracts rather than frightens away the young men at the ball. Her incorporeality will make her weaker and therefore more attractive. Some women went so far as to have ribs removed in order to have smaller waists. Girls' schools used corsetry to literally mold the girls into compliant, uncomplaining creatures of whom no young man need be frightened. The weakening of the woman's image was used to strengthen the man's by comparison. Thus the man did not have to fear humiliation by the woman; he could experience himself as more competent and more masculine by comparison with a weak woman.

In the same era visitors to China were reporting the shocking practice of foot-binding in Chinese women. It is my contention that both corseting and foot binding were used in the service of emphasizing women's masochism and bolstering men's sense of power. Humiliation is incompatible with erections; in order to be sexually competent, a man must feel self-respect and pride. The delicate, tender, harmless woman will not humiliate the man. Therefore she is attractive.

An important misunderstanding of Chinese foot-binding is that it was universal. Actually, it was a Han Chinese practice instituted some time after the Han people were conquered by the Manchu. When Han men were required by the Manchu to adopt the pigtail hairdo, Han women accepted the bound foot preferred by Han men. If the Han men felt humiliated because they had lost China to the Manchu, the Han women were subordinate to them; the women were disempowered by their bound feet.

Like Western women who have adopted spike heels, they were aspiring to a status of non-functional bodies. They were adopting a style that identified them as sex objects. For the modern Western woman, the spike heel says "I am not at work. I am not competing with any man. Therefore, a man can safely approach me for sex." The spike heel, like the bound foot also says "I cannot run away. You have power in this relationship." The Han woman sent the same message of reassurance to the defeated Han man, inviting him to approach her for sex. But the modern spike heel has another connotation. Its can serve as a weapon when the woman feels threatened by either unwanted sexual approach or aggression.

In the Arab world, women adopt the headscarf, *burka*, or other covering as a marker of sex as well. They see it as a sign of their loyalty to their men and their men's religion. Like the spike heel, the wrap also serves a defensive purpose. It shields the woman who wears it from the unwanted attentions of men. It allows the woman to invoke the power of the patriarchy against a man who would sexually attack her. Each of these forms of shackles also has the potential for being a weapon. Within each culture, the women adapt so as to maximize power of sexual attraction of the mate and defense against other men.

After the end of foot-binding in China came the issue of hair-bobbing. Long hair requires time and effort to keep clean, to brush and comb, to arrange in whatever is the then current style. Students led the way in bobbing their hairdo making it convenient to care for in order to have more time to study—or to make a revolution. Similar considerations led to controversy over whether to continue the Chinese tradition of breastbinding or to allow natural breasts, or even enhanced breasts in brassieres. Questions of health, modernity, and effect on breastfeeding were hotly debated. Breastbinding made women look more like men or boys. Yet it was traditionally Chinese in contrast to the brassière. The latter had been invented by the American corsetmaker Ida Rosenthal, and was meant to enhance rather than suppress the breasts. Freeing the breasts was as important to Chinese women as it was to the post-flappers of the West.

A recent controversy reported by Valeriya Safronova on November 9, 2015 in the *New York Times* was about the corn-row hairstyle that had just become fashionable for white women after being worn almost exclusively by blacks. This cultural appropriation looked exotic to the white wearers and was resented by some black women who regarded it as **unfair** that the style was labeled "ghetto" when they wore it, but "cool" when whites did. Context matters in fashion as in language. Fashion is that language expressed in clothes, jewelry and bodily adornment.

While Barthes (1990) analyzed the language of fashion from writing about it in magazines, the expression of a language through the material culture of actual clothes and actual body modification shows a multi-layered set of meanings with messages passed from society to the individual and from the individual to society. The possibility of setting boundaries, stretching them, and transgressing them are all avenues of

217

communicating values. As we have seen, economics, climate, gender, age, social class, culture, age and body type contribute to the language system of clothes and body presentation. The extreme complexity of this language belies the belittling notion that fashion is frivolous and exposes the sexist notion that it is a subject fit only for silly women.

Seeing fashion as an art form is relatively recent. Once understood as art, fashion is seen as expressive, serious, and part of a universal need to put feelings into a relationship to a viewer who receives the message of the piece. Created as an expression, fashion can indicate a sense of control, as in the "dandy" look, or a sense of being outside the boundaries, as in the "Bohemian" look (Breward 2003). The sense of control is defined by fine workmanship, smooth fabrics, solid colors, undraped lines and subdued pattern. The look is tailored, the sense classical. Bohemian style uses pattern, bright and varied color, draping, patchwork, ruffles, and floating bits to convey a sense of freedom, the unusual and the startling.

In this sense, the Chinese fashion of *qipao* is a dandy fashion in its simple, body-hugging lines, the high collar that emphasizes the wearer's face, and the fine tailoring. Its attention to the body veers toward the Bohemian when the leg slits expose the thigh and when printed fabric is used to make the dress. The *qipao* is a category of dress that says: "I am a Chinese woman of the 21st century." Within the cultural context and as a qualification of that statement, it can convey the power of modernity, or the nostalgia for the historical Mongolian man's tunic from which it evolved (Hansen, 1994), or both.

It can convey more specific and individual meaning within the culture. As fitted to the individual body a dress says I am thin or fat, curvy or trim, sexy in my high slits or modest in my pleated inserts, tall in my long dress or short in my petite one. It can convey attention to detail in trim or an attitude of casual inattention to detail in lack of trim. In red it can convey I am a bride today, in white, I am a widow. Sequinned, it can say "Look at me," and/ or "I am valuable, rich, powerful or want to be those things." Lace trim can make it, and its wearer, look delicate. Printed with fans or kittens, it can say "Look how cute I am, how harmless, how cuddly."

The flapper look that appeared in the West at about the same time

had a similar message. It promised freedom and power. No more corsets—let my legs show. I am doing what I want. For some women the
qipao and the flapper dress substituted for the freedom they promised.
In addition, the flapper dress, like the *qipao*, demanded bound breasts
and high heels, both restrictive and unfree. The complexity and context-
dependent nature of the art form of fashion rival that of any language.

At the same time, the individual designer expresses his or her own
history and that of the culture. Alexander McQueen, for example, expressed the bloody history of Scotland and his own tragic history of
being abused as a child in his designs that included metal braces forcing
the mouth open as if screaming.

That he was able to make such images acceptable by combining them
with designs of great beauty made them acceptable to women. Women
who wore his clothes could feel empowered to express their own pain.
Yet they also became beautiful in their acceptance of themselves, including the pain they had suffered in their own lives.

Or, as Ms. Guo, who created the 280 handmade theatrical designs for
the 2008 Beijing Olympics' opening ceremony, said via Skype from her
cavernous Rose Studio in Beijing, "Everyone wants to learn about China,
and fashion is the easiest way"(Abrams 2015).

She expanded on this later: "I don't consider my work to be within
the limits of conventional fashion, nor do I follow trends creatively or
commercially," she said. "My work displays feelings and emotions that
are precious enough to be handed down generation after generation, as
well as the experience of developing gowns directly with my clients.
They are reflections of myself, and of them, of the scale of my dreams
and the pride I have for Chinese culture" (Paton 2016).

Japanese dress adds another dimension to the language of clothes.
Dalby (1993) describes the 19th-century change from the kimono style
to Western dress as disavowal of Chinese-influenced clothing in favor of
Western influenced clothing as an attempt to absorb Western power and
divest from Eastern powerlessness. Nothing could signify identification
with the powerful.

Within the ancient tradition of being essentially Japanese, the *kimono*
makes a unique statement. No one can mistake *kimono* as coming from

another culture. It is purely Japanese. While everyone wears Western clothes for everyday, some occasions call for *kimono*. Within the *kimono*-wearing culture, the *geisha* tradition is the most conservative preserve of *kimono*. It is the dress that expresses womanliness as willingness to live for man's pleasure; it is a badge of loyalty to the patriarchy of Japan. Derived from the Samurai tradition, it speaks of continuity and of belonging to a tradition and a social class with enough money and leisure to learn how to wear it and to select the appropriate patterns for the wearer's age, the season of the year, and the degree of formality of the occasion.

Like the white wedding gown in the West, the *kimono* today is mainly worn by women wishing either to marry or to demonstrate their demure docility. It is the costume for marriage, for death, and for child-naming. For middle-aged women it is a costume for traditional hobbies such as flower arranging, tea ceremony and attending performances.

This is a cultural version of wearing what celebrities wear. It identifies with power. It makes a woman feel that she can be as strong, rich, talented or beautiful as the person who first wore a new style.

While clothing, accessories and grooming are considered frivolous or impediments by men like Freud (tk), John Donne (1997) and others, presenting the self to the world is the expression of how a person feels about herself and how she feels about the world she lives in. Paying attention to this gives the therapist valuable information about which the patient herself may be unaware. Being someone who notices is an important adjunct to being someone who hears. Noticing clothing and responding to its message enables the therapist to tell the patient things about herself that she was not aware of and that enables her to understand herself and her place in her world better than she could before.

What is plain in foreign cultures goes back to illustrate messages in one's own culture too familiar to be noticed at home. Exploring Chinese dress has enabled me to understand something about a patient that I could not see before. By seeing the woman who came to ask for a reduced fee while wearing a super-luxury, super-fashionable outfit as ridiculous, I was blinded to the fact of her helplessness in the face of a rich and powerful husband. Once I thought about how her clothes expressed his power and her powerlessness, I could begin to empathize with her. That empathy became the basis for a very valuable, if under-paid, treatment. It allowed me to see her penis awe, her self-denigration and depression as expressed in her luxurious clothes.

In thinking about what the elements of self-presentation such as clothing, hairstyle, accessories and jewelry convey to the observer, I came up with the following:

1. ethnic group
2. body type
3. a wish to be noticed—or not
4. season and climate
5. social status
6. mood
7. conformity—or non-conformity
8. value of beauty versus utility
9. comfort versus willingness to endure pain
10. age of wearer
11. occasion
12. degree of consistency, flexibility, or rigidity of identity projected
13. degree of identification with a celebrity
14. adherence to the past, keeping up with the times, or the push to move away from it
15. economic status

All of these influence what a person chooses to wear. Therefore, dress conveys a great deal visually. When you add the sound of taffeta, the hush of velvet, the smells of body effluents, perfumes and the appearance of comfort or discomfort displayed in the face of the wearer, paying attention to appearance creates the opportunity to know a lot about the person.

Fashion dictates clothing. It expresses the wearer's body, both how she wants her body to be feeling and how she wants her body to be perceived. Styles appropriate for one's social class, age, and status are prescribed by the culture. Clothing mediates between oneself, one's body, and social norms. Jewelry, hair styles, body painting, tattooing and piercing also signify belonging to an age group, social class and society. Uniforms impose belonging to an organization: team, school, military or business. They can indicate status within the organization and impose standards of behavior that correspond to the status.

Refusal of the organization or status within is defined as disruptive and is easily visible because of the uniform.

Current American fashion is produced in the service of women who want to be taller, thinner, younger and more beautiful. Fashion magazines and self-help books show women how to have a beautiful appearance. Some show how to do it on a budget; some parade clothing only affordable by a very few people. Some tell about how to pack, how to spot, plan, match or coordinate non-matching outfits. Some are directed towards teenage girls, some are full of advice about a decade- by-decade differentiation of clothes. Few feature styles for the overweight woman except in ads from stores specializing in clothing for the "plus-size" woman. Clothes for sport differ from clothes for work. Putting on weekend clothes that are not appropriate for work signifies a freedom from constraint that keeps both relaxation and play separate from the work week.

Within these rules, fashionable clothes are shown on young, some-times adolescent models. The clothing they display is meant to transform the potential consumer-wearer into someone like the model. The dress may make her look younger, thinner, taller or more sexually desirable than she sees herself to be when she looks in her mirror. Clothes on a hanger cannot project the dimensions and other attributes of a model. So the models are an image of the impossible: no woman can reverse her age to adolescence. Because it is impossible to succeed in looking like an adolescent, seeking for that must last forever. Fashion must be an impossible dream.

The essence of fashion is change. Each new season brings a new way of seeing the female body and a new sense of what is beautiful. Thus, characteristics of the person like age, size, social status, financial power and body type are seen differently each season. Often what once was underwear or informal dress becomes the style for more formal occa-sions. This makes for a complexity that is further complicated by the purposes for which the clothes are worn.

Analysts are untanglers of complexity. By thinking about the clothing and appearance of the person she is trying to understand, an analyst can help the person facing her to understand herself better. She can add what she knows about the current culture and what she has become aware of through observing other cultures, in order to understand what the person may not even be aware that she is saying in her appearance.

REFERENCES

Bai Shouyi (2010). *An Outline History of China.* Beijing: Foreign Language Press

Bancroft, A. (2012) *Fashion and Psychoanalysis: Styling the Self.* New York: Tauris

Barnard,M. (Ed.). (2007). *Fashion Theory: A Reader.* New York: Routledge

Barthes, R. (1990). *The Fashion System.* Berkeley: University of California Press.

Breward, C. (2003). Fashion: Oxford History of Art. Oxford: Oxford U. Press

Dalby, L. (1993). *Kimono: Fashioning Culture.* New Haven: Yale Univ.

Finnane, A. (2008). *Changing Clothes in China: Fashion, History, Nation.* New York: Columbia Univ.

Freidman, V. (2016, March 13). On her shoulders, a nation's pride. *The New York Times.* PST13.

Hanson, H. (1994). *Mongol Costumes.* New York: Thames & Hudson

Wilson, A. (2025). *Blood Beneath the Skin.* New York: Scribner

3. *Chinese Handwork in Fashion*

Dear Ruth,

Something happened which I am struggling to tell you. My boy-friend asked me to stop the treatment because I am getting worse. I fell sick again after that dream. Actually when I wrote it down: woman, beautiful hands, the BACK of her hand, sitting in a chair, suffering... I knew it was you. Remember I had noticed and made a comment on your beautiful hands? You canceled the next session because of your trip. From then on I started worrying you would suffer a lot by sitting up on the flight. Finally it became my nightmare.

You were right, I am very sensitive to people's pain. Lying on your couch, second by second, reminds me how much this living being has suffered during the past decade, no need to know the details. Just like my desire to save my mom, I automatically took your pain on my shoulders...

This letter was written after seeing my analyst for 5 months. In the third month, I almost left the therapy because she forgot my big secret: I lost my virginity in my early twenties to an old man who was 39 years older than me. I was finally abandoned after an abortion and attempted suicide.

I have been looking for a father-like partner for my lack of father's love. My father physically abused me when I was young. My memories of childhood were grey, gloomy. The image of father, to me, was a weak

224

vampire, deformed, greedy, cold, selfish...bleeding me dry. He destroyed many things: my concepts of maleness, authority, love... He is supposed to be a big tree who should have sheltered the tender grass under the strong branches. On the contrary, I, as a little girl, became the only outlet for his rage, about which he horribly suffered throughout his life. Misery robs a man of his integrity, his virtue—and even his soul.

My analyst's back was badly injured in an accident more than 10 years ago. Lying down during the sessions relieves her pain. Afterwards, I knew some medication also reduced her physical pain. I did not know how she felt telling me I could choose to work with another analyst with better memory. My tough exterior hid a broken heart at that moment. How cruel for an intelligent one to see memory fading! Later on withdrawing the medication assisted in recovering her memory. Also, I tried to make my talk impressive. So I chose some photos with different costumes, moods, times, places to present my different identifications. My boyfriend is a photographer; we love to spend time in taking photos together. In general I do the creative design and post-production, he does the tech part.

My mom was so dextrous that she used to tailor me a traditional Chinese-style attire for each Chinese New Year since I was 5 (#1). Even the Chinese traditional buttons were made by her skilled hands. People paid so many compliments on them. That was almost the only moment I could feel love from my mom, because she did not really take care of me. I was left in my maternal grandmother's care before school age, in my father's during school age. In my 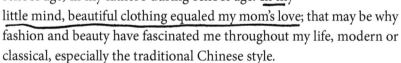 little mind, beautiful clothing equaled my mom's love; that may be why fashion and beauty have fascinated me throughout my life, modern or classical, especially the traditional Chinese style.

The background of the following series (#4-7) is the Han Dynasty (206 BC-220 AD), which was one of the most flourishing periods in Chinese history. Meanwhile, Ancient Rome emerged as the other most powerful part of the world. China has 5000 years of history and culture, the essence of which is the ancient part, rich, splendid, of which I am proud.

The typical colors in the Han Dynasty were black and red, which are still the representative colors of Japan. Japan retains more traditional Chinese culture in some ways, such as bowls in Japanese restaurants with red inside and black outside. Here is a face without makeup, because the flat face, small eyes and mouth are ideal classical features of Eastern women. Showing a plain face is enough. There is a picturesque term in Chinese to describe a woman's small mouth:櫻桃小口, meaning "cherry-sized mouth." Actually we tried to avoid post-production unless special effects were needed. Among all the photos, this was the only series with some post-production, so that the lips were tinged with red, through which people may get the sense of associating small red lips with the cherry—the old aesthetics in ancient China. I also recognized in this series the Japanese geisha girl, which is why I used post-production to make the skin paler.

I tried to cut all the connections with my parents. I had hated my mom for her absence as a caretaker; but how can we cut the roots of where we came from? My mom gave me her facial features, including a sweet smile, which made me find favor in people's eyes.

My grandma could've been a good psychological mother instead of my biological mother if she were full of love. Unfortunately, she always hated to look after kids, including me and her own seven children. Born into a peasant background in a rural poor area in 1935 (The Anti-Japanese War happened during 1937-1945,and the Chinese Civil War ended in 1950.), my grandma managed to marry my grandpa in order to move to the city for a better life; she had no desire to care for her 7 children. My mom was a premarital pregnancy. My grandma's sister went crazy because of her premarital pregnancy, which was absolutely unacceptable in those years. My grandma was extremely terrified. She tried to kill my mom when she was pregnant, such as jumping down from a roof. I suppose what my mom received from her mom was not love but fear and hatred. Fortunately/unfortunately, my mom survived. But my grandpa had been doubting my mom was his because my grandma had another lover before their marriage. It is imaginable that my mom didn't receive much love from her father: instead, beatings and scoldings happened often.

In this picture (#8), I am wearing traditional Chinese-style attire. The higher collar with three straight Chinese traditional buttons only appears in movies and on stage to highlight the lithe and graceful neck of the actress(In general there are 1 or 2 buttons on the collar.). The straight traditional buttons are usually for men, flowered buttons for women. I prefer the former, which is more plain and masculine(part of my personality), also more difficult for the tailor to conceal the stitches (in the flowered ones, it is relatively easier to conceal the stitches). The T-shaped  cut, without a shoulder seam, is one of Chinese traditional cutting techniques, which also appears in kimono cutting. It is my mom's favorite, so it is mine. I finally found an excellent custom tailor near the Forbidden City who was able to meet all my challenging requirements.

There are different butterflies embroidered on the dark purple lining (not shown in the picture), my inspiration was drawn from Cipai entitled Die Lian Hua蝶戀花. The Ci form of Classical Chinese poetry is especially associated with the poetry of the Song Dynasty(960 -1279 AD), during which it was indeed a popular poetic form. The literal translation would be Butterflies over Flowers. (Die:butterfly; Hua:flower; Lian:to love, to be enamored of, to long for, to be sentimentally attached to a person or place.). The ambiguity of Chinese, especially Classical Chinese, makes our language more picturesque and poetic.

Ci 詞 are a poetic form, a type of lyric poetry, done in the tradition of Classical Chinese poetry. Ci use a set of poetic meters derived from a base set of certain patterns, in fixed-rhythm, fixed-tone, and

*variable line-length formal types, or model examples: the rhythmic
and tonal pattern of the ci are based upon certain, definitive musical song tunes. Typically the number of characters in each line and
the arrangement of tones were determined by one of around 800 set
patterns, each associated with a particular title, called cípái 詞牌.
Originally they were written to be sung to a tune of that title, with
set rhythm, rhyme, and tempo. (From Wikipedia's entry on Ci, poetry)(Please find a sample in the NOTES.)*

I chose peony because it is the national flower of China, as well as one of
my mom's favorite flowers. The embroidery was done in Suzhou City.
There are different kinds of embroideries from different parts of China,
Suzhou, Sichuan, Hunan, Guangdong, for instance. Work from Suzhou
is the most sophisticated and vivid.

My mom has a talent for embroidery: she could do it pretty well
when she was young without any professional training. But in her original family, only boys had a chance to develop their interests; girls were
long-term unpaid helpers. The latter were asked to unconditionally take
good care of the former. As the oldest one, my mom's time at home was
completely occupied by taking care of younger siblings and endless
house work. Even when she was going to the cinema with her classmates, my grandma would force my mom to carry one younger brother
on her back. Mom, as a little girl, felt extremely ashamed with a baby on
her back in front of all her classmates. (It happened in the 1960's; the
Cultural Revolution was coming soon, films were a very rare entertainment. Those students could go to cinema only once per semester.)

The only happy time in my mom's childhood was before her school age
when she had a little freedom to visit her paternal grandparents. My mother's paternal step grandma was 18 years younger than my mom's grandpa;
she was a beautiful singer and was purchased by my mom's grandpa; she
had no children but was very nice to my mom. My mom told me about the
following episode hundreds of times: "Each Saturday morning when I woke
up I looked forward to the afternoon. I left for my grandma's place after
school, would stay there as long as possible, hated to go back to that hell on
Monday morning." When my mom was 7 years old, as she was physically

228

strong enough to carry a baby, she lost the only little freedom to visit her grandma over the weekends. Then her real disasters began, until she got married when she was 24. My grandparents absolutely did not agree with my mom's marriage for these reasons: before her marriage my mom had to give all her salary to my grandma who did not even leave my mom a penny to buy a sanitary napkin. To my mom, my grandma was not only a vampire bleeding her dry but also a schemer. Before my mom's payday, my grandma would be nice to her, until she managed to make my mom hand over all her salary. Mom would throw all the cash on the floor out of rage; my grandma picked each penny up unperturbedly. After the payday, my grandma would start to revile her own daughter with a stream of obscenities. My grandma was clear that she would no longer get my mom's salary after the marriage; that's why she incited my grandpa to thwart it. One very early morning, my grandpa went on a rampage, tore down my mom's quilt, yelling at her that she could marry my father without taking anything from the original family including underwear, and ordering her to get out of the house. My mom could not endure that humiliation, and tried to kill herself by taking pills; she fainted in the street and would have died if my aunt didn't trail after her. After the rescue, my grandpa did not comfort my mom at all; on the contrary, he chased her with a fire hook in the courtyard. Besides taking care of her younger siblings, my mom brought up the son of her youngest brother, who was for sure spoiled by my grandparents and returned evil for good. When my mom finally mustered all her courage to write him a letter in her late fifties, telling him what she did for him and the whole family, he could not even finish reading it; his invectives had already rained down on my mom (I dreamed of him many times in big explosions). There are innumerable youngest sons in China who usually are the worst ones among all the children for their serious lack of ability to compete. Mom received a THANK YOU neither from her siblings nor from her parents. When I was little I knew that no one but me could disentangle her from that veritable morass. It is a miracle Mom could survive such a horrible early life and the subsequent Cultural Revolution that lasted 10 years.

This is my mom's life story, which has become engraved in my mind forever. I have viewed my mission in life as saving my mom since I was a little girl. Maybe each child has such a wish to strengthen her parents just by going back to be that little kid again who is supposed to be protected and loved by parents.

My mom loves all kinds of flowers. This is her motto: "Each woman is a flower, even the smallest, simplest one is beautiful: you could be a peony in full bloom, thriving and prosperous; could be an orchid, elegant; could be a lily, pure; could be lavender, romantic; could be a daisy, simple...each one has its unique beauty, as long as it is a flower." These words were rooted in my little mind since maybe before I was born. This simple sentence may create a part of who I am. But where is my mom's florescence of life? She was a beautiful woman with a flair, and her life should have been blooming with color decades ago. Who can compensate for her loss during these decades? How many decades could there be in one's life?

These professional embroidery works (#9-12) were made by my mom. I finally was able to financially support her to take one-on-one professional training in Suzhou in her fifties. My mom said without me she would never have thought of learning it in her remaining years; it was me who encouraged her to make her dream come true. In her whole life it was the first time she discovered how talented she could be. It is a big pity that she can not do it any more in her sixties due to her poor eyesight, although she still has a beautiful wish to embroider a wedding dress for her only daughter. Whether or not she can achieve this goal, her life has flowered, even decades late, even like epiphyllum, a flash in the pan.

No one is likely to illustrate her mother's motto better than her own child's listening to her day by day, like the floral dress (#14) worn over a matching blouse (#13). Maybe each child's coming into the world is to fulfill its parents' desire.

In the 18th and 19th centuries, the open bell-shaped "pagoda" sleeves required engageantes (false sleeves). Instead, I chose the similar colour blouse (#13) worn under it(#14). Mom says raglan sleeves(#13) highlight narrow shoulders of women, it became one of my favorites. As a part of the blouse, the sheer scarf tied in a bowknot instead of a common collar was a centre of attention(#13). The stunningly imaginative blends of wool and silk lace (the whole back of the blouse was made of lace which is not shown in the photo #13) was another unique way of doing

design and making the winter magically grow pink flowers. In Chinese, bowknot is called "butterfly knot." Mom does love butterfly, butterfly knot as well. I like to match with purple stockings and purple shoes with bowknots. Sometimes straight hair with bangs is more suitable for the elaborate and intricate style with voluminous ornamentation.

I did not know if the designer was dreaming of butterflies (#15). The gauzy tulle dress embroidered in butterfly motif and wing-like sleeves associate with "The Butterfly Dream" – "Zhuang Zhou Dreams of Being a Butterfly" (莊周夢蝶) . Zhuangzhou/Zhuangzi was an influential Chinese philosopher who lived around the 4th century BC during the Warring States period, a period corresponding to the summit of Chinese philosophy.

"Once upon a time, Zhuang Zhou dreamed he was a butterfly, a butterfly flitting about happily enjoying himself. He did not know that he was Zhou. Suddenly he awoke, and was palpably Zhou. He did not know whether he was Zhou, who had dreamed of being a butterfly, or a butterfly dreaming that he was Zhou. Now, there must be a difference between Zhou and the butterfly. This is called the transformation of things." [1]

Am I a butterfly who one day shall finally wake up from this bitter life?

Both the color and the print are lavender: flowing rompers matched with a broad hat with brim; the pastoral attire is for outdoor scenes.

I was inspired by a line of a Chinese poem "那河畔的金柳是夕陽中的新娘"（徐志摩）meaning "the golden weeping willows by the riverside are brides in the setting sun." The solid-colored cotton strapless dress has a minimum of ornamentation, with the same simplest design, the pure white patent-leather high-heeled shoes manifest minimalism, which is used to maximum effect in which "less is more" (#18-21).

Mom says simple design always requires exquisite workmanship, it's true.

I had desired to be a tailor when I was a little girl. In my little mind, it was magic to make something beautiful out of nothing with those dextrous hands like my mom's. But Mom said students with high scores like me should go to college, not work as a laborer, a tailor for instance. I did hope I could be bad at school, then I could be a tailor, but I never reached that "goal," because my mom always complimented me in front of people. That little girl pushing herself too much to be good to strive for Mom's love was not psychologically healthy. Children cannot survive without love, after all. Mom stopped me from being a tailor, but couldn't restrain me from pursuing beauty and shaping my own taste in fashion. Like it or not, our families make us what we are. Even nowadays I still pay much attention to people's hands, skilled ones or beautiful ones. My boyfriend has such

hands by which some special photoflash lamps were made, by which my wounds healed. It is said a good partner can play a therapist role. It's true. He had been playing a parent saving my life from those fatal traumas by giving me unconditional love, shining the light of his love into the coldest corners of my heart. I cannot tell if I could survive without having him in my life.

Graceful hands can speak louder than words, like my

analyst's: slightly rounded nails with a little bit of growth slenderize her fingers, a nice glowing pink color of the nails appears naturally healthy and never needs polish. The milky, soft skin looks like Khotanese jade ,(Hetian jade,和田玉, nephrite jade). Hotan is a city in Xinjiang in western China). Such beautiful hands came into my dream, which is mentioned in the letter with which the chapter begins.

That dream was dark as usual, daytime. In the cruelest part, a white man was going to stamp a mark into the back of a woman's hand with a lathe. The lady was sitting in a chair which was being moved to the lathe by that strong guy. Her calm exterior hid her deepest fear, with her heart's beating faster and faster, helplessly waiting for bloody torture and mutilation. I saw him putting her beautiful hand under the dark green lathe; I looked away at the last minute because it was absolutely unbearable for me to see her suffering. I was waiting for her scream, which actually didn't come out from her throat. Then I wondered, staying still: What happened to her? Why didn't she scream? What a tough woman! I still couldn't look back at her hand joining the lathe together. My heart was desperately broken, imagining her beautiful hand was irredeemably destroyed.

Explosion/fight/war was a usual theme of my dreams, such as arena in ancient Rome, heroes with cold arms, battle steeds… disgusting bodies without head or limbs caused by explosions not frightening but exciting me, who unemotionally helped with disposing of the bodies in a dirty toilet. I wouldn't call them "nightmares" because I didn't feel cruel or uncomfortable; but that hand made me feel as if a knife were being twisted inside my heart.

I had quite a few dreams related to my analyst metamorphosing, for example, at the beginning of the analysis, into a ferryman punting me

across a pink sheet of lotus buds coming into full blooms wherever her pole led, which was one of the few dreams without darkness all my life. Another time a pretty healthy lady appeared in a sumptuously gorgeous silk robe with opulent peony and butterfly print, who witnessed my jumping down from a skyscraper with my long black hair fluttering freely in the air (after that dream I made some pictures #22-25 using some original photos to highlight the hair, which impressed me a lot). She turned into a super-smart crow preventing me from eating the toxic puffer fish from an underground river or into a goofy hedgehog fighting with me and finally falling down into a city moat… She could appear as the Maitreya Buddha on my way up to a grand temple or as a ferocious shark with  its soft underbelly (this signifies vulnerability to me. Churchill called Italy "the soft underbelly of Europe" in opening the second front of World War II)

In my mind, my analyst is a tough lady with a very strong will and vulnerability—her pain, by which my mom is characterized, keeps me in the sessions. It's been a long time since I fantasized if she had terrible scars on her back. In the fifth month of the analysis I had a dream demonstrating a direct link between my mom and me.

 There were 3 scenes in my dream, it was the last one. Dark, still. I was very ill, went to see a Taoist priest as a doctor of traditional Chinese medicine in the Taoist temple in my neighborhood (in reality I am living in a cultural village with all traditional Chinese-style architecture including that Taoist temple where these photos #26, 27 were taken).

After feeling my pulse he prescribed a shark (dead) to me (traditional Chinese medicine includes not only plant elements, but also animal parts and minerals.) A small fish inside the shark tried to come out of the shark's abdomen by break- 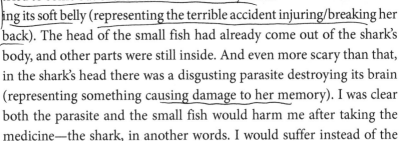 ing its soft belly (representing the terrible accident injuring/breaking her back). The head of the small fish had already come out of the shark's body, and other parts were still inside. And even more scary than that, in the shark's head there was a disgusting parasite destroying its brain (representing something causing damage to her memory). I was clear both the parasite and the small fish would harm me after taking the medicine—the shark, in another words. I would suffer instead of the shark (sacrifice myself), but I still ate it. As was expected, the parasite going inside my brain blurred my mind gradually, and the small fish came out of my body by trisecting my back with 2 horrible big wounds that would for sure become terrible scars.

In the tenth month, I dreamt of my mom with a similar theme—sacrifice. Dark, still. The last scene. I was a little girl, in bed, with a doll in my arm, very ill, dying. My mom came to see me with another man who was waiting for her outside. She wished I could understand her absence as a caretaker, because she had no choice. I knew she was in a hurry to leave me again as usual, leaving me to a man who should have been my protector. I was too weak to talk, saying to her in my mind: "No worries. I can understand you, mom, you may leave now." As my analyst said, death might be a way out. It's true. In my dream, my wish to die may relieve my mom of the burden of taking care of me, also giving me a way to escape from my father's hands.

It is an original shot (#28), no post-production at all. Different photoflash lamps were needed in the daytime for that effect. The golden trees are ginkgos, which are called living fossils. Autumn is the best season in Beijing, which is unfortunately very short. For the outdoor scenes—golden ginkgo woods with navy blue as opposition, chosen to be dominant hue to serve as a foil to the intoxicating gold. This woollen dress, made in Japan, implying exquisite workmanship, never let me down. The original dress was quite plain, with no white lace at all; it was my idea to add them on. Lace, dating from the 15th century in Europe, has been enhancing the beauty of collars and cuffs. Mom sewed them on;she is never tired of dressing me up, her own way to love, each stitch.

In the 20th century Coco Chanel pared down the opulent design. Minimalism then could be fashionable, whereas in the Middle Ages the aristocracy could demonstrate their affinity for luxury in dress and ostentatious living by wearing more fine laces, often denoting class or rank. My mom is always a big fan of lace. I once found a documentary about lace for her. I was impressed by the exquisite craftsmanship and sophisticated huge hand-operated looms. It happens everywhere in the world: many handmade industries have disappeared. It has become increasingly difficult to keep the technique alive. Similarly, Yunjin, also called cloud brocade, the World Intangible Cultural Heritage, dating from 417 AD, is a traditional Chinese silk brocade. The most sophisticated type of cloud brocade is still made on hand-operated looms. about two inches can be made per day by two craftsmen working together.

Elbow-length sleeves rich in elaborate fine lace and a neckline trimmed with flounces; a gown decorated with vertical rows of floral lace (#29-31) serves as an impressive reminder of the Rococo artistic trends of late 18th century.

Lace adds a touch of elegance to the fur (#32-34). The open bell-shaped "pagoda" sleeves, Sèvres blue (*bleu de roi*) coming from Sèvres porcelain, which was a French court art of the 18th century, constitute the retro items.

Lace with jeans also creates Romantic style (#35,36). The bell-bottom is another element of mine. Light blue short silk jacket with trumpet-shaped full sleeves gathered at the wrist and an

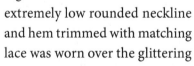

extremely low rounded neckline and hem trimmed with matching lace was worn over the glittering light-blue velvet partlet edged in ivory-gold filigree neckline and hem. The Rococo artistic color scheme of blue, white, and gold is light and stylish.

I fell in love with the dress (#37-39) at first sight, I love those "fish scales" swimming in freedom, (the shape also look like the petals of lotus) which inspired me to form a strange match—a skirt consists of four angles including two long ones(not shown in the pics) and two short ones (#39). It could be put on in any direction, long ones at side for instance, but I prefer long ones stay back, associating with fishtail. There are many different measure words in Chinese language. "A slice of bread": "yi(one) pian(for thin and flat) mianbao(bread)"; "a bread"; "yi ge (used before a noun which does not have a fixed measure word of its own) mianbao"; "a snake": "yi tiao (for long narrow or thin) she". Some nouns have different measure words— "a fish": "yi tiao yu(fish)" or "yi wei (it is a noun, meaning tail, also a measure word used for fish) yu". The measure word "wei" makes fish come alive. I never heard people say, "I ate yi wei yu"(people say "I ate yi tiao yu"). Peep-toe is called "fish-mouth shoes" in Chinese. I do love things related to fish associated with freedom. For many years I often had the same dream: I had full-fledged wings, which were too large to be contained by my room, and I had to huddle my pinions against the ceiling, and I could not fly out of the house. Curling myself into a ball against the ceiling of the dark room made me feel I was a nasty ghost.

I can not find a Chinese term, zhigu桎梏 for instance, to replace the connotational term "pinion," which includes the meaning of the flight feathers of the bird's wing and cutting off those feathers to prevent it from flying. ("Zhigu," comes from a Chinese ancient work entitled Records of Grand History of China 《史記》 (104 -91 BC), meaning fetters and handcuffs, ancient instruments of torture, and the figurative meaning is "mental shackle.")

I was pinioned. I could not be in high school, even though I did extremely well in my middle school and got an offer from one of the best high schools. My parents did not have enough money for my further study; they became laid-off workers of state enterprises that had been privatized in the 1990's. It was a part of the Chinese economic reform led by Tong Shau-ping. Instead of high school, I went to a normal school so that I could work earlier to financially support my original family. Actually I still had a chance to be in college after the normal school. It was my father again who cut off my pinions by hindering my college study. More than 10 years of my youth was spent in working to benefit my family. Meanwhile I studied on my own and became an autodidact. When I finally got a hard-earned opportunity to study in the US in my early thirties, my failures to get a visa (with all documents the US embassy required) made me learn there was a causal connection between freedom and race. Having spent my youth, in years of arduous effort could be reduced to nothing in a blink of an eye. Despairingly, I realized what could pinion me was not only my father, who might be surmounted by my growing up and redoubling my efforts; but also my color, which I can never change (writing down these words, a line from the film *Tale of Tales* is right now hovering in my mind: "Flay me!") This may be why I ached for freedom and have been having the same dream for many years, even after getting my master's degree.

The longing for freedom was not only from me, but also from my mom. I am not the only one who loves fish and birds symbolizing freedom (my mom's embroidery works (#40,41). They (#42,43) were taken in April, 2012 in Zhongshan Park, a former imperial garden, which lies just southwest of the Forbidden City. The Zhongshan Park houses numerous pavilions, gardens, and imperial temples such as the Altar of Earth and Harvests社稷坛, which was built in 1421 by the

Yongle Emperor. It stands symmetrically opposite the Imperial Ancestral Temple, and is where the emperors of the Ming (1368-1644) and Qing(1644-1912) Dynasties made offerings to the gods of earth and agriculture.  (From Wikipedia's entry on Zhongshan Park, Beijing). There are many kinds of flowers in the park. I liked to take my mom to the parks in springs to enjoy the flowers: this was one of few joys I could bring her.

I love this ankle-length khaki robe made of cotton; to me khaki is a symbol of nature. But I don't have milky skin: a sheet of khaki would drown out my dark skin tone without any makeup and the white woven band and flouncing collar of a white shirt echoing each other would brighten my face.

The design of tiered skirt with round collar is that of a baby-doll dress. I always liked to be hidden beneath a loose robe, which made me feel safe. Many people could not understand why such a slim me wouldn't like the garments flattering to my hourglass-figure, they would persuade me by saying: "If I were you, I would wear…" If they were me, they would understand I almost never felt secure, due to the trauma of my early life. Wide silhouette shelters me from the outside world, from danger.

The similar loose outerwear also appeared in the following photos  (#44,45). Champagne is one of my favorite colors. Abundance of layers, like a flared skirt, broad, high-waisted silhouette with a large bowknot on the back, fine sheer silk decorated with filigree embroidery scattered on the elbow-length sleeves, tiers edged in gold filigree plus ivory woollen stockings—all these elements were my favorites.

Oversized pants (#46-48) also could function as a shelter. Baggy jeans plus a backless (#46-48) top under which butterfly bones (a popular Chinese term for shoulder blades) bloomed up,  wearing neither makeup nor bra, with a bit of tanned skin and natural straight hair; youth itself is beauty. Unfortunately wearing no bra is not fashionable in today's China. White and blue are my favorite color schemes; these colors are from nature and I associate them with sky and cloud.

Besides loose style, I have a strong attachment to soft cloth, such as cotton, wool, and artificial furs (I am a born vegetarian. In recent years I would not buy fur and leather if I had other options) just like the Rhesus macaques in Harry Harlow's best known experiment: the surrogate mothers.

For this experiment Harlow presented the infants with a clothed mother and a wired mother under two conditions. In one situation, the wire mother held a bottle with food and the cloth mother held no food. In the other situation, the cloth mother held the bottle and the wire mother had nothing. Overwhelmingly, the infant macaques preferred spending their time clinging to the cloth mother. Even when only the wire mother could provide nourishment, the monkeys visited her only to feed.

They (#49,50) were taken in Olympic Forest Park in fall. Canary woollen one-piece dress, grayish blue artificial furs coat with hood, fluffy material always made me feel warm and secure, such as the following (#51-53):

Van Gogh was a colorist, seeking oppositions of blue with orange, red and green, yellow and violet. The oppositions of red with green were also a Chinese traditional color scheme. For the outdoor scenes—

Confucian temple, dark green tartan coat and crimson corduroy shorts with plaid were chosen.

Peking Temple of Confucius, the second largest Confucian Temple(built in 1302 AD), after the one in Confucius' hometown of Qufu in Shandong Province (established in 479 BC), officials used it to pay their respects to Confucius until 1911. Inside the temple there are 198 stone tablets positioned on either side of the front courtyard, and they contain more than 51,624 names of jinshis进士 (advanced scholars) of the Yuan(1206-

1368), Ming(1368-1644) and Qing(1644-1912) Dynasties, and 14 stone stele pavilions of the Ming and Qing dynasties that hold various historical documents of ancient China. Of all glories, I can think of none more honorable than what those intellectuals achieved!

They (#54,55) were taken in August, 2012. The two similar white dresses were my favorites, tiered-skirt style, round collar with ruffle(#55), which were bought in 2006 when I was 27 years old. I got my driving license in that year. I remembered I was in this white

dress (#55) for my driving license exam, and the examiner thought my age was not old enough for the exam until I showed him my ID card.

This is how I looked (#56) in 2006 when the photo was taken unnoticed. That natural unadulterated state set off by the Dalmatian print on the pajamas was more childish.

The similar childish look also appeared in the photos taken in October, 2012. Sometimes we took photos along

 Chang An Avenue, the main street in Peking, where the Forbidden City is located in. The indoor shot was taken at MacDonalds when we had a rest in there. I was not posing for the camera. I was quite comfortable with those cutesy, girlish pink clothes and  hair bands. Apparently my psychological age adhered to childhood because of traumas in my early life.

At the beginning of 2013, I had my first therapy because of depression. That therapist suggested me to study psychology in order to recover myself. I took the advice and then I fortunately passed the qualifying exam for a psychotherapist certificate. Both the therapy and study helped me to come out of the depression. Study also helped me to psychologically grow up. From then on I gradually ceased to hate my parents. In contrast, I could put myself in their shoes to feel what they suffered.

My father is tiny, 162cm (5.3feet), 45kg (99pounds), who should have been much taller and stronger like my paternal grandparents were. His being undersized was triggered by nutritional deficiency which was "fortunate" during the Three Years of Great Famine (1958-1961) characterized by widespread famine. Drought, poor weather, and government policies contributed to the famine, although the relative weights of the contributions are disputed due to the Great Leap Forward大躍進 led by Mao Zedong (From Wikipedia's entry on the Great Chinese Famine). Chinese journalist Yang Jisheng concluded there were 36 million deaths due to starvation, while another 40 million others failed to be born. My father was born in 1951. He and his father had shared food with pigs. When he was 7, he lost his mother, who died of tuberculosis in her thirties. His stepmother was a devil who pocketed most portion of the rice and wheat flour for her biological son, which should have been allotted to my grandpa and the twochildren (my father and his younger sister). Many things were rationed during those years of scarcity: food for instance. According to my parents, one's monthly allowance included 250g of oil, 1500g of rice, 1500g of wheat flour, 10.5kg of coarse food grain such as maize, sorghum, millet, etc. My

242

father got a serious stomach illness in his teens, which has never been cured all his life. My aunt has had lung disease since age two. She died of heart disease, emphysema, diabetes etc. when she was 47 with a displaced heart in the right chest caused by emphysema. Of course, my step-grandma never took them to see a doctor. My grandpa was a talented man of few words. He was not really educated but could read ancient Chinese medical works with a dictionary, could play any tunes whatever he heard on an Erhu (a two-stringed instrument), and could do Chinese painting on brown wrapping paper from cement with pulverized brick as color (he was working as a top-lever plasterer). But he was so weak that he fell victim to bullies throughout his life; the only outlet for his rage was my father as a child, who was beaten up a lot by my grandpa. Adults who have been subjected to physical punishment as children are more likely to abuse their own child or spouse and to manifest criminal behavior (Gershoff 2008).

People knowing me would say my personality was not as feminine as how I look. If the feminine part is from my mom, the masculine part may be attributed to the lack of an ideal father who should be a strong backbone of the whole family. On the contrary, my father never regarded it as his responsibility. When I was young, I knew I was the only candidate who had to take his place. In fact, my father stopped working as soon as I got my first job as a school teacher after I graduated from that normal school. It was I who bought my mom social insurance and a flat. During those working years I passed the self-study exams to earn a qualification for full-time grad school. It was extremely hard for me, but I was never allowed to be vulnerable by myself.

I bought the jacket (#59) only because it looked like a racing suit. I have different peaked caps (#60-62) for different clothes. Wearing them, I identified myself with a boy. They (#63,64) were taken in April, 2014: the same pink jacket served as a foil to the fuchsia pink flowers, but I no longer felt comfortable with those girlish stuff, instead, hot pink peep-toe high- heeled shoes were chosen to echo the jacket. The white stockings with big yellow, blue, and pink polka dots were a clever match for the jacket's white lining with the similar color-scheme flower print.

 They (#65,66) were taken at the end of 2013 at Beijing Ancient Observatory, built in 1442, one of the oldest observatories in the world.
The two instruments built in 1673 were for astronomic observation during Ming(1368-1644) and Qing(1644-1912) dynasty. The one right behind me is a celestial globe for determining the time in which the celestial bodies will rise and set as well as the altitude and azimuth of them at any given time. The other one is an ecliptic armillary sphere for determining the coordinates of celestial bodies as well as the solar term. (From Wikipedia's entry on Beijing Ancient Observatory)

Lapel and cuffs are turned back to reveal the contrasting linings with leopard print for mature ladies, which is also shown in the following (#67,68) taken at the end of 2014.

That childish look has gone in the sexy shots taken in 2014. My dreams are still dark and full of terrors and resplendent trappings, my being destroyed and loved by white and yellow race are still going on in my pajamas. I am not sure if one day my dreams will be sprinkled with sunshine. But as my analyst said, psychoanalysis is a journey in which people need to be brave. It is worth a try, isn't it? I didn't drop out, maybe because I was not sure the next analyst would have beautiful hands and blue eyes; sound ridiculous? Maybe. However, I know it's she who makes me regain the sense of decency, virtue (she tried to dramatically reduce my fee for my mom's eye surgery) and the universal language—LOVE, despite the seemingly insurmountable cultural conflicts and language barrier.

POST-CREDITS SCENES

My paternal step-grandma became a widow when she was eighteen. Bringing up her biological son by herself, she became a burden for his marriage. Therefore, he intentionally discarded her somewhere far away from their hometown, and afterwards she met my grandpa. Carrying the docked rice and wheat flour, my step-grandma teetered with her bound feet back to her biological son once a year or every two years after her remarrying. But her daughter-in-law disowned her, since her son had asserted he was an orphan before their marriage.

When my maternal grandma was a little girl, her whole family shared a pair of pants temporarily belonging to whoever went out. She and her sisters were naked while weeding the fields lest their underwear rip. My mind sometimes flashed back to scenes of the past that I never really saw: the farmland resounded with giggles of the innocent children mixed with the rustles of leaves in the wind, with several naked little girls appearing and disappearing in the crops.

NOTES

All the photos (#1-73) in this chapter are taken by Xiangyu Chen; the post-production (#4,5,6,7,22,23,24,25) is done by Tina Tian. The embroidery works (#9,10,11,12,40,41) are made by Yazhi Chiang.

A SAMPLE OF CIDIÉ LIÀN HUĀ TUNE

Butterfies over Flowers[4] 蝶 戀 花 Yàn shū Yan Shu

晏 殊 jiān jú chóu yān lán qì lù Orchids shed tears with doleful asters in mist grey.

檻 菊 愁 煙 蘭 泣 露, luó mù qīng hán How can they stand the cold silk curtains can't allay?

羅 幕 輕 寒, Yàn zǐ shuāng fēi qù A pair of swallows flies away.

燕 子 雙 飛 去。 míng yuè bù ān lí hèn kǔ The moon, which knows not parting grief, sheds slanting light 明 月 不 諳 離 恨 苦, xié guāng dào xiǎo chuān zhū hù Through crimson windows all the night. 斜 光 到 曉 穿 朱 戶。 zuó yè xī fēng diāo bì shù Last night the western breeze

昨 夜 西 風 凋 碧 樹, Blew withered leaves off trees. dú shàng gāo lóu I mount the tower high

獨 上 高 樓, wàng jìn tiān yá lù And strain my longing eye

望 盡 天 涯 路。 yù jì cǎi jiān jiān chǐ sù I'll send a message to my dear,

欲 寄 彩 箋 兼 尺 素, shān cháng shuǐ kuò zhī hé chù But endless ranges and streams sever us far and near. 山 長 水 闊 知 何 處？

246

References

Graham, A. C. (1981). Chuang-tzu, The Seven Inner Chapters and other writings from the book Chuang-tzu. London: George Allen and Unwin.

Suomi, S. J. & Leroy, H. A. (1982), In memoriam: Harry F. Harlow (1905–1981). *Am. J. Primatol., 2*, 319–342.

Mirsky, J. (2012, December 9). "Unnatural Disaster: 'Tombstone: The Great Chinese Famine, 1958–1962,' by Yang Jisheng". The New York Times Sunday Book Review. p. BR22. Retrieved from http://www.nytimes.com/2012/12/09/books/review/tombstone-the-great-chinese-famine-1958-1962-by-yang-jisheng.html.

Yuanchong, Xu. (2013). Version of Classical Chinese Poetry.

V

Shopping for Clothes

1. Clothes and the Couch

ARLENE KRAMER RICHARDS

Every morning, suit,
you are waiting on a chair
to be filled
by my vanity, my love,
my hope, my body.
In bad moments
you cling to my bones
— from "Ode to My Suit" by Pablo Neruda

The enormous size of the garment industry is a reflection of how important clothes are to the women who live in them. The activities of making, shopping for, and wearing clothes provide an almost unparalleled opportunity for women to work, to express their creativity, to define themselves. For those women who experience shopping for clothes as an endless temptation, preoccupation, and sometimes torture—a never-fulfilled quest—shopping for clothes seems to be at least as important as wearing them. How does the ordinary pleasure and necessity of buying clothes become a compulsive, driving need?

In this chapter I will consider clothes shopping in the context of a psychoanalytic understanding of women's interest in dress, discuss some issues related to how shopping compulsions develop and what they can mean, and provide clinical material to illustrate four different manifestations of this symptom. Touching as it does upon so many issues of sexuality, narcissism, safety, and power, shopping for clothing is a natural venue for

251

symptomatology in many areas. One case that I will use to illustrate this idea appears to me to have clear aspects of sexual perversion. I will discuss it at length, because it is relevant to important work being done now on female perversions (Richards 1989, 1990, 1997) and other particularly female manifestations of sexuality.

PSYCHOANALYTIC VIEWS OF CLOTHING

Clothing has many different meanings for women, far too many even to hint at most of them here. Dressing and display are multifaceted acts. A woman can display her body temptingly as part of courtship; flaunt it aggressively to frighten and humiliate men and/or other women; or experience it privately as the comfortable center of her sense of self. Freud's comment (Rose 1988), that not even the most intelligent woman is free of the dictates of fashion, suggests that the motivation for that interest is not frivolous, as some contemporary critics of Freud would have it, but has real psychological import.

There is a long tradition of clothes' being taken seriously in psychoanalytic theory. But clinical interest in clothing has been hampered by societal biases and gender stereotypes, and in the recent past psychoanalysts have noticed dress primarily as an indicator of feelings and thoughts of which a person is not necessarily aware. It was a commonplace for case reports to indicate that a patient began treatment sloppily or inappropriately dressed and came to look better groomed as treatment progressed. Bergler (1953) cited many cases of what he believed to be improper or unfashionable dress as evidence of the presence of neurosis. As late as 1985, Bergmann used "femininity" of dress and adornment as an indicator of her patient's comfort with her gender identity and therefore of her mental health. But increasingly, theory and clinical observation are being applied in ways that include the importance of aggression and androgyny in female development and do not regard "feminine" as equivalent to "normal" for females.

Flügel (1930) has been an influential writer on the meaning of clothes, not only for psychoanalysts but for historians of fashion as well. He believed that clothing was used to enhance the body by enlarging salient features of it. Skirts, for instance, he noted as making the female body appear wider and therefore more powerful, especially when extended by crinolines, hoops, or bustles. He also noted negotiations over the protective functions of clothes as part of the currency between parent and child, in that a mother tends to suggest to a child that he or she wear more, but rarely less, clothing (see the case of Mary, below). Bergler believed that clothing was always used to draw attention to female sexuality, and that even when apparently modest, it was used to enhance attractiveness by allaying men's fears of the unclothed female genitalia.

Dress is at one and the same time a clue to unconscious fantasy (Arlow 1971) and an enactment of it. Clothing can be costume as well as apparel, and as such is an actualization of the life of fantasy that keeps young children playing for hours on end and continues to operate in adults in subtler ways. (See Sally, below, and her fantasies: both the conscious one of being the wife of a rich and powerful man and the unconscious one of sadistic teasing with her parents.) Fashion can embody a fantasy of being younger or older, a cowboy or an Arab, any role of interest that is not available in ordinary life. For Freud (1908) this kind of fantasy was the kernel of creativity and the center of psychic life, not only consoling its creator for the necessary restrictions of the real world, but also providing the basis for psychological change and ongoing development. Unconscious aspects of these fantasies may play a large part in the development of compulsive shopping. Again, this is illustrated in the cases of Sally and Annie below.

Clothing demarcates the individual body. It outlines its contours and also suggests the physical uses to which it will be put. Hollander (1994), for instance, believes that the trouser suit worn by western men since the 18th century contrasts with the skirt in that it emphasizes the possibility of activity rather than the capacity for reproduction.

But most important for my purposes here, clothes are the covering of the erotic female body. An analytic patient dreamed of looking at some silk blouses on a rack. In the dream her sister told her that cheaper blouses were just as good as expensive ones; they didn't show because they were worn under jackets and the good ones were almost as expensive as the suit itself. The patient had complained the previous day about a suit she had been given by her mother. When her analyst interpreted that the patient would prefer a sexier one, the analyst hit upon a truth that changed the patient's view of herself. It countered her unconscious fantasy that her analyst had been trying to desexualize her. By allowing her to want what she believed others did not want her to have, this interpretation also helped her to feel entitled to have her own ideas about other aspects of her life. Clothing was the accessible metaphor for this woman's genital issues of sexiness, desirability, and assertion of the positive value of female sexuality. It can equally be a metaphor for protection, power, or other such important psychic constructs, and as such is a likely area for symptom development.

De Lauretis (1994) believes that clothing can function as fetish when the sense of the female body as erotic object is damaged. A fetish is a not-necessarily-sexual object, body part, or activity that is invested with profound sexual meaning, giving rise to extreme erotic excitement because it includes a strong, hidden aggressive component. As such, it itself becomes the object of desire, obligatory for sexual pleasure and taking precedence over genital sexual activity with another person. According to De Lauretis, the image of her own female body as erotic may be lost when the mother refuses to leave the father's bed for the little girl's, resulting in a woman with a permanent longing for her mother's affirmation of her worth and a need to use clothing to represent her lost, erotic, female body. Neither De Lauretis nor I imply that people are aware of such things. In most cases they are not. The psychoanalytic view is that organizing fantasies are not conscious until brought to awareness by the analytic process.

Clothes may serve women as a means of psychological negotiation with men, who also have complex but not necessarily conscious feelings about the female body as an erotic object (De Lauretis 1994). Male reactions of envy and fear of the vulva are sometimes experienced by a woman as devaluation of her feminine fullness. Sometimes a woman anticipates envy and fear and develops her own fear of being envied. Transvestites and female impersonators use feminine clothing in ways that can flatter or frighten women, but always express this envy. Clothing serves as a flexible barrier, allowing a woman to remove a bit at a time, testing whether the other will be further attracted or repelled by her femaleness. Removing clothing in stages can be part of courtship. And the changing in the dressing room is a rehearsal of the taking off and putting on of clothing that enhances the body. It both anticipates and prepares for the removal of clothing as seduction. Meanwhile, it provides the exhibitionistic pleasure of imagining oneself's being seen.

Theorists from Freud through the postmoderns have suggested that a woman wants her body to be admired and desired by both men and women, just as little girls want their bodies to be admired and desired by the people they love: their parents. When she feels that it is, she may enjoy the pleasures of clothing as a way of expressing her valuation of herself. When her sense of desirability is damaged, however, and she wishes to make herself desirable again, she may turn desperately to clothing as a means to that end or even sometimes as a fetishistic substitute for the devalued body itself.

THE PLEASURES OF SHOPPING

Shopping for clothes, especially sexy ones, includes pleasures beyond the acquisition of the clothing itself. The shopping itself can be a part of feeling desirable and attractive. One woman commented that every time she tries on new clothes it feels as if she's getting a hug. The physical sensation of the clothes on her skin—a pleasurable feeling that becomes less intense with familiarity—is noticed again and the sense of pleasure is renewed with new clothes. The experience of looking in the mirror also increases sensory awareness, the excitement of the newness heightening the physical sensation of something touching the skin.

There are social pleasures to shopping as well as these more sensual ones. Women shop with friends, mothers, or daughters. Someone else's seeing the new clothes can elicit the same heightened awareness that the woman above noted. An observer can respond erotically to the highlighting and/or concealing of erotogenic zones. Another person's reaction gives the wearer a mirror more faithful than the one on the wall to supplement her experience of herself. An observer provides criticism, judgment, discrimination, compliments. And there are pleasures of power: of demanding, rejecting, returning, competing, spending.

HOW SHOPPING COMPULSIONS DEVELOP

These types of pleasures are related to longings for sensual pleasure, closeness, and intimacy, and to desires for endless supplies, endless love, and endless dependency. Since possession of a garment cannot fulfill such longings, the shopping itself may become the object of desire and a shopping compulsion may develop. Yet this attempted solution is also illusory. Longings and desires of this kind are doomed to frustration, especially when their owner is not aware of them. Shopping, with its promise of a quest fulfilled, serves well to stir them up. But it has little capacity to satisfy. It inflames but cannot assuage. A salesperson may temporarily seem a dispenser of longed-for parental love and approval, but ultimately the shopper is left unfulfilled and/or guilty rather than satisfied. Unfulfilled because the salesperson is not a sufficiently important object; guilty because of the stealthy nature of the covert transaction, or because the attainment of the forbidden wish requires an equally great punishment (these dynamics will be clarified in the case material below). The expenditure of large sums of money may briefly offer a consoling fantasy of control and power, but that is quickly deflated when the bills come due. To the extent that the shopper does not recognize that what she is looking for cannot be found where she seeks it, she may return to the site of a former partial success and seek it there again and again.

Compulsive shopping as a symptom has only lately appeared in the psychoanalytic literature. Schwartz (1992) has described such a compulsion in a woman with borderline pathology, Lawrence (1990) theorized a neurotic etiology, and Kaplan (1991) associated it with personality disorder of a sociopathic kind. Krueger (1988) considered shopping compulsion in terms of narcissistic psychopathology. All of these writers postulate, in the analytic tradition, the existence of unconscious fantasies that drive the quest, and they recognize the resulting paradox: that although the conscious goal may be clothing, in the unconscious quest a different object is sought.

It is my belief that this confusion of unconscious needs with the conscious wish for clothing gives rise to compulsive shopping symptoms. The complexities of these constructions are beautifully illustrated by Winestine (1985), who described a woman whose compulsive shopping was eventually traced to a childhood seduction. This had resulted in a feeling of helplessness that she attempted to overcome by shopping in fancy stores and imagining herself the wife of a powerful rich man. The patient could not afford the clothes, but she enjoyed using credit cards, which she then would not pay, thus being able to cheat the bankers while blaming them because they kept extending credit to her.

It is important to recognize that the realities of wealth or wardrobe are not particularly relevant in these matters. If her resources for buying are insufficient or conflictual, shopping or shoplifting may give a woman a feeling of power, but a woman who appears to have the money to buy anything she wants still may not believe she has enough since what she really wants cannot be bought. If she experiences her needs as contemptible, the literal possession of any given object will not suffice to relieve her. If she considers clothes, accessories, or cosmetics the guarantors of beauty, yet believes she can never feel beautiful, she may understand this as not being able to buy enough. If buying things is her only experience of being loved, it will avail little against a black hole of endless unreciprocated desire. These needs are so frightening in their apparent boundlessness that a woman may provoke authority figures into setting limits in the hope of obtaining protection from her own painful longings and the powerful and menacing impulse to satisfy them (see Krueger [1988]; also Winestine, above, and the case of Elinor, below).

A word here in preparation for the case material. This driven quality can arise in any area of a person's emotional life where a commanding need is secretly going unmet. When such needs conceal aggressive wishes behind a screen of sexual or flirtatious wishes, the compulsion may take on the quality that we tend to identify as "perverse."

Psychoanalytic schools differ regarding how perversions come about, but fundamentally agree on what they are. Perversions, in psychoanalytic terms, are a form of compromise between intense sexual and aggressive wishes and the fears and moral judgments that require their suppression. They are defensive in that they keep the unacceptable wishes hidden from the person's awareness. They take the form of highly ritualized scenarios in which disguised forms of these impulses and fears are repetitively acted out. The scenarios retain the intensity of the primitive wishes, but are very tightly scripted. They allow the individual to experience the intensity fueled by aggression, while avoiding the dreaded aggressive reaction from a potential partner who might have his or her own needs, both libidinal and aggressive. In return for this pleasure the perversion exacts a price: the perverse behavior itself may become a source of shame and guilt; and the possibilities of other kinds of sexual pleasure diminish. Because the perverse behavior is obligatory for arousal, it ends up replacing other forms of sexuality, coitus included, as the sole desired goal. In a "successful" perversion this complex balance protects the aggressive aspects of the underlying wishes from exposure, allowing them expression in relative safety.

Representations of (unconscious) attempts to master overwhelming childhood experiences of excitement and terror, perversions have as much to do with rage as with sexuality. The specific form of the perverse scenario for any individual is determined by his or her own particular fantasies, but all perversions depend on a sense of alienation as a shield against the power of other people. To the extent that it works, it does so by permitting, requiring, and enforcing maximum distance from the dangerous "others" who are mistakenly believed to be the source of the overwhelming feelings.

This concept has widened steadily since Freud's original formulation. He defined perversions as "sexual activities which either (a) extend, in an anatomical sense, beyond the regions of the body that are designed for sexual union, or (b) linger over the immediate relations to the sexual object which should normally be traversed rapidly on the path towards the final sexual aim." (Freud 1905 p. 150). That is, they indicate a deflection of interest away from the primary sexual organs and away from the goal of coitus. Freud, starting with his acceptance of Sabina Spielrein's 1911 concept of the death instinct (Freud 1920), came to consider aggression as a major source of human motivation, as important as loving or libidinal wishes within the context of the personality as a whole. Correspondingly, perversion has been seen as less motivated by loving and fear of loving, and more as a sexualized response to the sometimes intolerable intensity of these aggressive wishes toward potential sexual partners. Etchegoyen (1991) showed how perverse symptoms could occur in people who were not sexual perverts. He showed how the idea that aggression could be disguised as erotic excitement could clarify the perverse aspects of people who seemed on the surface to be more neurotic or even normal. Kaplan (1991) specified the concept of perversion in a way that is particularly relevant to this study. She focused on the preoccupying psychological attachments to material goods and their acquisition that are so common in contemporary society, and which she understands as fetishistic in nature (see above). She then proposed a connection between these preoccupations and perverse phenomena, and has extensively elaborated the uses that may be made of apparently nonsexual phenomena for perverse purposes. The difference between Kaplan's position and mine is that I see a spectrum of degree of pathology, so that one person's perversion is another person's pleasure, with many degrees of fixity and restriction between the poles.

CASE ILLUSTRATIONS

Annie

Annie began compulsively shopping after her husband died. She felt that shopping for clothes was the only thing that could satisfy her. She talked to salespeople in the stores constantly, soliciting their advice on how to put outfits together and how to choose the ones most flattering to her. She enjoyed finding flaws in the things she chose, bringing the items to the salesperson and asking for a discount to compensate for the flaws. A lipstick mark on the inside of a dress or a pulled thread in a hem gave her pleasure, because she could talk to the salespeople about them. She engaged them in discussions of how the clothing was made, why there were flaws in it, and whatever other reasons she could find for why she should get it for less. For her, shopping was a demonstration to others that she had been cheated and deserved reparation. She had never used shopping in this way before. It was the death of her husband that precipitated her need to console herself with material things.

She had always enjoyed having her husband look at her and appreciate her body. She talked about how helpful saleswomen were in advising her which clothes looked best on her. It occurred to me that these saleswomen were providing her with an audience like the audience that her husband once provided for her. She talked of how she did not want to be in the singles "scene." She did not want to meet new people. She had enough of that before her marriage when she was younger and had a better figure. As I interpreted her shopping compulsion as a fear that her body was no longer young and attractive enough to get her a new man, Annie's shopping symptom slowly receded. Later she began to understand that she was complaining to the salespeople about her feelings of having been damaged herself by the loss of her husband. What she was actually looking for was someone to love and someone to love her. Now that she was no longer using the symptom of shopping to get what she could never again have (the sense of being loved as a young woman, the feeling she had with her husband when they were young) she was able to look for something that she could have: a sense of being wanted and appreciated for what she was now.

The symptom was relatively easy for her to give up and replace with a new hobby: she began taking care of a group of teens who had no place to be together away from their parents. Annie began to look forward to the after-school hours when they would come to her home and watch television, play games, or bake cookies. She also found comfort in working for an organization that collected money for research on the disease her husband had died from. She met people and gradually established a new life for herself. Like most patients who are thought of as neurotic, Annie managed to achieve a new balance in her life more easily than can people like the patient I will talk about next.

Elinor

Elinor had a passion for shopping that usually ended up in her acquiring nothing. Her weekend hobby was shopping for clothing and jewelry that she would then return during the following week. She constantly yearned for clothes, and felt satisfied when she was buying them, but she hated them once she "felt trapped" into keeping them. Old clothes, "antique" clothes, were more acceptable to her. She liked knowing that the antique dealers she bought them from would not accept returns. For Elinor the only way to avoid the cycle of buying and returning was to deal with people who would not allow it.

The first phase of her symptom giving way began when she discovered that I was wearing new shoes exactly like ones she had bought the previous week. She regarded this as a triumph of taste. We liked the same things. She did not have to return the shoes even though she had been keeping them in the closet while deciding when to return them. I suggested that she think about why it was so important to her that we had chosen the same shoes. We talked about the beginnings of her pattern, and it turned out that her mother had established the pattern by encouraging her to buy several things at the same time, bringing them home to her father for his opinion and then sending back the ones that did not meet with his approval, keeping only those he liked best. She was harboring a childhood fantasy that she too could be returned if she were not a good enough child. She avoided making long-term commitments for a similar reason; as long as she did not choose the other person, if she could still return him; she would not be the one who was returned as not good enough.

Months after Elinor had begun to experience some relief from her continual need to shop and return things, one of her uncles died. At the funeral. the uncle's daughter thanked her for coming. Elinor felt terribly sad, even as she reflected that the death of her relative would not make much difference in her own life. But although her mourning for her uncle appeared to be minimal, still she resumed shopping in a way she called an addiction. The pattern was so severe that she became extremely embarrassed at causing the salespeople so much trouble with her constant demands on their time and energy, both to sell her the things and to issue the credits to her for returning them. Sometimes she would give the clothes away to relatives or friends rather than take them back to the store where she had bought them. The symptom had been so severe before treatment that Elinor had worn the same winter coat for a decade. She could not find anything that she felt comfortable in. It was only late in her analysis that we were able to understand why a coat had such significance to her.

Trying to understand what had caused her to relapse into her old shopping ways, I suggested to Elinor that it might have something to do with her uncle's death, but she thought it had to do with her father's death. It then became clear to us that the pattern became pronounced after her father's death, and that her uncle's death had only brought it back. I interpreted that she felt her father was back with her when she bought things to return, the way she had when he was alive to approve her choices. This intervention allowed the return of memories of being taken to a large city near her hometown to buy new clothes for each new season. She and her mother would choose many things, but would return most of them.

Further analysis from this point was able to make it clear that in their shopping both she and mother had been doing and undoing: that is, acting and then undoing the consequences of the action. What was being undone related, for her mother, to the early death of her own father. Elinor herself, we found, had been undoing what she herself feared most, the possibility of her own mother's early death. Her identification with her mother, and fear of her loss, was concretely embodied in the buy-and-return cycle, and provided its driving force. They had participated in it together, and it provided comforting proof that anything could be undone, nothing was final, nothing was irreversible, not even death. But when death itself (her father's and then her uncle's) proved this fantasy untrue, her anxiety increased, and so did the undoing necessary to contain it. This triggered the intensified shopping-and-returning. Note that it was the apparently superficially felt death of her uncle that first alerted us to the connection of this behavior with death and loss. We were able to pursue the pattern from her uncle's death through her father's and from there to its deepest and most encompassing level, the identification with her mother and her need to undo the possibility of losing her.

This fear of loss was fueled by Elinor's unconscious rage at her parents; she feared their death because she also longed for it. Her rage at them stemmed from a sense that they had deprived her of the most important thing, their love and attention, while showering her with material objects that served only to prove to her and the world that they had the money and the power to provide these things, not to satisfy any wishes of hers. The winter-coat symptom now became clearer to me. A coat is something that the world sees: it is outdoor wear. In this regard it was like her parents' gifts in that a new and expensive one would show the world that she was like her parents, exhibiting her buying power. Yet a new cheap one would not satisfy her, either because it would show the world that she did not have her mother's elegant taste or her father's money. To have either was impossibly painful, so she kept herself in a threadbare coat, looking, she thought, like someone who did not have what she needed, and thus shaming her parents.

This complicated set of thoughts covered up and displayed her rage simultaneously. Her rage had to be discovered over and over again as Elinor saw how she was displacing her rage onto the shopkeepers who had to take back what she did not want just as she had wished that she could make her parents take back their gifts and spend time with her instead. It is because of the intense aggressive aspect of her shopping compulsion and the substitution of shopping for the pleasures of loving another person that I see Elinor's symptom as perverse.

After several years of analysis, Elinor felt less worthless. She could relax her fear of being "returned" herself, rejected by her parents as unacceptable. She allowed herself her rage at them and was no longer so ashamed of it that she had to hide it from herself. She felt better able to cope with eventualities such as loss or death, and, feeling safer, was able to allow herself more material things as well. She became able to use clothing for pleasure rather than as a seasonal sacrifice in the service of the denial of death.

Annie and Elinor, it may be seen, used their compulsive shopping in different ways to protect themselves, in fantasy, from object loss. Lawrence (1990) has elaborated this theme provocatively. Individuals who for whatever reason find the risks of object loss too great, she says, may shift their focus away from the wish to be loved onto the love of material things. In this way they free themselves from dependency on an autonomous object whose love they desire but might lose. She also points out that a sense of psychological linkage with a concrete thing may provide a sense of shared permanence to a person who is dismayed by the evanescence of his or her own human state. She points out that the linking of oneself with concrete objects allows an individual "to transcend the death fear and impose the feeling of immortality and permanence on the ephemeral individual. In this way the object lends the individual a future" (p. 68).

Mary

Mary went shopping for clothes in preparation for each new season. She had dozens of similar outfits in a range of colors that she thought fit each time of year. She wore a dazzling array of dresses, making it clear to her co-workers that she had more than any of them. She chose dresses with the most feminine details she could find, always describing her style as "girly." She enjoyed being dressed in bright or pastel shades, wanting always to look cheerful and prosperous. From her point of view, the show of prosperity was the most important purpose of her life. Her mother had been a European orphan, picked up by American soldiers and brought home as a kind of mascot by the young men who had found her starving and dressed in rags. One of them had adopted her but had been unable to keep her; his wife found the little girl unmanageable because she had temper tantrums and would steal from neighbors, friends, and family. She had gone from foster home to foster home until she married the patient's father. Her mother had always dressed herself in modest somber colors, but had taken great pride in her daughter's large, varied, and very colorful wardrobe.

Mary understood early on that her mother maintained a depressive conviction of being worthless and pitiable. She knew that her clothing in some way compensated for this for both of them. But it took the exploration of other unconscious beliefs to release her from the constant need to amass more clothes. Two other intertwined fears were connected to her constant and exhausting consuming. These had to do first with her uncertain relationship with her own femininity and sense of attractiveness to either men or women, and second with the relative value she placed on women and men.

Her sense of her own femininity was attached to her awareness of her father's attraction to her as a woman. Ambivalent about his attraction to her, at times he denigrated and disparaged her feminine charms, which led to a conviction on her part that she was unattractive. When other men responded to her as attractive she was plunged into uncertainty over whether her father really had admired her. Answering this question affirmatively allowed her to believe that he had secretly preferred her to her mother.

Her confusion about the relative value of men and women had to do with her belief that her mother, who constantly disparaged Mary's father, was the powerful and nurturing one in the family. Mary's mother required her to be loyal to her exclusively. Mary was confused by the fact that her mother had remained with her father despite what the mother presented as his supposedly unacceptable behaviors.

Every time she surpassed either her mother or father in any way, she felt more alienated from them. Any achievement tasted of ashes, as it made her feel that she was losing her parents' love. Yet her way of feeling better about herself was to achieve still more. The only way out of this dilemma that she could find was to buy clothes. It felt good, and it did not in any way diminish her parents' achievements. In fact, it enhanced them, because it was their achievements that provided the money that bought the clothes. Mary could buy clothes to reassure herself that she was still a pretty and nice girl, still a valued part of a family that saw her other accomplishments as unfeminine and threatening.

When her doctor told her that she was entering menopause, she had the thought that she would go and spend a month's salary on clothes to cheer herself up. She then told me that before her treatment she would have actually done it, but now she could notice the impulse and think about what had triggered it. She had spent most of her life worrying about her parents, both of whom had been chronically ill since she was a little girl. Yet she had taken loans from her parents continually, never paying them back, because she needed the money for clothes. I was finally able to connect the shopping with a fantasy she had talked of years earlier of having a rich and powerful father who would always be there to protect her. In the fantasy, as long as she remained a dependent little girl, her parents would be safe from the encroachments of time. The clothes- buying had maintained for her this sense of secure dependency.

In the course of her treatment she made sure to outdo me by having many more outfits than I did, by being more in step with current styles, by being more feminine in dress and grooming, and by changing her makeup so that she was more youthful looking. As we painstakingly explored her need to compete with me and be sure that I did feel bested in these ways, she taught me how she felt. As long as she was able to depend on me, as she had on her parents, as long as she needed to overspend in order to be in debt to them and to me and to the credit card companies, she was sure that none of the parties would die. She was repeating in her current life the fantasy of keeping her parents alive by depending on them and being in debt because she continually bought more clothes than she could afford. The interpretation of the dependency fantasy and how it had played out between us in the transference was what enabled her to stop the compulsive shopping.

Sally

Sally was a tall, long-limbed, 30-year-old blonde. She was a saleswoman in a high-fashion optometrist's shop, and had been in analysis for several years. One of her most puzzling symptoms was her need to constantly "improve" her looks. She spent hours each morning on makeup, on selecting clothing, and on doing her hair. She was beautiful, but was convinced that she was "a dog." Handsome boyfriends made her frantic because she believed that they were always looking for a woman more beautiful than she was. She could not believe what people told her about her attractiveness. In the analysis we wondered about her belief that she was so ugly and worthless.

Sally's attitude toward her clothing reflected her attitude toward her body. She would buy many pieces of cheap clothing at a time, be interested in them for a few days, then want more. She frequently borrowed her mother's clothes and those of her friends. She seemed to be searching for another body. She was, I think now in retrospect, expressing with her clothes both a restless disappointment with her own body and a wish to be able to change it at will, having it now thinner and more childish, now fuller and more womanly.

This preoccupation was connected with the shopping, and it encapsulated some old conflicts with her mother. Sally's mother had fought vigorously against Sally's early attempts to be very thin, and the wardrobe changes that were necessary to match her changing bodily shape played into their mother-daughter drama. As Sally lost and gained weight, she complained that nothing fit her, and she used this complaint to justify buying new clothes constantly. In this she identified with her mother in the way the latter dealt with changing weight. But while her mother changed wardrobes only once a season, Sally needed new things constantly. In order to have them she spent much of her weekends shopping. It became her hobby, her passion, and her constant companion when she became a teen.

It became clear in the analysis that Sally was ashamed of the erotic aspect of buying clothing. She punished herself for the pleasure she took in it by depriving herself of the other things she "could have bought" with that money. She understood her shopping as "a release," and expressed it in highly charged language, far more fully realized than her descriptions of any of her sexual encounters with men. "I choose the store. 1 like the ones where they let you sit there and they show you the stuff. I can hardly afford those. They're too expensive. But I get someone to help me in the other kind. I like them to want me to want it. I like to leave them with it. I like it best when it's just a little too expensive, and I can't get it."

Similarly, when the analysis had first started, Sally had reported shopping trips with both her parents that repeated a sadomasochistic pattern extending back to her childhood. She described it as an almost sexual teasing:

When it's my birthday or something, they won't get me a present. But my Mom says I can have a new thing, whatever it is I want. So I go to a store and I find something. Then I go call my Mom and ask her. She won't let me have it. But she says: "Okay. We'll go for a walk on Saturday." My Dad comes on these trips with me sometimes. I hate it when she says "Yes" and he says "No." I hate when they both do it. She says "Yes"; he says "No." He can't stand it, but he's the one who says he wants to get me a present. They make me beg for it.

Sally's struggle of impulses came to a head after a disastrous love affair with what she called "a poor, dirty, low-class man." She became pregnant and had an abortion, which recalled to her attention a prior abortion when she was 16 years old, which she concealed from her mother. When her mother found the pamphlet on contraception Sally had gotten from the abortion clinic, she slapped her daughter and called her a whore. Sally was appalled at this, became very docile, and stopped going to nightclubs. In the ensuing years of her early adulthood she followed her mother's advice on most things, spent much of her leisure time with her mother or with both parents, and called her mother every day, sometimes several times in the course of a single day.

During this period of compliance to and intense contact with her mother, and of suppression of her own desires, shopping together was the main activity they shared. Sally described these outings as teasing glimpses of a world of luxury. Her mother would ask Sally whether she "needed" something to wear. Sally would think of something. They would go to a boutique. Mother would try on clothes, Sally would try on clothes, and each would critique the way the other looked in her outfit. Sally complained that her mother would insist on buying only the highest-priced designer clothing while restricting Sally to lower-priced items. At the same time she would make a paradoxical but oft-repeated remark that Sally found chilling but believed to be true: "Well you will never find a man who can give you as much as I can." This statement touched on Sally's own fantasy that she was her mother's beloved but still worthy only of second-class clothes. The fantasy, we discovered as analysis progressed, had been nourished by her belief, echoed by her mother, that the mother had held her marriage together for her daughter's sake; that she loved her daughter as much as she hated her husband; and that her husband, Sally's father, was a detestable man who contributed nothing to the family. This belief was so strong that Sally had real difficulty remembering that it was her father who earned all the money in the family. Over the seven years of the treatment, Sally sometimes realized this and sometimes did not, in an alternating pattern.

Before the second pregnancy, Sally had been exploring her relationship with her father, and had become aware that all the lower-class, immigrant, and married men she chose, including her current lover, were in the image of her father. By having an abortion, she felt she was renouncing an incestuous baby. This kind of multilayered structure is characteristic of perversion. The overt impulse of the perversion, the "stealing" of love and security from sadistic and controlling parents, was sufficiently scary to distract Sally from her much more horrifying wish for a baby, or at least a close and loving connection, with a sadistic and controlling man. The perversion protected the underlying wish, allowing it to flourish unchallenged while all of Sally's attention went into her embattled relationship with her clothes.

The analytic work on this issue led to a renewed shopping spree, although by then the shopping symptoms had begun to abate. The increase in anxiety that came up with the pregnancy wish required stronger compulsive measures to contain it. At first the spree seemed to me to be a regression or a negative therapeutic reaction. I later came to understand it as a reaction to her new attempt to make restitution for having lived on stolen goods, and to earn for herself a place in what she saw as my world. (She believed that I lived in the world of the adults, those who did not need to depend on others to sustain them.) The shopping spree defended her from depression over her abortion and the emptiness of her life of living out her mother's fantasy of her as mother's "girl." It also served to placate her self-condemnation about the fantasy of being her father's "girl" through identification with him and his power. Even though shopping reminded her that she was not the rich wife, she found it thrilling, because the use of cash reminded her of the power she thought her father had when he paid for things that way. The fantasy was complex, multilayered, and changed with each deepening of the treatment. As the symptom of shopping decreased, the fantasy took one turn; interpreted, it turned protean and became something else.

Sally's mother doled out money to her grudgingly. She treated Sally as her husband treated her, and with a similar result. Sally took money from her mother's purse or bank account whenever she was desperate for cash or wanted luxury items she could not afford on her own allowance when she was not working or even her earnings when she had them. Money became the focal point of her guilt and her anxiety.

Early in her treatment, she had paid me in envelopes of dollar bills. I worried about what this might mean, and I told her to tell her parents that I reported cash as income. She told me that she believed I looked down on them for this. She told me that they habitually bought things that they called "wholesale" or "factory extras," but which were, in reality, stolen goods. They got more than they paid for in many illicit ways and in all of them they had to use cash so there would be no record of the transactions. I really did find that less than admirable and I had to admit it to myself and to her in order to feel comfortable asking her to trust me. Cash thus became a symbol not only of power, but also illicit power. Furthermore it became a way that she could defy what she thought was my prissy moral code and assert her identification with her parents. Yet my assertion of principle did, I believe, act as a comforting limit set on her and on her family. She settled down into treatment after that intervention, stopped missing sessions and coming late for them, and seemed more relaxed.

Over time she stopped buying stolen goods. Since her guilt at having things that were stolen had always made her feel bad about herself, and the only way she could feel better was to have things that she believed made her look good, she had been trapped in a vicious circle. She finally got out of the circle by understanding that the things she wanted to have in order to feel better were exactly the things that made her feel worse. This was not instantaneous: she repeatedly had to go through the experience of having something illegally gotten, feeling disgusted with it, and analyzing why she felt so disgusted. There was no one-time revelatory experience that changed her life, but a series of repeated understandings: each time with another nuance, each time with a bit more memory of previous times, until she finally was able to satisfy herself with something reasonable and wear it with some pleasure.

Her own resources could not provide the luxury items that went with the fantasy that she was a rich lady. She had only the fantasy that her mother's money was hers, a fantasy that echoed her mother's fantasy that the father's money really belonged to her. It turned out that her lack of satisfaction with the items she bought related to this fantasy. To suppress her awareness that the money was not really hers, she had to prove that it was by spending more. Her constant round of spending and becoming dissatisfied with whatever she had bought was both exhausting and saddening. She could not enjoy the fantasy because it was really her mother's money she had spent, and her mother would inevitably taunt her with that fact. Their shopping expeditions and her mother's insistence on buying luxuries for herself while allowing Sally only low-priced clothes reminded Sally that she was not the rich wife, just the little girl who got what the mother did not want. This situation has lasted years into her analysis.

Our work over money and power was tested as we proceeded to work on matters pertaining to the second pregnancy and the renewed sprees that accompanied it. Sally's conflict over her dislike of her father was complicated by her sense that without him she had to remain her mother's "girl" forever. This fear reactivated her need to shop. Eventually, however, these impulses became manageable. Once, she felt an impulse to buy a duplicate of an item her mother had bought for her years before. This time it was from someone who had gotten it when it "fell off a truck." But she was able, to her pleasure, to resist any illicit buying, and she was even able to stop herself from buying something on the grounds that she already had it. This was something she had never been able to do before then.

Sally needed new clothes so often because she believed that her body was ugly. She was able to give up the very frequent shopping when she recognized that new clothes always seemed to offer hope of changing, but did not ever really change the body beneath. Sally's analysis offers an illustration of the generalization that clothes that conceal the body beneath them also take on the body beneath them. Thus patients who hate their own bodies will hate their clothes soon after they buy them.

For Sally the erotic interaction around buying clothes was part of a sadomasochistic character disorder of the sort Arlow (1971) described as a "perverse character." Arlow defined perverse character as the substitute for perverse sexual practices. Sally's perverse character was a perverse expression of her sexuality; that is, it was a way of simultaneously experiencing sexual pleasure outside the realm of actual sexuality, and also of expressing the hate-filled and humiliating aspects of her relationships with the other people involved. In the analysis this interaction became dystonic and she became more aware of how it replaced all other forms of excitement and pleasure for her. It was confused with a mingled longing for and rage at her depriving and teasing father. Her erotic experiences with other men were tainted because they did not want to engage in her shopping and in the teasing, demanding, yielding, and recriminating that had characterized the shopping trips with her parents. Men she encountered did not find this ritual erotic, usually experiencing it as boring or even disgusting. She mourned giving it up even as she understood that it was precluding her pleasure.

The analyzability of perversions has sometimes been questioned on the grounds that in many cases their possessors do not wish to let them go, but this is not always the case. In Sally's case, she was able to establish less convoluted modes of contact, and eventually shopping became a way to relate to other people as she made a career in a retail business.

DISCUSSION

The women discussed in this chapter use clothing for "normal" purposes, but the *seeking* of it became a compulsive symptom for each one of them. They illustrate some of the many kinds of fantasies and motivations that can result from or help form a compulsive shopping symptom. For Annie, shopping was a way of dealing with loss and finding an audience with whom to share her sense of being damaged. Elinor's shopping demonstrated her wish to outmaneuver the intolerable reality of death. For Mary, it was a way to protect valued ties to her parents from her own conflicted ambitions to be an independent woman. Sally's shopping allowed her to displace a pattern of enraging, but exciting, teasing, and frustration away from an incestuous sexual arena to a safer place.

All four women were using the search for clothing to express old needs and wishes of which they were initially unaware, trying to fill in adulthood an emptiness they had been carrying around with them unwittingly since their early years. All of them managed to gain some peace with themselves and some control over their shopping as they became able to recognize and understand their own needs and wishes less fearfully and less judgmentally.

These women wanted more love than they had or could allow themselves to wish for. All used clothing, and shopping for clothing, to express fantasies of loving and being loved by their mothers and/or fathers. Because shopping for clothes is so predominantly a female occupation in our culture, girls of ten experience shopping with their mothers as the sharing of a close and acceptably erotic experience. When there are fantasies about the mother-daughter relationship or the father-daughter relationship that cannot be expressed in words, and particularly when they bear with them frightening aspects of rage and fear, they may be enacted in compulsive, and sometimes "perverse," scenarios. Rather than trying to stop the scenarios, I think that good treatment consists of gaining a conscious understanding of what satisfaction is really being sought in the compulsive behavior, and what can and cannot be satisfied by shopping for clothes. Longings for sensual pleasure, closeness, and intimacy cannot really be satisfied by shopping, and wishes for endless supplies, endless love, and endless dependency cannot be fulfilled by objects bought, so the longings and wishes are better directed toward activities that can satisfy them. When shopping enacts an unconscious fantasy of endless fulfillment, a vicious cycle of disappointment followed by a frantic search for another chance is established. When shopping is a search for something nice to wear well, then the pleasures of shopping can be enjoyed without guilt and shame.

REFERENCES

Arlow, J. (1971). Character perversion. In *Psychoanalysis: Clinical Theory and Practice,* ed. I. Marcus, pp. 177–193. Madison, CT: International Universities Press, 1991.

Bergler, E. (1953). *Fashion and the Unconscious.* New York: Brunner/Mazel.

Bergmann, M. V. (1985). The effect of role reversal on delayed marriage and maternity. *Psychoanalytic Study of the Child,* 40:197–219. New Haven, CT: Yale University Press.

De Lauretis, T. (1994). *The Practice of Love: Lesbian Sexuality and Perverse Desire.* Bloomington, IN: Indiana University Press.

Etchegoyen, H. (1991). *The Fundamentals of Psychoanalytic Technique.* London: Karnac.

Flügel, J. (1930). *The Psychology of Clothes.* London: Hogarth.

Freud, S. (1905). Three essays on the theory of sexuality. *Standard Edition* 7:125–245.

—— (1908). Creative writers and daydreaming. *Standard Edition* 9:143–153.

—— (1920). Beyond the pleasure principle. *Standard Edition* 18:3–65.

Kaplan, L. (1991). *Female Perversions.* Northvale, NJ: Jason Aronson.

Krueger, D. (1988). On compulsive shopping and spending: a psychodynamic inquiry. American *Journal of Psychotherapy* 42(4):574–584.

Lawrence, L. (1990). The psychodynamics of the compulsive female shopper. American Journal of Psychoanalysis 50(1):67–70.

Hollander, A. (1994). Sex and Suits. New York: Knopf.

Neruda, P. (1990). *Selected Odes of Pablo Neruda,* trans. M. Sayers. Berkeley: University of California Press.

Richards, A.K. (1989). A romance with pain: a telephone perversion in a woman? *International Journal of Psycho-Analysis* 70:153–164.

—— (1990). Female fetishes and female perversions: "A case of female foot or more properly boot fetishism" by Hermme Hug-Hellmuth reconsidered." Psychoanalytic Review 77:11–23.

—— (1997). Perverse patients and perverse analysts. *Psychoanalysis and Psychotherapy* 14:145–156.

Rose, L. (1988). Freud and fetishism: previously unpublished minutes of the Vienna Psychoanalytic Society. *Psychoanalytic Quarterly* 57:147–160.

Schwartz, H. (1992). Psychoanalytic psychotherapy for a woman with diagnoses of kleptomania and bulimia. *Hospital and Community Psychiatry* 43:109–110.

Winestine, M. (1985). Compulsive shopping as a derivative of a childhood seduction. *Psychoanalytic Quarterly* 54:70–73

2. Clothes, Inside Out

EVE GOLDEN

In *Seeing through Clothes,* art historian Anne Hollander (1978) says that "all nudes in art since modern fashion began are wearing the ghosts of absent clothes" (p. 86). And not only in art, she points out, since people with no clothes on still hold their bodies as the fashions of the day have taught them to. "Clothes, even when omitted, cannot be escaped" (p. 87).

The development of dress was a great cultural achievement. Like cooking, clothing is a crude necessity that we have transformed into expressive art. But, again like cooking, it has shaped us as irrevocably as we shaped it. Eating is more than a simple response to hunger, and clothing ourselves has long been much more than a simple response to cold or sun. It is more even than a way to "express ourselves," honestly or not, to other people. It is a deep reservoir of accumulated cultural, social, and personal meaning. Anyone who doubts this, or thinks clothing a trivial concern among our many loftier ones, can turn for pleasure and enlightenment to Thomas Carlyle's 1833 novel *Sartor Resartus* (that is, *the tailor retailored*). This satirical "spiritual biography," constructed metaphorically upon a Philosophy (the capitals are Carlyle's) of Clothes, is a bravura demonstration of the symbolic richness of clothing, and of the depth and pervasiveness of the psychological experience of Dress.

I want to examine that experience as we live it in our own postindustrial Western society, and to offer some ideas about how clothes work on us and in us. I will point to important references in other fields where they seem appropriate, so that they may compensate for necessary omissions and facilitate further exploration. Finally, I will consider some possible links between clothing and obsessional symptomatology. My topic is clothing as concept—the *idea* of clothes—as distinct from the particulars of what any person chooses to wear. By definition, fashion is ever-changing. But although dress varies, "clothes" are a physical and psychological constant, stable and relatively independent of style.

HISTORICAL VIEWS

The origins, forms, and purposes of clothes have preoccupied people for centuries. The first two categories I leave to more expert commentators (for example Hawes 1942, Hollander 1978, and Laver 1969). The third has not always been handled with much psychological sophistication, and the resulting explanations are mostly too general to be satisfying. Still, a few have been important or useful enough to warrant mention.

Until the mid-nineteenth century, for example, literal and figurative interpretations of Genesis enshrined modesty as the primary "reason" for clothes. James Laver (1969), an eminent British historian of fashion, defines *modesty* as "the enemy ... of Swagger and Seduction" (p. 13), noting dryly that moralists have tended to be alert for offenses against the latter sin in women, and the former in men. Victorian commentators spoke of hygiene as the fundamental concern; this austere assumption of restrained healthfulness is the one that was politically correct when Freud came along.

J. C. Flügel (1930) was the first psychoanalytic thinker to attempt a systematic study of dress. He concluded that its purposes were *decoration, modesty*, and *protection,* and his investigation of the complex and ambivalent interrelationships between these three desiderata was influential in its time and still attracts interest. Laver too proposed three "principles" of clothes: *utility, hierarchy* (or *dominance*), and *seduction.* As Hollander (1994) puts it: "We put on clothing for some of the same reasons that we speak: to make living and working easier and more comfortable, to proclaim (or disguise) our identities and to attract erotic attention" (p. 27). This last, the seduction theory of clothing, remains popular, although some follow Laver in the belief that women have traditionally dressed for seduction and men for dominance, because those reflect their respective chief values as mates. More recent theoreticians of clothing, however, Hollander and fashion historian Valerie Steele among them, have challenged the seduction theory altogether. Hollander thinks that dress is governed by the same rules that govern the other visual—in other words, that clothes are primarily a way of experiencing form. Steele, in her 1985 *Fashion and Eroticism,* takes a parallel but more psychological approach, believing that people strive in their dress less for seduction than for beauty.

CLOTHING AS INTERFACE

For psychologists, explanations like these oversimplify the complex motivations and awarenesses that exist in real people. They also fail to address the essential fact that clothing—"so different from flesh but so necessary to it" (Hollander 1994, p. 85)—doesn't just reflect our psychology. It forms it. It influences how we see ourselves, and as the interface between ourselves and the not-self world it is not passive. It is an active membrane that regulates what we allow in and out.

Concretely, for instance, a fur coat is a device for keeping body heat in and wind and cold out. It covers up our sexual parts. It pleases the touch with its softness and the eye with its beauty. Psychologically, however, the coat serves far more intricate purposes, and they will be different for different people. For one owner, mink may contain the insecurities of an impoverished childhood and ensure respect. For another it may be an instrument of intimidation. A timid person may feel that fur attracts (lets in) too much anger, or displays (lets out) too much arrogance, and therefore may choose not to wear it at all. But a person who isn't conflict-averse and thinks that any attention is better than none will flaunt the coat and let the devil take the hindmost.

Clothing figures prominently in the vocabulary of images that we use to think of and speak to ourselves. When we are picturing ourselves as healthy, businesslike, or sexy, or as mother, or lover, or violinist, we likely distinguish each of these versions of "me" from all the others by

277

the way we dress its image. Clothing is intimately associated with every aspect of our lives, including (perhaps especially) the ones where we take it off. It therefore carries great symbolic and metaphoric weight.

This is intensified by a paradoxical quality in clothing that runs very deep. Clothes are elective, in that we choose what we wear. But they are also compulsory, in that we have to wear *something*. Clothes are concrete physical things, yet endlessly plastic in their psychological uses. Above all, although clothing never becomes materially part of us the way food does, we know ourselves to be incomplete without it. We feel ourselves so strongly as dressed beings that the moments when we don't wear clothes are the ones when we are most aware of them. We don't yet have a study of how this comes to pass in children, but we all know that it does. So when a friend of mine objects: How about nudists?, I answer that nudists know better than anyone the depth of the convention they challenge. The decision to undress in front of another person, for whatever reason, is a momentous one.

Thus clothing functions psychologically both as artifact and as idea. As artifact—that is, in its material form as garment—it protects and delineates. As idea, it symbolizes and expresses our representations of ourselves and serves, like all ideas, as the raw material for art and imagination. We wear the thing, but the idea structures our thinking.

THE TRANSITIONAL NATURE OF CLOTHES

Clothing differs from most of our other contrivances in that we experience it as self and not-self—always, and at the same time. Some people feel their clothing as more intimately a part of themselves than their own dreams and fantasies; the rest of us notice that even in our dreams and fantasies we are almost always dressed. This built-in ambiguity makes clothing an elegant device for modulating the tensions between us and the "outside" world. Separation and merger, inclusion and exclusion, conformity and individuality, closeness and distance, concealment and display, truth and fiction: clothing helps us keep these adjusted to tolerable levels.

Because of this curious self/not-self status, the psychological home of clothing is neither the inner nor the outer world, but what Winnicott

(1971) called the potential space: "the area of experiencing, to which inner reality and external life both contribute" (p. 2). In this, clothes have much in common with the transitional phenomena of infancy, in which use is made of "objects that are not part of the infant's body yet are not fully recognized as belonging to the external world" (Winnicott 1958, p. 230). Like teddy bears and security blankets, our clothes protect us from the full impact of a frustrating environment, and in various ways increase our capacity to take care of ourselves. Also like bears and blankets, they have no psychological value (however elegant they may look on the model) until we have chosen them as our own, and endowed them with meaning and power.

Consider this curious statement from the 1959 *World Book Encyclopedia,* a reference authority with which I and many other children of my generation grew up. Although other land animals depend on body hair to keep them warm, the *World Book* says, people "do not need hair because we wear clothes. Neither do whales because they have blubber" (p. 8729). This is a vivid, if befuddled, demonstration of how deeply we feel clothing as intrinsic, and how uneasily we balance it between what is self and what is not. It also shows why the question Winnicott (1971) raised about transitional objects—"Did you conceive of this or was it presented to you from without?" (p. 12)—is the question that must drive any psychological study of clothes.

I emphasize this because transitional phenomena (the abstract kind as well as the stuffed ones) are so important in developing our capacity to reflect upon, rather than just undergo, internal and external experience. To be able to reflect, one must be able to imagine, and then retain the imagination of, experience in symbolic form. Ultimately, the confidence that one can reflect upon and contain what one feels allows risk-taking in the object world. But that confidence requires us to be able to recognize and tolerate the separateness of self and other, thought and reality, inside and out—and so does imagination.

Transitional objects are one means by which a baby explores (some say "denies" [Muensterberger 1994, p. 3], but I think it is not only that) these elements of separation. He allocates comforting not-me attributes to an object that he can control, and this allows him to experiment with not-me-ness more safely than he could with an independent other person. Winnicott's (1958, 1971) eloquence on this matter is built deeply into the thinking of most psychotherapists. Clothes resemble babies' blankets in that they too are half-discovered and half-created: that is, the physical garment is already there, but it has no psychological potency until its wearer invests (a clothing metaphor) meaning in it. Once meaning is invested, though, a garment has great potential as a more or less permanent transitional object. It is always available (unlike a teddy bear, it need never be "outgrown"), and society actively encourages us to use such things to reinforce and extend our sense of ourselves. The advertising world is an inexhaustible source of illustrations of this encouragement, but I'll limit myself to one example: an ad for men's underwear that declares: "Family jewels shouldn't be housed in a slum" (http://adsoftheworld.com/media/print/bonds_slum).

The psychological importance of clothing is invented by individual wearers in the service of safe exploration of the self and not-self worlds. When courage is lacking for any reason, clothes may be enlisted to try to compensate for it (see Muensterberger 1994). It is convenient to talk about the external and internal manifestations of what clothes "mean." But however they manifest themselves superficially (in cotton, in fantasy, in art), their psychological roots are always in the area of transition between the "me" and the "not-me."

CLOTHING AND BOUNDARIES

Clothes in the outer world delineate and maintain boundaries: bodily ones for physical protection and psychic ones for safety in relationship. "Hast thou always worn [clothes] perforce," asks Carlyle, "and as a consequence of Man's Fall; never rejoiced in them as in a warm movable house, a Body round thy Body, wherein that strange THEE of thine sat snug, defying all variations of Climate?" (1833, Book I, chapter ix). Many students of fashion dismiss physical protection as a matter of no importance, believing that such primitive functions have long since been superseded by more sophisticated ones. But psychologists know that primitiveness is no guarantee of irrelevance—quite the contrary— and that the persistence of archaic needs is a testament to their strength.

A clinical example: A young woman who feared and dreaded winter stayed inside as much as possible, isolated and depressed, as soon as it began to get cold. Her mother had preached a moralistic and idealized asceticism, and had discouraged the daughter's attempts at self-soothing, which she considered regressive. The daughter grew up expecting herself to be unflinchingly self-reliant, and knew that she succeeded poorly in this. As she worked in analysis she became aware that she was acting out her guilt over, and anger at, impossibly harsh standards by failing to dress appropriately for the weather. Chattering teeth and blue lips exposed her mother's demands as unrealistic and cruel. At the same time, her cowardice in avoiding the cold, and her suffering when out in it, provided both the reasons and the means to punish herself for her weakness and her rage. When she finally began to challenge her unattainable standards, she acquired a warm coat and boots that didn't leak, and winter began to lose its terrors. But it was the symptomatic denial of her need to keep warm that provided the clue to deeper problems of separation. Hollander (1994) says correctly that it is Nature herself who "ordains that human beings be completed by clothing, not left bare in their own insufficient skins" (p. 5).

However carefully we choose our clothes, we can't choose not to wear them. Remember Hobbes the tiger's outburst when Calvin wonders why people are never content with what they have. "Are you kidding?" cries Hobbes. "Your fingernails are a joke, you've got no fangs, you can't see at night, your pink hides are ridiculous, your reflexes are nil, and you don't even have tails! Of course people aren't content! Now if *tigers* weren't content, that would be something to wonder about" (Watterson 1966, p. 157). From the superior vantage point of his tigerhood, Hobbes has no problem recognizing what we usually deny—that we want because we don't have. Our skins, whatever their color, are so insufficient that we are driven to supplement them. Our attention to what we wear distracts us from the humiliating knowledge that in a world of poison ivy, wind chill, ultraviolet, and yellow jackets we alone among animals must wear *something*. The lack of distinction between blubber and clothing in the *World Book* quotation above illustrates this denial perfectly.

Clothes provide nonphysical protections, too. The lover's sweater, the mirrored shades, and the talismanic "power suit" provide a psychological safety that we all understand. Then there are the more potent kinds of sartorial magic (Lurie 1981). Seven-league boots and cloaks of invisibility may be in short supply, but basketball great Michael Jordan was famous for never playing a game without his lucky shorts. And Elizabeth Hawes, a game-changing dress designer of the 1930's and 40's, thought that we use clothes to protect ourselves against "what we conceive to be moral danger" (1942, p. 38)—perhaps the danger of too much exhibitionism. This is not to say that we don't exhibit ourselves even as we hide—in translucent negli-gées, for example, or the short face veils of the '40s; clothing is *nonpareil* at that sort of paradox. But whatever the threat may be, our clothes demon-strate our vulnerability even as they remediate it. And they do so tactfully, never confronting us with Winnicott's numinous question about whether the protective power lies in us or in them.

Clothes and groups. Along with the boundaries between inside and out, clothes also delineate boundaries among and within groups, and among and within individuals. They are very effective in this, allowing quick, broad identifications from a great distance, and very fine ones from closer in. Consider the information, large-scale and small, con-veyed by army uniforms. They distinguish among groups (American *vs.* British *vs.* French soldiers, for example), and among the ranks those groups encompass. They integrate (a group of American officers) and differentiate (the British lieutenant among them) the individuals within them, all at the same time. This is no minor matter; we place great reliance on such information. That is why we condemn an enemy who attacks us in his own guise much less harshly than we do one who disguises (that is, dresses) himself to conform with a group not his own in order to attack it from within. The former is an adversary who may still be treated with honor; the other is a traitor or spy.

The gate-keeping aspects of clothing are easy to see, especially among groups of kids where an uncool brand of sneakers or the wrong prom dress may spell ostracism and catastrophe. Conversely, any person who doubts his welcome in a desired group may turn to clothes to prove that he belongs and to hide that he doesn't. The Duchess of Windsor (1956), by her own account a compulsive clothes buyer, seems to have operated like this. Cultural anthropologist Ted Polhemus's *Street Style* (1994) is a wonderful guide to the group—*styletribe*, he calls it—dynamics of clothes. Polhemus traces the rise and fall of urban cultural groups through the development of their garb, documenting their lifecycles in clothing. The photographs are a treasure trove for anyone interested in clothing as communicative display.

What an individual does with his group's basic uniform provides still more information. Hollander points out that clothes address simultaneously the need to belong and the need to be separate. They help us balance, in our different ways, the safety of conformity with the risks and pleasures of individual notice. In *Gone with the Wind*, Scarlett defies the fashion rules of her society to make sure she is seen; the elegance of Robillard's mother transcends the conformity Scarlett fears even as she and her peers dictate the rules with which others (including her daughter) are expected to comply. Scarlett's father Gerald tries to conform but never quite can, which his friends find delightful and his wife contemptible. Melanie, a shy traditionalist, sincerely values conformity, but her brother Charles conforms because he hasn't the imagination to do anything else. Ashley can imagine, but not act. Hollander (1994) reminds us that "the social laws that govern choice in fashion are both unwritten and slippery, and wearing the right thing requires the right instinct and judgment instead of plain obedience to the rules of custom" (p. 20). The green silk bonnet that Scarlett does not dye black is the first real step toward her rejection by "genteel" Atlanta; it proves that she is not truly one of the group, however expert her disguise.

Clothes and distance. Endless variations of this kind show how sensitively dress reflects fine degrees of merger and separation. It also reflects, and sometimes enforces, distance. Concretely, our clothes interpose layers of matter between us and other people (rubber gloves and johnnies in the examining room); metaphorically, they send signals (the flannel nightgown instead of the silk one). Above all, they give us alternative sets of boundaries that we can take up and put aside as we need them, in most cases so automatically that we never even have to notice that we are enlisting auxiliary troops. Thus the legend about Frank Sinatra, who is said to have snapped "Hands off the threads, creep!" when then-Speaker of the House Sam Rayburn put an arm around his shoulder at the 1956 Democratic National convention (Page 1998). Ordinarily we say, "Don't touch me," or "Keep your hands to yourself." Sinatra's extreme, if apocryphal, verbal separation of himself from his clothes apparently gave him the sense of extra space that he (or the threads) needed right then.

Biographer Marian Fowler offers detailed studies of five great dressers in her intriguing but disappointingly documented work of "fashion biography," *The Way She Looks Tonight* (1996). One of these is Jacqueline Kennedy Onassis, whose use of clothing Fowler sees as an incomparably successful device for regulating distance. Fowler believes that Onassis developed for herself a style of dress so perfectly tailored (another clothing metaphor—they are extremely common) to her needs that, by itself, it managed to garner for her both the notice she craved and the distance she needed. It riveted the attention of others on her clothes and away from herself in a kind of sartorial bait-and-switch.

Fowler points out that in her clothing Onassis combined impersonal drama with the obscuring of personal cues. She concealed her eyes, for example, with veils and sunglasses, and the lines of her body with stiff fabrics—what Hawes (1942) called "hiding behind clothes." This balance bound so much anxiety, if Fowler's sources can be believed, that Jackie preferred acquiring clothes to wearing them, and was driven to near disgrace by smuggling Paris originals into the White House when she was supposed to be wearing only American-made clothes. ("'Jesus, Jackie,' yelled Jack. 'The New Frontier is going to be sabotaged by a bunch of goddamned French couturiers!'" [p. 257]). In contrast with Marlene Dietrich's "generous desire to fully gratify, or even satiate, the eye," Fowler understands Jackie's clothing as austere and unwelcoming, as if to say: "Look at me! But don't get too close" (p. 276).

CONCEALMENT AND REVELATION

After the need to fit in, which we take so much for granted that we're usually not much aware of it, comes the matter of how we are seen. Manipulations of distance tend to be unconscious, but we think consciously about showing and hiding, pride and shame, truth and disguise. (Of course, we also don't think about them. Both show in our dress). This dialectic, including as it does the great sexual tension between the wish to expose and the wish to hide, is the aspect of clothing that until recently has most exercised psychoanalysts and historians, and is therefore the one that has accumulated the wildest collection of interpretations— shoes as female genitalia, shoes as phallus, shoes as both, and so on (Freud 1920, p. 129; 1927, pp. 152-157).

The main thing about exposure and concealment in clothes is that it's hard to tell them apart. The fig leaf is a fitting symbol because, as has often been pointed out, it draws attention to the genitalia by the very act of covering them. Clothing always hides, and it always reveals — frequently the same things, and always at the same time. To reveal one thing is to conceal another, and vice versa. Layers of dissimulation lie (and lie!) beneath the surface of any array of "manifest clothes."

Just as psychoanalytic theory gradually and fruitfully extended concrete early observations about sexuality to include more abstract aspects of desire and need, we can extend the fig-leaf metaphor beyond the actual sexual organs to the body and then to the self. This makes the ambiguous connection between hidden and exposed even more acute, and not only in the sexual arena.

Flügel (1930) comments epigrammatically that "the very word 'personality' . . . implies a 'mask (persona=mask)' which is itself an article of clothing" (p. 16). When the boundaries between personality and clothes are so fluid, how can we know which characteristics belong to the clothes and which to the person? It is the baby's use of a blanket for soothing, not the blanket itself, that ultimately effects the change in his psychic structure. But for the baby who has attributed power to a particular blanket, that blanket has to be there for the change to happen. When a scared medical intern derives confidence from his first white jacket, his use of it changes him. Where, in those first weeks, does his confidence reside? Not in himself, not in the jacket, but in his use of the jacket. Did he conceive of that jacket? Was it presented to him from without? Either way, the use of clothing as talisman is very common and may be an aspect of compulsive clothes-seeking.

Flügel (1930) points out another paradox: "When we wear a mask, we cease, to some extent, to be ourselves; we conceal from others both our identity and the natural expression of our emotions, and, in consequence, we do not feel the same responsibility as when our faces are uncovered . . . The masked person is, therefore, apt to be freer and less inhibited . . . and can do things from which he might otherwise be impeded by fear or shame" (p. 51). So when we are masked, says Flügel, we are both more and less ourselves. And we are *fully* ourselves only when masked.

Obviously "mask" is a metaphor for clothing. Garments not only cover us; they also provide alternate façades with readable meanings of their own (Lurie 1981; see also extended examples in Fowler 1996). The disguise may not necessarily be known to its wearer. Hollander (1994) quips that "the famous messages of dress, the well-known language of clothes, is very often not doing any communicating at all; a good deal of it is a form of private muttering" (p. 189). My mother once observed that the common experience of buying something and then finding it so "not right" as to be unwearable shows not only how intimately we identify with our removable skin, but also how our interactions with it instruct us about our internal selves. And who among us has not had experiences, at times when we felt estranged from ourselves, of shopping frantically and unsuccessfully for some necessary (or not) garment, hoping that in the process we'd learn to recognize ourselves again?

A great deal has been made of the disingenuous aspects of dress. But most of us know from experience—sometimes to our relief, and sometimes to our dismay (see Richards 2000, for example)—how limited in fact are the powers of clothes to transform. Even while they conceal, they must reveal. In any case, clothes are not primarily aimed at the outside world. "Clothes cannot be altogether dramatic or theatrical because people are not always acting or performing, even though they are always appearing. It is the inner theater that is costumed by the choice in clothes, and this is not always under conscious management. The public may not always be intended, much less able, to get the picture" (Hollander 1978, p. 451). Hawes (1954) addresses the same question with her usual hardheaded practicality: "You, too, can learn to use your dressing for play-acting, but in my opinion it gets to be a bore" (p. 199).

CLOTHES AND SEXUALITY

Theoreticians seem to agree that there is something intrinsically sexual in the experience of *wearing* clothes. This can be allowed, I think, even if one rejects the reductionism of the clothes-as-seduction theory, about which more in a moment. Steele (1985) says simply that "because clothing is so intimately associated with the physical body, at the deepest level all clothing is erotic" (p. 9). Hollander (1994) concurs: "Clothes address the personal self first of all, and only afterwards the world" (p. 6). The autoerotic, not the seductive, aspects of clothing are the deeper ones. Anti-theoretician Hawes (1954) takes this as a matter of course. "There is, of course, plenty of pleasure to be derived from looking decorative in the bedroom even if no one else is about. I doubt if even those psychologists who dub this kind of pleasure narcissistic and, in their opinions, bad, would deny that the pleasure of finding one's self pleasing to look at is real" (p. 24). (Hawes is alone in reliably distinguishing between dressing to attract and dressing for display, while Steele reliably distinguishes between the desire for beauty and sexual desire.)

The seduction, or attraction, theory of clothes is usually attributed to Flügel, whose work has a great deal of charm. It is dated by its very early Freudian point of view, but Flügel himself was considerably more subtle a thinker than he has sometimes appeared in the interpretations of psychologically inexpert followers. He knew ambivalence to be a weighing of risks, not a simple power struggle. And he didn't consider the choice of clothing the passive fallout of psychic unrest, but rather an active contribution that we make in our efforts to resolve it: "an ingenious device for the establishment of some degree of harmony between conflicting interests" (p. 20). He understood very well that modesty and exhibitionism transcend sexuality, and he believed that the autoerotic aspects of clothing are rooted in a confusion of the sense of self with the physical object.

So we can extend the fig-leaf metaphor yet another degree. Steele (1985) paraphrases Flügel: "The unconscious conflict between exhibitionism and modesty is displaced from the naked body onto clothing, which then functions as a 'compromise,' since it both covers the body and attracts attention to it" (p. 25). This same conflict holds true in all areas where exhibitionism and modesty coexist: the social, the artistic, the intellectual—in short, wherever people maintain narcissistic investment in themselves. And in these areas, too, clothing can function as a compromise; people who feel narcissistically deficient, for instance, may seek garments that make good the lack, relying on them at once for proud display and for the concealment of shame.

A last comment on this: clothing is erotic in part because it arouses curiosity. This is an inevitable result of the conceal-and-reveal counterpoise. In fact, some people consider fashion essentially a device for nurturing curiosity, as endless change constantly restores the jaded eye and causes it to look again, keeping interest and engagement high. Hollander (1994) says: "One basic modern need is to escape the feeling that desire has gone stale. Fashion therefore depends on managing the maintenance of desire, which must be satisfied, but never for too long" (p. 49). Steele's (1985) book *Fashion and Eroticism* is an intricate and extensive study of this subject, so I will leave further commentary to her, and turn from the internal reflections of external clothes to the outward manifestations of clothing-as-idea.

CLOTHES AS CONCEPT

Clothes-the-idea is an imaginative enrichment of the conception of the self, as Carlyle amply demonstrates. In most of our experience of life we are clothed; the concept of clothing seems to be nearly inseparable from the concept of self in the representational machinery of the mind by which we picture ourselves in our own thoughts. Making images of ourselves—imagination—has two primary uses: to portray ourselves to ourselves (unconsciously in psychic structure, for instance, and consciously in fantasy); and to portray ourselves to others (for instance in art). But what counts as "ourselves"? That is not an easy question to answer.

INTERNAL REPRESENTATIONS: SELFOBJECT FUNCTIONS

Kohut (1971, 1977), described how infants depend on other people for the restoration of narcissistic equilibrium, the elusive state of psychological well-being that we all desire but lose too easily under stress. He called the internal representations of such restorative experiences archaic or transitional selfobjects, and he considered them precursors of psychic structure. His idea of selfobject experience shares three characteristics with Winnicott's idea of transitional phenomena: they are efforts to maintain psychic equilibrium; they are temporary functional fusions of the self with an object not fully differentiated from it; and they require the child's investment of his own psychic powers in the object. In both cases, the result is not a relationship with an object, but a strengthening of the experience and boundaries of the self.

Non-infants use related techniques for pulling themselves together when they fall apart (restoring the cohesiveness of the fragmented self, as Kohut calls it). But as we mature we tend to seek out nonhuman sources of selfobject functions, among other reasons because they are convenient and because we can control them. Food and sleep are commonly used in this way, and I wish I could remember who once wrote about hot baths as selfobject phenomena. Any sufficiently steadying and reorganizing experience (gardening, running, shopping, listening to music) can serve, and all people establish preferred techniques; the need for selfobjects is common to everyone and not pathological in itself. But when narcissistic vulnerability is especially great, the need for restoration is more frequent and feels more desperate. Very vulnerable people may therefore seek selfobject support from things, which are safe and predictable, rather than from people or experiences, which may not be. Muensterberger (1994; 2000) addresses this theme specifically.

Clothes by their nature possess extremely powerful, near-universal selfobject potential. Although we keep the *idea* of clothing very close to the idea of self, actual clothes themselves are not vulnerable to the psychic fragmentation that selves undergo; as concrete matter they possess a semi-permanent cohesiveness that the self in need can draw upon. How much we *do* draw upon it becomes apparent when their permanence fails and those favorite jeans finally get beyond mending. When we feel fragmented enough, we too "come apart at the seams." In a beloved hymn, the poet John Greenleaf Whittier entreated God to "reclothe us in our rightful minds," another exquisite illustration of the metaphor of clothing-as-cohesive-self. A third variation on the theme is the frequently cited (but provenance contested) aphorism that "the consciousness of being perfectly well dressed may bestow a peace such as religion cannot give." My own clinical experience leads me to think that many clothes-related symptoms are best understood as extensive dependency on clothing as selfobject. Krueger (2000) and Muensterberger (2000) have much more to say on this subject.

INTERNAL REPRESENTATIONS: FANTASY

The same conflation of idea-of-self with idea-of-clothing means that clothing appears in almost all of our fantasies and dreams. People in them are conceived to be dressed. Even though the conceptual presence of clothing is not always worthy of note or recollection, our reaction to its absence demonstrates how powerful that presence is. The rarity of dreams of nakedness, and the dismay and mortification that they occasion, betray how strongly we feel our inner selves as clothed. And because clothing is conceptually present in all our experiences (including—probably especially—the ones for which we take it off), it has associative attachments to everything in our lives.

This is remarkable. Try to think of any single other not-self element, however important, that is present explicitly or implicitly in virtually all encounters, virtually all activities, virtually all locales, virtually all fantasies. I can't. Richards (2000) further demonstrates the flexibility and vitality of clothing as symbol and metaphor in fantasy.

The fundamental psychological "fact" of clothing, therefore, is that in Western culture, clothes and the representation of the self can never be definitively separated. Like language, its only rival in this, clothing is an ever-present lens through which we see ourselves: more, it is a device by which we learn to see ourselves in the first place. Clothes and self form each other in an invisible and eternal spiral. "In human life the dressed

290

state, though it may be a lower condition than theoretical ideal nudity, is also the best emblem of corporeal existence . . . Clothes stand for knowledge and language, art and love, time and death—the creative, struggling state of man" (Hollander 1978, p. 448).

EXTERNAL REPRESENTATIONS: CLOTHES AND ART

Elizabeth Hawes, the radical designer and fashion critic, wrote a series of perceptive books on the relationships of people (both sexes—she really was a radical, and got into serious trouble with the FBI during the McCarthy years) with their clothes. She was a tough-minded pragmatist as well as an artist in clothing, and she had a rude but canny grasp of psychology where it intersected with her own medium.

Hawes thought that most people get little pleasure and a lot of grief from their clothes. Influenced by Flügel's psychoanalytic theories, but possessed of a practical understanding of clothing-as-artifact that he didn't have, she tried to bring the notion of what clothes "mean" down to earth. She considered the act of dressing a route to self-awareness, and she agreed with Carlyle that "the beginning of all Wisdom is to look fixedly on Clothes . . . till they become transparent" (1833, Book I, chapter x)—an ambiguous statement if ever there was one. She concluded that the confusion of boundary between self and other is what clothes and art have in common; for more on this, Hollander's *Seeing through Clothes* is an admirable and exhaustive study of the relationship of clothes to the other visual arts.

One further twist in the helical relationship between ourselves and our clothes, and, incidentally, a confirmation of Hawes's idea, is illustrated in a passage from *The Seduction of the Minotaur,* by Anaïs Nin (1961):

She no longer sat before an easel, but before a dressing table . . . Sometimes her dress seemed painted with large brushstrokes, sometimes roughly dyed like the costumes of the poor. Other times she wore what looked like fragments of ancient Mayan murals, bold symmetrical designs in charcoal outlines with the colors dissolved by age. Heavy earrings of Aztec warriors, necklaces and bracelets of shell, gold and silver medallions . . . all these caught the light as she moved. It was her extreme liveliness that may have prevented her from working upon a painting, and turned a passion for color and textures upon her own body (p. 33).

There are real people for whom, as for Nin's imaginary woman, getting dressed is an act of deliberate personal art. Fowler provides extended studies of several of these (in this context see especially the chapter on Marlene Dietrich). Both Nin and Fowler, I think, validate Hawes, and illustrate Hollander's provocative statement that mirrors let us see the self as a picture. Valerie Steele, who tends to be more interested than Hollander in the experienced (as opposed to the perceived) meaning of clothes, notes that the eyes as well as the skin are a primary erogenous zone. The experience of seeing the self as a picture adds yet another dimension to the endless interplay between self and not-self that is clothing's special dynamic.

Whether we do it deliberately or not, we are constantly making what Hollander calls visual fictions of ourselves. Every time we get dressed we create images that represent us to the outside world and to ourselves, reflecting our existing inner representations and informing new ones in an infinitely recursive process. The wearing of clothing both demonstrates and undermines the truth of ourselves as we know it, and at the same time it constructs new fictions and new truths that can be used internally as self-knowledge or externally as art.

CONCLUSION: CLOTHES AND COMPULSION

Why are clothes, like food, gambling, and drugs, such a common object of obsession? Certainly they are fascinating and attractive, and one way or another they address a wide variety of human needs. Still, most clothes-loving people are not compulsive, and when they are, the causes of their compulsiveness—poor affect tolerance, narcissistic depletion, and so on—generally have little to do with clothing *per se*. This raises questions: Under what conditions does an ordinary interest in clothes become compulsive? And what is it about clothes that makes them such a potent magnet when compulsions do arise?

I think the answer lies in their transitional nature. Winnicott (1971) believed that the use of the "potential space" between self and other evolved with maturation away from magical thinking and toward the purely symbolic. As the boundaries of the self strengthen, the "space" retains the uniqueness of its intermediary position, but it becomes increasingly the venue of what he called "play," the symbolic ideation that allows us to see and reflect upon inner experience and to act with awareness in the outside world.

When symbolic capacity is limited for any reason, concrete modes of thought may be enlisted to contain anxiety. Clothes lend themselves to compulsive scenarios because of their metaphoric richness, their unsurpassed selfobject potential, and their conceptual location in the same transitional area that harbors magical thinking and its vicissitudes. In addition, they can substitute concretely, at least to some degree, for unreliable internal resources—provide a look of self-confidence, for instance, for a person who cannot feel it—and so they offer a kind of tempting transitional mimicry when the need arises. (See also Muensterberger 1994 for an extensive study of acquisition and transitional phenomena, and Barth 2000.)

In short, both compulsions and clothing enable the outward staging of interior dramas. Compulsions are external reflections of pressing inner needs and conflicts, while clothes, as Hollander (1978) has said, "give a visual aspect to consciousness itself. . . . They produce its look as seen from within" (p. 451). They are natural partners when complex feelings cannot be contained internally and spill over into action. When we can't see ourselves in our imaginations, we turn to clothes to show us ourselves. That's what they do.

REFERENCES

Barth, F. D. (2000). When Eating and Shopping are Companion Disorders, in A.L. Benson. (Ed.). *I Shop Therefore I Am: Compulsive Buying and the Search for Self* (pp. 268–287). New York: Jason Aronson.
Carlyle, T. (1833). *Sartor Resartus.* New York: Holt.
Flügel, J. C. (1930). *The Psychology of Clothes.* London: Hogarth.
Fowler, M. (1996). The Way She Looks Tonight. New York: St Martins Press.

Freud, S. (1920). *A General Introduction to Psychoanalysis,* tr. G. Stanley Hall. New York: Horace Liveright.

Freud, S. (1927). Fetishism. *The Standard Edition of the Complete Psychological Works of Sigmund Freud,* tr. J. Strachey, v. XXI. London: Hogarth, pp. 152-157.

Hawes, E. (1942). *Why Is a Dress?* New York: Viking. (1954). *It's Still Spinach.* Boston: Little, Brown.

Hollander, A. (1978). *Seeing through Clothes.* New York: Viking. (1994). *Sex and Suits.* New York: Knopf.

Kohut, H. (1971). *The Analysis of the Self.* New York: International Universities Press. (1977). *The Restoration of the Self.* New York: International Universities Press.

Krueger, D.W. (2000). The Use of Money as an Action Symptom, in *I Shop Therefore I Am: Compulsive Buying and the Search for Self,* ed. A.L Benson. New York: Jason Aronson, pp. 288–310.

Laver, J. (1969). *Modesty in Dress.* Boston: Houghton Mifflin.

Lurie, A. (1981). *The Language of Clothes.* New York: Random House.

Muensterberger, W. (1994). *Collecting: An Unruly Passion.* Princeton, NJ: Princeton University Press.

Muensterberger, W. (2000). Collecting as Reparation, in *I Shop Therefore I Am: Compulsive Buying and the Search for Self,* ed. A. L. Benson. New York: Jason Aronson, pp. 157–167.

Nin, A. (1961). *The Seduction of the Minotaur.* Chicago: Swallow Press.

Page, T. (1998). *The Washington Post,* May 16, 1998; p. D01.

Polhemus, T. (1994). *StreetStyle.* New York: Thames & Hudson.

Richards, A. (2000). Clothes and the Couch, in *I Shop Therefore I Am: Compulsive Buying and the Search for Self,* A.L. Benson, ed. New York: Jason Aronson, pp. 311–337.

Steele, V. (1985). *Fashion and Eroticism.* New York: Oxford University Press. (1996). *Fetish.* New York: Oxford University Press.

Watterson, B. (1966). *There's Treasure Everywhere: A Calvin and Hobbes Collection.* Kansas City, MO: Andrews and McMeel.

Windsor, W. (1956). *The Heart Has Its Reasons: The Memoirs of the Duchess of Windsor.* New York: David McKay.

Winnicott, D. W. (1958). *Through Paediatrics to Psycho-Analysis.* London: Tavistock. (1971). *Playing and Reality.* London: Tavistock.

World Book Encyclopedia (1959). Chicago: Field Enterprises Educational Corporation.

VI

*Conversation with
Simon Doonan*

What is the first dress you remember your mother wearing?
My mother was very into tight pencil skirts and fitted blouses. She always wore seamed stockings and high heels. Her hair-do was a hangover from the 1940's, upswept like Bette Davis in 'Now Voyager'

Did you like it?
When I was very young I was embarrassed by my mum's vampy appearance. All the other mums in the street looked like QE 2, and my mum was determined to be different. BY the time I was a teen I was digging the fact that she was unconventional.

Vivienne Westwood said, "People who wear impressive clothes have better lives." This was very true of my mother.

She benefited enormously from her sartorial efforts. She talked her way into jobs and situations which might otherwise have been out of her reach.

Clothing is nonverbal communication, and her stylish clothing communicated confidence and optimism both of which served her well.

What is the first outfit you remember wearing? How has that affected your taste now?
I recall being obsessed with flowery shirts. I saw them on swinging dandies like Mick Jagger and Jeff Beck and became obsessed. I still wear flowery shirts.

How are men's fashions and women's fashions related?
Men are more likely to adopt some kind of uniform. Even stylish men often have a formulaic approach to dressing. Women look to clothing to

299

fill emotional voids and fulfill dreams. For women there is a strong element of fantasy and emotion. In recent years there has been a boom in the men's designer clothing business. I would not be surprised if some of these men's designer shoppers were to adopt more complicated emotional attitudes towards their clothing.

How did you react to how other kids were dressed? And how did they react to how you dressed?
When I was a kid we wore school uniforms, often on the weekends too. Money was tight. I was only able to indulge my fashion impulses once I got a job at the age of sixteen. I promptly spent all my earnings on mod clothing.

What is your ideal outfit? How would you care to see your ideal woman dressed?
I don't have any ideals or any limits. Fashion should be about creative expression and surprise.

How should the ideal man dress? Is this different for gay or straight?
Men should dress how they want to. I have no dictatorial impulses. The only thing I would suggest is that men (and women) should try to look like themselves. Since clothing is nonverbal communication then it's best to dress in a way which reflects who you are, or at least who you wish you were. If you are a very demure gal then I would not recommend that you dress in a louche or trampy fashion, unless of course you are heartily sick of being demure and looking to reinvent.

Do you think there is a relationship between psychoanalysis and fashion?
Freud made many interesting observations about clothing. For example: he suggested that women's handbags, if they appeared in your dreams, were vaginal symbols. Every piece of clothing has psychological resonance. It's all about codes and symbols.

What would you like to own that you do not have now? Why?
When I lived in L.A. in the 70's I met Nudie, the amazing Country and

Western show-biz tailor. He made those incredible embellished suits for Tammy Wynette and Johnny Cash. I wish I had had the dough to buy a Nudie suit. He is no longer around, or I would order one asap.

How has your relationship to fashion evolved during the course of your life so far?
I am still excited by newness. I still covet things. I fixate on styles and obsess about particular items. Fashion has always worked like an antidepressant for me. I am in my 60's but feel the same tingle of excitement when I encounter some snappy must-have item.

How is dressing a window different and similar to dressing yourself?
There are similarities. Both represent opportunities to communicate ideas and nuances. A window should complement and express the philosophy of a particular store. With your clothing you have the opportunity to communicate aspects of your personality as you see fit.

How do you wish people would react to how you dress?
Lots of people compliment my clothing, especially my flowery shirts. But lots of people clearly think I look like an idiot. Taste and style are subjective. If you go out on a limb style-wise you have to be prepared for the occasional burst of derision. Being unconventional and standing out are very important to me, but not to the majority of people.

I got interested in fashion in the early 1960's when the futurist trend arrived. I was a young teen living in a gritty factory town. When I saw the images of girls wearing insane space-age clothes—Courreges and Cardin—I freaked. Suddenly anything seemed possible. I understood the transformative power of fashion. Anybody could be anything. Fly me to the moon. You just needed to wear white go-go boots. It was about this time I realized that clothing had played a huge role in my mother's life. She was born into Irish agrarian poverty and left school at 14.

With the aid of style and glamour and peroxide she had transformed herself into Lana Turner and left the cows and sheep behind. Style equals transformation and transcendence.

VII

*Interviews with
Fashion Professionals*

1. Karlo Steele

What led you to choose fashion as a career?
I worked in retail nearly my entire life but was offered an opportunity to start a boutique and act as the creative director and buyer.

What do you want to accomplish in Fashion?
There wasn't a goal as such. I just wanted to do a good job.

What are the gratifications?
The money, obviously.

What are the frustrations?
Many. Fashion is unjust, cruel and dangerous. The massive carbon footprint, toxic pollution and enormous waste in fashion are endemic. Cheap laborers, usually in third world countries, often work in unsafe and unsanitary conditions for excessively long hours. Fashion is racist, ageist, weightist, ableist, ultra-exclusive and deeply conservative.

2. Ildi Marshall

What led you to choose fashion as a career?
Because I grew up with custom-made clothes, and my mother used to tell me that, after coming back from camp, I would remodel all my clothes, and my mother was very upset that I would do that, because they were very expensive custom-made clothes. Basically, I would go after school to my grandmother's lingerie factory and start playing with fabrics, and sometimes I would sit at the sewing machine, and I would break all the needles because I didn't ask for help, just thought I could do it. I still have my fashion-design of clothes from when I was 12, and my mother saved it. I took very good care of it because I put wax paper in between pages so that one page of drawings wouldn't rub off on the other page.

What do you want to accomplish in Fashion?
In the 60's I was on the cover of Vogue magazine, and I got a letter from Polly Mellon how much Diana Vreeland loved the blouse—modeled by Verushka, the German model.

Now? What I have accomplished all through the years—when people ask who your favorite designer is—some people say I am—(Ildiko label now). Sometimes I go to places and expect that no one would hear about me. But doctors I go to etc. give me a lot of recognition that I don't expect—blogs about me—because I don't advertise my product—word of mouth and repeat customers to specialty stores.

What are the gratifications?
The compliments on my clothes and the reorders by stores. The acceptance of my designs by customers. I enjoy the creative process. I enjoy what is unique about the process of creating fashion. I design on a wholesale level.

I take pride in that I try to create clothing that complements—flatters most body types—or most women—not only models, and my styling works for petite people to plus size. It's just a style that looks good on everybody. When I design, I try to think of things that won't go out of style next year. They are not throwaway clothes. I think things should be classic and elegant. The downside of that is that people keep them and don't buy more. Good fabrics and good fit are very important.

What are the frustrations?
The frustrations for a designer who owns her own company is customer's who don't pay on time. Also late fabric deliveries.

3. Puck

PUCK, Designer, manufacturer,
retail business owner where she sells her clothing

Puck sees fashion as art. It's the same process as creating a piece of pottery or a painting or a garden or a sonata (or, the authors add, a better life for people who have the courage to enter psychoanalysis).

What led you to choose fashion as a career?
I was always attracted to adornment and beauty. I'm always attracted to beauty and art and to making other people look more beautiful.

What do you want to accomplish in fashion?
In my opinion most designers create for their own fulfillment. Many designers are not interested in making women look beautiful. It is a creative act for them to create something beautiful or interesting. Like a painting. Their own fulfillment. We're talking about top designers. For most designers it's a business.

What are the gratifications?
Fame and fortune. I'm not really a designer. In my case I'm continuing a look. The Koos look which is multi fabrics and collages. Karl Lagerfeld designs for Chanel. So he is continuing a look. That's what happens in most fashion houses. They are continuing a look. A lot of top designers have designed and collaborated with H & M.

What are the frustrations?

When you create and are not pleasing your clientele. If you are out of sync with the clientele. That's why some of the brands go belly-up.

4. On Becoming Thakoon – Two Friends Talk

Interview with Thakoon by Carolyn Tate Angel

Thakoon Panichgul is a fashion designer who moved to Nebraska from Thailand when he was 11 years old. We worked together at Harper's Bazaar until 2004 when he started his own clothing line. Starting August 2016, Thakoon is relaunching his namesake brand adopting a direct-to-consumer, designer-fashion now model. We sat down together this past summer to discuss all things fashion.

Carolyn: What led you to choose a career in fashion? What are your goals as a fashion designer? What are the gratifications of working in the fashion business? What are the frustrations?

Thakoon: So, what led me to fashion? Um, I remember when I was like nine, in Thailand, I remember that there was a certain way that I was interested in, like watching people dress and how they styled themselves, and I was very much consciously aware of that experience. And it wasn't so much what they were wearing, but it was more about how they were tucking their shirt, or how they put it together. So I was like "I think that I can understand that," at nine, and I was like wow that's interesting, I was aware of being intrigued by what I'm feeling. And at the time I had a cousin who was doing seamstress work too, and I would see her sew all of these things. Her friends would bring tear sheets to her and have her copy them for them. So she would sew full garments and I was really interested in how she did that. This was in Thailand. So then cut to when I moved to Nebraska.

Carolyn: How old were you?

Thakoon: I was 11. And basically we had gone from Bangkok, which is like the biggest city, it's such a metropolitan city, to Omaha, which had nothing. So I was kind of not depressed, but I just didn't know what the outlets were—like there were no outlets to do anything. So I discovered the magazine store— the newsstand. And then I started looking at books, photography books, but then I started looking at magazines and I discovered fashion magazines. Then all of a sudden it was sort of, you know, like I had this dream of America and then I saw images by fashion photographers Bruce Weber, Patrick Demarchelier, Steven Meisel and Peter Lindbergh. All of those images from Vogue at the time were incredible imagery of fantasy fashion. This was sort of a way for me to kind of escape Omaha a bit. I started collecting fashion magazines at a very young age. I remember the first magazine I bought was a GQ with Tom Cruise on the cover, and then I bought a Christy Turlington *Vogue* cover. I was like "Oh my God, these are amazing," so I would make my mom take me every weekend to the magazine store, and then I started subscribing to magazines. And then I started having tear issues every-where. I would put them all over the place.

Carolyn: My bedroom in high school was covered in fashion magazine clippings too, I wonder if nowadays kids do that.

Thakoon: I don't think so, it's not the same.

Carolyn: It was like that for me as well. I loved looking at fashion maga-zines, taking out images and I put them all over my wall. For me, I remember the year Marissa Tomei won the Academy Award for *My Cousin Vinnie*, and I created a mood board around the dress she wore. I made my own layout of a page for a magazine. What are your goals as a fashion designer?

Thakoon: So, I mean it continues to evolve. But in the beginning my goal was to basically put my voice out there, because I felt like I had such a voice and nobody was kind of listening to it. I think I was just frustrated. I think that I'm driven by frustration a lot of times. And it was almost like,

when you're working at a magazine there's almost sort of this hierarchy that happens, but when you have creative ideas, sometimes it's shot down. And I think that because of that, it redirected my creative desire elsewhere. And so, in the beginning when you and I worked at *Harper's Bazaar* together, it was as if I wanted to have a voice in fashion. So that was my passion. When I launched the first collection, it was a very distinct collection and it was a distinct point of view. Looking back, the collection wasn't too many pieces, I knew exactly what the message was. And thankfully, at the time, it was actually new. It felt new to people. We did a presentation, and presentations weren't done then at all as well as a tableau, which was beautiful. It felt new and I was happy about that. And then it shifted to, okay, now that the voice is out there, what do I want out of the Thakoon brand. I like to design because I love to put clothes on people, that's ultimately what I think a designer should be. I'm not a stage designer, I don't do costumes.

I like to design clothes for people. And then for me, it's shifted to: I want to make clothes that people can wear. I want to create a lifestyle for people. And now we're doing that. It's like, my prints, people love. And I can translate usually to home and lifestyle. There are just a lot of things I have to do still.

Carolyn: What are the gratifications of working in the fashion business?

Thakoon: I think the gratification is the newness. I think that I get so bored, and I have such short attention span that I don't have the same process for working every season. If there's a same process I kind of want to reinvent it and do something different.

Carolyn: And what you're doing right now is on the cutting edge.

Thakoon: I like working against constraints so it's almost as if I kind of put that against myself. But I admire the newness that fashion brings, so every season you can do something new. It's inspiring that way. There are not that many industries where you can actually say that.

Carolyn: And you can constantly be reinventing yourself.

Thakoon: Exactly. And fashion will accept that.

Carolyn: And that's what you love. That's what every story used to do in a fashion magazine. It was something new, new ideas, and you can always be reinventing the wheel.

Thakoon: Right, and what was ugly is now cool. There's no rule for what can be cool. The problem is, which is a frustration now, is that we've rehashed so many ideas, and the fashion industry is changing so quickly right now from media to design, to the way fashion is manufactured, to the way fashion is consumed by people and social media and digital. There's so many changes within all of those elements that it's a moving target, you don't know ever what you're doing. And on top of that, there's so much supply, and people are bored so quickly. It's such a frustration actually. It's like, how do you introduce something new?

Carolyn: And even I think shopping, for me as a consumer, has become so hard. Am I supposed to be going online to buy something new; am I supposed to go to a store? As a shopper I'm trying to get the best thing, but am I getting the best thing at this one place? Should I be going somewhere else? And then I think maybe I should just shop my closet!

Thakoon: In a way it was easier before, because it was, not a set of rules, but there was a theory behind it in that it was coming from the top down. If you bought that Balenciaga dress, if you got that Celine item, if you subscribed to these fashion brands then that's it. Somebody was telling you.

Carolyn: If you understood the rule, and were able to do it, then it showed "I know what I'm doing."

Thakoon: And it was coming down from somewhere. It was disseminated from the powers that be from above: who you were either working for or who you were reading about. Now, that power's all gone. Now it's social media, and kids only pay attention to what's happening there. They're just getting into their own groove of, "I'm interested in Fila sneakers" all of a sudden. And that doesn't come from high fashion, that just comes from the street.

Carolyn: And not the "street" of the 60's, because it's so different... because the street could be so many things.

Thakoon: It's power to the people now, and people have the ability to make their own voices. So because of that there's so many voices that you don't know what's collectively trending, because everything trends. So how do you cater to an audience that big that has so many variables to consider? You can't. Or you make one thing. That's the frustration of fashion right now. Fashion has become all about these flashy trends. Like super-quirky or super-distressed. It's so trendy, we're talking in the trend level because they recycle so quickly now. There's no inherent sort of classic thing that runs through at the bottom level. The cycle of trends are faster now, whereas before it wasn't that fast.

5. Pamela Weekes

What led you to choose fashion as a career?
It was a bit accidental. I've always loved fashion but never considered it as a career. I was working at an international engineering and architectural firm as an assistant to one of the partners, hoping that perhaps they would pay for me to go to graduate school in architecture. The day-to-day was not very exciting, so I would always be looking for other opportunities "just in case." When I saw an ad in the *New York Times* for a position with Norma Kamali, I figured I had nothing to lose by trying to get an interview. I had long been a fan of Norma Kamali and this felt like one of those amazing New York opportunities. I have a liberal arts degree as an art major with a concentration in painting, and a minor in arts management; and I loved the creativity that abounded in fashion at that time.

What do you want to accomplish in Fashion?
I wanted to have fun and to learn as much as I could about running a business. At first a smaller business, and then later a larger business. I was interested and willing to do as many different things as possible, which opened up a lot of different opportunities everywhere. I knew eventually I wanted to have my own business. (But a bakery was not a thought at that time!)

What are the gratifications?

Fashion was a very interesting business. It offered the opportunity to help women feel good about themselves in a very surface way that could lead to a much deeper confidence for them. It also could be incredibly frustrating, because it could be very shallow as well. The day-to-day could be a lot of fun as well as hard work. I made many good friends that I still have today. I'm not certain if it was the time, the industry or our demographic, but I remain in touch with many of the people I worked with in fashion. Also fashion is an industry that has some really good female role models, so for an ambitious woman it was a good place to be rather than in a more male dominated industry.

What are the frustrations?

It has always been a business, but now most companies are driven first by numbers and then by creativity, which I understand but disagree with. A bit like the way we run the bakery: we believe in putting product and people (staff & customers) first and then the numbers will follow and fall into place.

Above: Anita Weinreb Katz
Below: Arlene Kramer Richards

CONTRIBUTORS:

Carolyn Angel has worked in the fashion industry for 15 years—as a stylist, a fashion editor at *Harper's Bazaar* and *W Magazine,* and currently as a consultant. She did her undergraduate honors thesis, titled "Are We What We Wear? Fashion from the 1940s and 1960s," at Tufts University, and her graduate coursework on visual culture at the NYU Steinhardt School. A native New Yorker, Carolyn is an avid lover of contemporary art, music and culture. Recently she and her husband, art consultant and director Adam Shopkorn, opened an art gallery and cultural space in the Meatpacking District called Fort Gansevoort, which blends both of their talents in one building. Carolyn currently lives in NYC with her husband and two children.

Valerie Tate Angel, MSW, LCSW is the Deputy Secretary- General of the International Federation of Psychoanalytic Societies (2008-2016) and Co-Chair of the IFPS XIX Forum("Violence, Terror, and Terrorism Today: Psychoanalytic Perspectives," May 2016 NYC) ; Director of the Supervisory Training Program, Institute of the Postgraduate Psychoanalytic Society. Training Analyst and senior supervisor, the Institute of the Postgraduate Psychoanalytic Society. She is also faculty, senior supervisor, and training analyst at the Training Institute for Mental Health, NYC. Regional Editor of the International Forum of Psychoanalysis (IFP). Publications include articles on psychoanalytic supervision, dreams, the mourning process and group supervision. Co-editor IFP,1995 Vol.4, #4, "Contemporary Perspectives in American Psychoanalysis," IFP 2006, Vol.15, #2 "Women and Success: The Unconscious Saboteur," and IFP 2011,Vol.20,# 4 "Creative Dialogues: Clinical, Artistic and Literary Exchange." IFP2015, Vol.24 #1 Evoking Freud's Memory: Pribor, editorial, Private practice in New York City.

Elsa J. Blum, PhD is a clinical psychologist and has co-authored articles in books and peer reviewed journals. She is a visual artist as well, and has worked in a variety of media, including painting and sculpture. At present she designs and crafts jewelry and does fine-art photography. She is an exhibiting member of Soho Photo Gallery.

Harold P. Blum, MD, Training and supervising psychoanalyst, Institute for Psychoanalytic Education, affiliated with New York University School of Medicine, Department of Psychiatry; Distinguished Fellow, American Psychiatric Association; Executive Director, Sigmund Freud Archives (1987 - 2014); President, Psychoanalytic Research and Development Fund (2008 to present); Editor-in-Chief, Journal of the American Psychoanalytic Association (1973 - 1983); Vice President, International Psychoanalytical Association (1993 - 1997). Author of more than 150 psychoanalytic papers and several books; Recipient of numerous awards and lectureships including the inaugural Sigourney Award, Mahler, Hartmann, and Lorand prizes; Sigmund Freud lectures in New York, London, Vienna, and Frankfurt; Anna Freud, Hartmann, Brill, Friend and Sperling lectures, two plenary addresses to the American Psychoanalytic Association; Chair of five Symposia on Psychoanalysis and Art in Florence, Italy; Clinical Professor of Psychiatry, New York University School of Medicine (1972 - 2013).

Hilda Catz. PhD, Miembro titular en función didáctica Asoc. Psicoanalítica Argentina, Directora del Departamento de Niños y Adolescentes de APA, Artista plástica. She lives and practices psychoanalsyis in Buenos Aires, Argentina.

Simon Doonan is an Author, SLATE columnist, and Creative Ambassador for Barneys New York. Writer, bon-vivant, window dresser extraordinaire and fashion commentator Simon Doonan has worked in fashion for over 35 years.

He has written six books: Confessions of *a Window Dresser, Wacky Chicks,* a memoir entitled *Beautiful People* and tongue-in-cheek style guides entitled *Eccentric Glamour* and *Gay Men Don't Get Fat.* His latest book *THE ASYLUM: a collage of fashion reminiscences...and hysteria,* is a collection of stories from his 35 years in the fashion industry. He has written regularly for *The New York Observer, The Daily Beast,* and currently writes a biweekly humor column for SLATE.com.

Simon is a regular guest at The MOTH, the well-known storytelling series. His contributions have consistently become their most popular podcasts and NPR broadcasts.

A TV comedy series based on *Beautiful People* has aired in the UK, the US and Australia. Simon has been a featured guest on late-night talk shows such as Chelsea Lately and The Conan O'Brien Show. He has regularly appeared on America's Next Top Model, VH1, Full Frontal Fashion and Bravo.

Simon has won many awards for his groundbreaking and unconventional window displays, including the CFDA Award. In 2009 he was invited by President and Mrs. Obama to decorate the White House for the Holidays. In 2010 Simon was commissioned by Target to design the season's Halloween costumes. Simon Doonan lives in New York City with his partner, the ceramicist and designer Jonathan Adler.

Ada Frumerman LCSW is on the staff of the Outpatient Center for Mental Health at Lenox Hill Hospital. Her previous papers on gender issues are Fathers and Daughters: The Origins of Masculine Identifications in Women and A Psychoanalytic Exploration of Cross Dressing in the Novel The Well of Loneliness.

Eve Golden, MD is a writer, editor, and independent scholar specializing in twentieth-century cultural and intellectual history. She lives in Cambridge, MA.

Charlene La'May Humber, LMSW, pursued her Bachelor of Science degree in Psychology at Tuskegee University with a minor in Journalism and acquired her graduate degree with a Masters in Social Work from New York University. She holds training certifications with the N.Y.S. Office of Mental Health Education Consortium in Evidence-Based Practice; Columbia Psychiatry, N.Y.S. Psychiatric Institute, Center for Practice Innovations in Motivational Interviewing and with Boston University, The Center for Aging and Disability Education and Research, in N.Y.S. Case Management.

As a licensed Social Worker, specializing in Gerontology, she serves as a Case Management, Social Work Supervisor, in Bronx, N.Y. Charlene also attends the Metropolitan Institute for Training in Psychoanalytic Psychotherapy's Adult program while, gaining clinical training as a therapist at the Metropolitan Center for Mental Health. She serves as a board member for the Metropolitan Society of Psychoanalytic Psychotherapists.

Anita Weinreb Katz, PhD is a Training and Supervising analyst at NYU Postdoctoral Program in Psychoanalysis and Psychotherapy, and at the Metropolitan Institute of Psychoanalytic Psychotherapy. She is a member of IPTAR, a fellow of IPA, and Clinical Supervisor at City University of New York. Her publications include: *Paradoxes of Masochism, Fathers Facing their Daughters Emerging Sexuality; Healing the Split Between Body and Mind: Structural and Developmental Aspects of Psychosomatic Illness*; and a chapter on "Loneliness in Two Men" in *Encounters With Loneliness*, edited by AK Richards and L Spira. She has presented on enactment in the psychoanalytic situation, envy and jealousy, and a case study on fashion and psychoanalysis. In addition, she has presented and published several psychoanalytically oriented studies of movies. These include the following: *The Vanishing, A Woman Under the Influence, Proof, American Beauty*, and *Utzz*. She is a member of CAPA (China-America Psychoanalytic Alliance), and a Supervising Psychoanalyst of candidates in China. She has one daughter, Jennifer Melissa Katz, who is a veterinarian. She is a Clinical Psychologist and Psychoanalyst and she maintains a private practice in Manhattan.

Linda A. Mayers, PhD is past Director of Training, Training and Supervising Analyst of the Institute of the Postgraduate Psychoanalytic Society; Adjunct Associate Professor at La Guardia Community College, City University of New York; former Director of Continuing Education, faculty and supervisor at Washington Square Institute; faculty, senior supervisor and former President of the Professional Board of the Postgraduate Center for Mental Health; former Adjunct Clinical professor at City University, Teachers College- Columbia University and Yeshiva University. Member of the Editorial Board of Journal of Infant, Child and Adolescent Psychotherapy; Editorial Reader, International Forum of Psychoanalysis. She is a founding member of Psychoanalysis, Art and Creativity, a member organization of the International Society for Art and Psychology. She has published in the areas of adoption, art and psychoanalysis, the history of mental illness and infant-parent disturbances. She is in private practice in New York City.

Ildi Marshall's love of fashion began in Budapest, where as a child , after school, she would go to her grandmother's lingerie factory and watch the fabrics turn into beautiful undergarments.

She came to the US in 1956, during the Hungarian revolution, and enrolled in school to study fashion. She started out as an assistant designer and worked her way up to designer for various companies on 7th Avenue, including one that marketed Christie Evert's name for tennis outfits. Being a player herself, it was one of her favorite parts of her designing career.

In 1982, she started her own company and now she caters to woman with sophisticated tastes who look for timelessly elegant clothes.

Arlene Kramer Richards, EdD is a psychoanalyst and a poet. She is a Training and Supervising Analyst with the Contemporary Freudian Society and the International Psychoanalytic Association and Fellow of IPTAR. She is currently faculty at the NYFS and Tongji Medical College of Huazhong University of Science and Technology at Wuhan, China. Her psychoanalytic writings have helped clarify and bring to life issues of female development, perversion, loneliness, and the internal world of artists and poets. Most recent publications include "Gambling and Death" in E. Ronis and L. Shaw (Eds.), *Greed, Sex, Money, Power and Politics,* (IP Books, 2011) and Little Boy Lost. In A. Adelman and K. Malawista (Eds.), *The Bereaved Therapist: From the Faraway Nearby.* (Columbia University Press, 2012), "The Skin I Live In" In A.K. Richards, L. Spira and A.A. Lynch (Eds.) *Encounters With Loneliness: Only the Lonely* (2013) and a book of her papers, *Psychoanalysis: Listening to Understand: Selected Papers of Arlene Kramer Richards.* She recently also published a book of poetry (2011), *The Laundryman's Granddaughter:*

Poems by Arlene Kramer Richards, New York: IP Press. She has been elected a representative from North American to the IPA. She is in Private Practice in New York City.

Karlo Steel was born in New Orleans, lived in San Francisco, currently resides in New York City. Founder, creative director and buyer for Atelier New York. Aesthete, flâneur, post-dandy fashion obsessive, art and architecture groupie, queer-homo, retro-futurist, analogue synth freak, Warhol acolyte, frustrated stylist, neurotic and insecure, Leo.

Claire Beth Steinberger, EdD, JD is senior faculty of the National Psychological Association of Psychoanalysis, faculty Object Relations Institute and Training Program in Family Law and Forensics; Clinical Member American Psychological Association, Psychoanalysis and Family/Couple Section and Supervisory Member American Association of Marriage and Family Therapy; Adjunct Associate Professor Long Island University, Graduate Department of Counseling and Development. Publication highlights: an interdisciplinary approach, psychoanalysis and family systems, cultural, interpersonal and intrapsychic interface, and therapeutic jurisprudence. Moderator / Presenter Dances of Intimacy: Psychoanalysis and Couples (NPAP, Spring Series 2017).

Thakoon Panichgul's Thakoon brand is a reflection of the diverse background of founder and designer, Thakoon Panichgul. Born in Thailand, raised in Omaha, and New York-based, Panichgul's creations are a skillful blend of distinct influences.

After earning a degree in business at Boston University, Panichgul moved to New York where he cultivated a deep working knowledge of the industry, spanning production, merchandising and communications. After several years as an editor at Harper's Bazaar, Panichgul enrolled at The Parsons School, and began to establish the pillars of his design approach, laying the foundation for his namesake label.

In September 2004, Thakoon presented his debut collection, and quickly became one of the industry's most celebrated new talents. In 2006 he was a recipient of the Vogue/CFDA Fashion Fund award.

Based on innovative construction and unique textile development, Thakoon's concentration revolves around the nuances of classical design and the continued reexamination of its process, where subtleties take center stage.

Tina Tian, has three education backgrounds: Education, Literature and Chinese Philology related to linguistics (Master's Degree). Before becoming a psychotherapist, she worked for both public school and international school(dean). She was also in charge of a Mandarin training school. Her previous work experience on dealing with people from different cultures and different parts around the world included the elites, such as an ambassador and people in Fortune 500. This resulted in her gaining an international perspective. She is now taking training at IPTAR to be a licensed psychoanalyst and get IPA membership. She is well-read and very much interested in arts. She learned piano, dance, horse riding and sword dancing when she was young. She was awarded a prize in hard-tipped pen calligraphy and made art work using butterfly wings. She has enthusiasm for photography, classical music and movies.

Pamela Weekes grew up on the North Shore of Long Island, graduated with a BA from Sweet Briar College as a Studio Art Major with a concentration in painting and a minor in Arts Management. Pam enjoyed working at Norma Kamali as well as at Adrienne Vittadini prior to founding Levain Bakery with her partner Connie McDonald. The bakery has outlets in Manhattan and East Hampton. A competitive swimmer when younger, Pam still swims as well as practicing yoga regularly.

Sara Zarem, PhD is a psychologist and psychoanalyst in private practice in New York City. She is also an adjunct assistant professor at LaGuardia Community College and supervises at the Lexington Center for Mental Health.

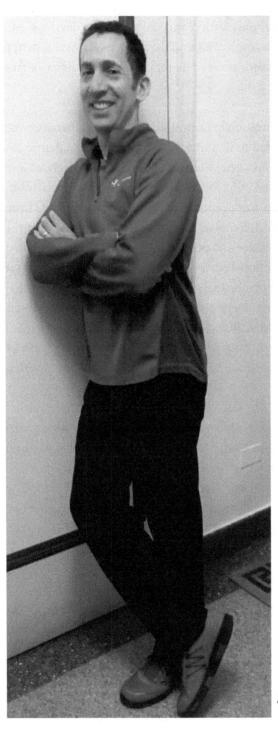

**Joel Matalon, a fashionable
personal trainer**

CPSIA information can be obtained
at www.ICGtesting.com
Printed in the USA
FFHW011801111118
49324438-53580FF